Upstream

HOW TO SOLVE PROBLEMS
BEFORE THEY HAPPEN

DAN HEATH

BANTAM PRESS

TRANSWORLD PUBLISHERS
61–63 Uxbridge Road, London W5 5SA
www.penguin.co.uk

Transworld is part of the Penguin Random House group of companies
whose addresses can be found at global.penguinrandomhouse.com

First published in Great Britain in 2020 by Bantam Press
an imprint of Transworld Publishers

A CIP catalogue record for this book
is available from the British Library.

ISBN 9781787632745

Printed and bound in Great Britain by Clays Ltd, Elcograf S.p.A.

Penguin Random House is committed to a sustainable
future for our business, our readers and our planet. This book
is made from Forest Stewardship Council® certified paper.

MIX

To my brother,

Chip, who kept me out of law school.

Contents

CONTENTS

Note from Author
on Sourcing

Over 300 interviews were conducted for this book. If a quote appears without a source listed ("Smith said"), then it's from one of those interviews. If a quote comes from another source, that source is made explicit ("as Smith told the *New York Times*," etc.).

When I use details or facts from other sources, they are cited in the endnotes. If a particular story draws more substantively on someone else's reporting, then that source will be cited in the text.

CHAPTER 1

Moving Upstream

You and a friend are having a picnic by the side of a river. Suddenly you hear a shout from the direction of the water—a child is drowning. Without thinking, you both dive in, grab the child, and swim to shore. Before you can recover, you hear another child cry for help. You and your friend jump back in the river to rescue her as well. Then another struggling child drifts into sight . . . and another . . . and another. The two of you can barely keep up. Suddenly, you see your friend wading out of the water, seeming to leave you alone. "Where are you going?" you demand. Your friend answers, "I'm going upstream to tackle the guy who's throwing all these kids in the water."

> —A public health parable (adapted from the original, which is commonly attributed to Irving Zola)

In 2012, Ryan O'Neill, the head of the customer experience group for the travel website Expedia, had been sifting through some data from the company's call center. One number he uncovered was so farfetched as to be almost unbelievable. For every 100 customers who booked travel on Expedia—

reserving flights or hotel rooms or rental cars—58 of them placed a call afterward for help.

The primary appeal of an online travel site, of course, is self-service. No calls necessary. Imagine a gas station that allowed you to swipe a credit card right at the pump—and then, about 60% of the time, something went wrong that forced you to go inside the store for help. That was Expedia.

Traditionally, the call center had been managed for efficiency and customer satisfaction. Reps were trained to make the customer happy—as quickly as possible. Short calls minimized expenses. "The lens we were using was cost," said O'Neill. "We had been trying to reduce that cost. Instead of a ten-minute call, could we make it a two-minute call? But the real question was: Why two minutes? Why *any* minutes?"

When you spend years responding to problems, you can sometimes overlook the fact that you could be preventing them. O'Neill shared his findings with his boss, Tucker Moodey, the executive vice president of global customer operations. Together, they dug into a basic but neglected question: Why in the world are so many customers calling us? They compiled a ranking of the top reasons customers sought support.

The number one reason customers called? To get a copy of their itinerary. In 2012, roughly 20 million calls were logged for that purpose. Twenty million calls! That's like everyone in Florida calling Expedia in one year.

At a support cost of roughly $5 per call, that's a $100 million problem. So why weren't customers receiving their itineraries automatically? The answers were pretty simple: The customer had mistyped her email address. Or the itinerary ended up in her spam folder. Or she deleted the itinerary by accident, thinking it was a solicitation. Compounding the problem was that there was no way on the website for customers to retrieve their itineraries.

O'Neill and Moodey took their data to Dara Khosrowshahi, then the CEO of Expedia. "We've got to do something about this," O'Neill recalled saying. Khosrowshahi not only agreed with their focus on reducing call volume, he made it the customer experience team's top priority. A "war room" was assembled, where people from different operating groups met on a daily basis, and the group was given a simple mandate: *Save customers from needing to call us.*

The war room group deployed solutions for the top drivers of customer calls, knocking off one at a time. The fixes for the number one issue—the itinerary requests—came relatively quickly: Adding an automated option to the company's voice-response system ("Press two to resend your itinerary"); changing how emails were sent to avoid spam filters; and creating an online tool to allow customers to handle the task themselves.

Today, virtually all of those calls have been eliminated. Twenty million support calls just vanished. Similar progress was made on the other "top 10" issues. Since 2012, the percentage of Expedia customers who call for support has declined from 58% to roughly 15%.

The effort to reduce call volume at Expedia was a successful *upstream* intervention. Downstream actions react to problems once they've occurred. Upstream efforts aim to prevent those problems from happening. You can answer a customer's call and address her complaint about a missing itinerary (downstream), or you can render that call unnecessary by ensuring that she receives her itinerary up front (upstream).

Surely we'd all prefer to live in the upstream world where problems are prevented rather than reacted to. What holds us back? Looking back on Expedia's success, what's particularly hard to understand is why it took so long to act. How could the company have reached the point where 20 million people were calling for itineraries? Shouldn't the alarm bells have been ringing rather loudly by the time, say, the 7 millionth call was logged?

Expedia's executives were not oblivious. They were aware of the huge volume of calls. It's just that they were organized to neglect their awareness. Like most companies, Expedia divided its workforce into groups, each with its own focus. The marketing team attracted customers to the site. The product team nudged customers to complete a reservation. The tech group kept the website's features humming along smoothly. And the support group addressed customers' issues quickly and satisfactorily.

Notice what was missing: It was no group's job to ensure that customers *didn't need to call for support*. In fact, no team really stood to gain if customers stopped calling. It wasn't what they were measured on.

In some ways, the goals of the groups actually encouraged more calls. For the product group, whose goal was to maximize bookings, the best move was to ask for a customer's email only once, because asking her to type it a second time would add friction. They might lose 1 person in 100 who'd be annoyed enough to abandon the transaction.

But the side effect of that decision, of course, is that some customers would mistype their emails, and they'd end up calling for an itinerary. That's a system failure. That customer never needed to call. Yet both teams would still look like heroes according to their goals: The product team closed a transaction, and the support team handled the resulting call quickly.

Mark Okerstrom, who was Expedia's CFO in 2012 and became CEO in 2017, said, "When we create organizations, we're doing it to give people focus. We're essentially giving them a license to be myopic. We're saying: This is your problem. Define your mission and create your strategy and align your resources to solve that problem. And you have the divine right to ignore all of the other stuff that doesn't align with that."

Okerstrom's point is that focus is both the strength and the weakness of organizations. The specialization inherent to organizations creates great efficiencies. But it also deters efforts to integrate in new, advantageous ways. In *upstream* ways.

And this is true in many parts of society. So often in life, we get stuck in a cycle of response. We put out fires. We deal with emergencies. We handle one problem after another, but we never get around to fixing the systems that caused the problems.

Therapists rehabilitate people addicted to drugs, and corporate recruiters replace talented executives who leave, and pediatricians prescribe inhalers to kids with breathing problems. And obviously it's great that there are professionals who can address these problems, but wouldn't it be better if the addicts never tried drugs, and the executives were happy to stay put, and the kids never got asthma? So why do our efforts skew so heavily toward reaction rather than prevention?

Back in 2009, I spoke with a deputy chief of police in a Canadian city; it was one of the conversations that sparked my interest in upstream thinking. He believed that the police force was unduly focused on reacting to crimes as opposed to preventing them. "A lot of people on the force want to play cops and robbers," he said. "It's much easier to say 'I arrested this guy' than to say 'I spent some time talking to this wayward kid.'"

He gave an example of two police officers: The first officer spends half a shift standing on a street corner where many accidents happen; her visible presence makes drivers more careful and might prevent collisions. The second officer hides around the corner, nabbing cars for prohibited-turn violations. It's the first officer who did more to help public safety, said the deputy chief, but it's the second officer who will be rewarded, because she has a stack full of tickets to show for her efforts.

That's one reason why we tend to favor reaction: Because it's more tangible. Downstream work is easier to see. Easier to measure. There is a maddening ambiguity about upstream efforts. One day, there's a family that does not get into a car accident because a police officer's presence made them incrementally more cautious. That family has no idea what didn't happen, and neither does the officer. How do you prove what did *not* happen? Your only hope, as a police chief, is to keep such good evidence of crashes that you can detect success when the numbers start falling. But even if you feel confident your efforts accomplished something, you'll still never know *who* you helped. You'll just see some numbers decline on a page. Your victories are stories written in data, starring invisible heroes who save invisible victims.

In this book, I'm defining upstream efforts as those intended to prevent problems before they happen or, alternatively, to systematically reduce the harm caused by those problems. Teaching kids to swim, for instance, is an excellent upstream way to prevent drownings. But sometimes even experienced swimmers can find themselves at risk of drowning. That's why, to me, a life preserver is also upstream technology. At first glance, life preservers seem reactive—anyone who needs a life preserver tossed to them is already experiencing a problem, after all. But if the "problem" we want to solve is *people dying from drowning*, then the life preserver can prevent that.

A telltale sign of upstream work is that it involves systems thinking: Because authorities are aware of the risk of drowning, life preservers are purchased and distributed to locations where they will be readily available if an emergency happens. By contrast, a father frantically diving into the pool at the waterpark to assist his struggling son—that's reactive. (There is usually an interplay between downstream and upstream: After the father saves his son, the waterpark will likely review the incident and make systemic changes to ensure something similar doesn't happen again. The downstream rescue leads to the upstream improvement.)

I prefer the word *upstream* to *preventive* or *proactive* because I like the way the stream metaphor prods us to expand our thinking about solutions. This chapter began with the parable of the drowning kids, which contrasts two locations: downstream and upstream. But the reality is that we can intervene at many points along an almost limitless timeline. In other words, you don't head Upstream, as in a specific destination. You head upstream, as in a direction. Swim lessons are *further* upstream than life preservers. And there's always a way to push further upstream—at the cost of more complexity.

To consider the spectrum of upstream action, let's take a specific problem: In 2013, burglars broke into my parents' house in College Station, Texas. My parents were taking a walk around the neighborhood, and while they were gone, the burglars kicked in the back door and stole a wallet, two iPhones, and some jewelry. My parents filed a report with the police, but unfortunately the thieves were never caught. The downstream response failed.

What might have prevented the burglary altogether? Seconds before: a deafening alarm. Minutes before: the visible evidence of an alarm system—like those security-company signs you see in people's yards. (Or maybe this would have only deflected their attentions to a neighbor's house.) Hours before: a more palpable police presence.

Months before: If the thieves had been arrested previously, they might have been enrolled in certain kinds of behavioral therapy that can break the cycle of recidivism. Years before: Let's keep in mind that no kid grows up aspiring to burgle homes. So a far-upstream solution to theft would be: Create a community context where theft seems pointless because of the plentiful opportunities available. (If this seems Pollyanna-ish, by the way, wait until chapter 5: There's a country that practically eliminated teenage drug and alcohol abuse by embracing a similar philosophy of opportunity.)

Could we imagine preventing a burglary *decades* before it happened? Yes. We'll never run out of room upstream. The psychologist and child development expert Richard Tremblay argues that the best time to prevent aggressive behavior is when the criminal is still in his mother's tummy. Tremblay points to a cluster of risk factors involving the mother that predict a child's chronic physical aggression: maternal poverty, smoking, malnutrition, anger, and depression, plus poor marital relations, low education, and having the baby as a teenager. These factors tend to come together, according to Tremblay—and more important, they can be *changed*. Tremblay is currently working on a program that helps pregnant women in these high-risk situations. "To solve the aggression problems, which are mainly a male problem, we need to focus on females," Tremblay told *Nature*. "If you ameliorate the quality of life of women, it will transfer to the next generation."

If we could assume that all these solutions worked, we'd

prefer the solutions further upstream—the ones where fewer kids ever became criminals. But while upstream solutions are generally more desirable, they're also more complex and ambiguous. Think of it: Tremblay is proposing to improve a pregnant mother's environment so dramatically that she'll be prone to fewer risk factors (poverty, anger, depression), which means that her child will be less prone to aggressive tendencies, which could in turn lead to a reduced risk of criminal activity. Maybe 18 years later, the woman's child will end up going to college instead of breaking into a house. Downstream efforts are narrow and fast and tangible. Upstream efforts are broader, slower, and hazier—but when they work, they *really* work. They can accomplish massive and long-lasting good.

So, what's right, upstream or downstream? Should we stop a burglary with an alarm system—or by nurturing the mother of the future "criminal"? The first and best answer is: Why in the world would we choose? If corporations can mount multiple levels of protection to *prevent network downtime*, then surely, we can invest in multiple levels of protection against crime and other important problems.

If, in a world of scarce resources, we absolutely must choose one point of intervention, then here's the uncomfortable answer: We don't know which one is right. The world hasn't gathered enough evidence (let alone mustered the will) to pick the right point on the "stream" for crime—or, for that matter, on the stream of almost any major problem. That's one of the main reasons I wrote this book. Because, while we have a wide spectrum of available options to address the world's problems, we've mostly confined ourselves to one tiny stretch of the landscape: the zone of response. React, react, react.

We spend billions to recover from hurricanes and earthquakes while disaster preparedness work is perpetually starved for resources. There are hundreds of agencies and organizations that exist to help the homeless, but how many organizations are dedicated to *preventing people from becoming homeless*? When Ebola starts to spread in a foreign nation, it becomes an international priority—and afterward it's hard to attract funding to support the local health systems that could prevent the next outbreak.

It's not that the upstream solution is always right. And it's certainly not the case that we should abandon downstream work—we will always want someone there to rescue us. The point is that our attention is grossly asymmetrical. We're so focused on saving the drowning kids in the river that we fail to investigate why they need saving at all.

~~~~~~~

Nowhere is the need for this shift more evident than in the $3.5 trillion health care industry, which constitutes almost a fifth of the American economy. The US health care system is designed almost exclusively for reaction. It functions like a giant Undo button. Blocked artery? We'll unclog it. Broken hip? We'll replace it. Impaired vision? We'll correct it. If all goes well, you will be restored to your baseline health. But it's hard to find someone in the system whose job it is to address the question *How do we make you healthier?* (As distinct from *How can we respond to the problems that make you unhealthy?*)

Could the health system shift upstream? To do so would require major changes in policy, and health care policy is a notoriously partisan issue. Hoping to understand more about the underlying values of conservatives and liberals, an organization called The Health Initiative, led by Rebecca Onie and Rocco Perla, convened two focus groups in Charlotte, North Carolina: one with African American Democratic women and one with white Republican women. Each group was asked, "If you had a hundred dollars, how would you spend it to buy health in your community?" They were given the option to spread the hundred dollars across several categories.

The African American Democrats allocated about a third of the funds to the formal health care system (hospitals and clinics) and the great majority outside it: $25 to healthy food, $19 to affordable housing, and $14 to childcare, for instance. What about the white Republican women—how did they spend their funds? In almost exactly the same way; they agreed nearly to the last percentage point. The same findings held up in other focus groups conducted around the country—with men, with Latinos, with swing voters, and more. "The similarities in the spending patterns were stunning," said Perla. "That stopped us in our tracks."

So, even as we engage in fierce fights with people across the aisle, we're all secretly in agreement about how our spending *should* be allocated. Across the political spectrum, we think the best way to "buy health" is to invest two-thirds of our money into systems that make people healthy (food, housing, etc.) and one-third into systems that heal sick people. To say it a different way, for every $1 we spend on downstream health care, most of us think it would be wise to spend $2 upstream.

As it turns out, that ratio is pretty close to the global norm for developed countries. The average spending pattern over time, across other developed countries, is that for every $1 a nation spends downstream, it spends between $2 and $3 upstream. There is one outlier among those nations and, yep, it's us. In the US, for every $1 spent downstream, we spend roughly $1 upstream. That's the lowest proportion of upstream spending to downstream among our peer countries.

The narrative we're used to hearing about health care is that the US "spends too much." That's oversimplified. It's true—by a long shot—that we spend more on formal health care as a percentage of GDP than any other developed country. But if you add together what nations spend on health care plus what's called "social care"—which is basically upstream spending, ranging from housing to pensions to childcare support—you find that the US is unremarkable. We're 9th out of 34 countries in total spending, according to data in a 2017 study by Elizabeth Bradley, Heather Sipsma, and Lauren Taylor.

As Bradley and Taylor point out in a book called *The American Health Care Paradox*, what's really distinctive about the US approach to health isn't so much the *quantity* of spending but the *way we spend it*. Compared to other countries, we spend more money fixing people's ailments and less keeping them healthy. We're downstream; other countries are upstream.

In fact, it's even worse than that: Even our *upstream* spending is not as upstream as other countries. According to a RAND research report, other developed countries spend almost triple what we do, as a percentage of the upstream budget, on supporting families (child credits, childcare assistance, etc.). Meanwhile, we spend about 30% more than they do on "old age" spending.

Where the US health system excels, as a result of this downstream focus, is in treating patients with serious diseases such as cancer or heart disease. That's why Saudi princes fly to Houston or Boston to have their cancer treated. But it's not just princes who benefit—it's anyone with those diseases.

The US is a world leader in knee replacements, and bypass surgeries, and the number of people living with kidney transplants, and the percentage of seniors who get hip replacements within six months of needing one. These are the fruits of investing in downstream action.

What about the flip side—the disadvantage of our downstream focus? Let's consider some evidence from Norway, which makes for an interesting comparison because our total spending on upstream and downstream health is similar as a percentage of GDP. But Norway's spending priorities are radically different than ours: For every $1 spent downstream, they spend roughly $2.50 upstream.

What do Norway's different priorities buy? Take childbirth as an example. A pregnant Norwegian woman will pay nothing for all prenatal visits. Nothing for the delivery. Nothing for the visits after the baby is born. It's all covered.

Assuming the parents are employed for 6 of the 10 months before their baby is born, they are entitled to a whole slew of leave: The mother takes 3 weeks before the expected delivery date. Then, both parents can take off 15 weeks afterward. After that period ends, the family still has an additional stash of 16 weeks to divvy up between parents as they see fit. And, Americans, you better sit down for this one: All of this leave is paid. That's 49 weeks in total. (By the way, if the mother or father don't meet the work requirement, they don't receive paid leave, but they do receive a lump-sum check of roughly $9,000.)

When the child turns one, he or she is guaranteed a place in a full-time, high-quality day care, and parents are charged on a sliding scale capped at a few hundred dollars a month. And families are sent a small monthly payment—a little over $100 per month per child—that continues every month until they turn 18. That money could help pay for diapers or food or school supplies. Or it could be used to start a college savings fund—though that would be somewhat pointless, since college tuition is free in Norway.

Which country's population is healthier: Norway or the US? It's not a close call: In infant mortality, Norway has the 5th best results internationally; the US is 34th. Life expectancy: Norway is 5th, the US 29th. Least stressed: Norway is 1st, the US is 21st. Happiness—surely that's where we vault ahead? Nope: Norway is 3rd, the US is 19th.*

Remember, both countries spend roughly the same on health (upstream and downstream) as a percentage of GDP. Norway is not spending more; it's just spending differently. We cranked up the treble, Norway cranked up the bass. Our choice as a nation has been to get better and better at fishing drowning kids out of the river.

We could choose differently.

~~~~~~~

---

* Some qualifications here to avoid oversimplifying. Even if the US matched Norway's level of upstream spending, there's no guarantee we'd see comparable population outcomes. Making an entire citizenry healthy is complicated, and the legacy of inequity and racism in the US makes it harder than in the (comparatively) homogenous Norwegian population. The other issue is more of a math point. It's not that there's anything sacrosanct about these "ratios" of upstream-to-downstream spending. (You could make the US's ratio look better, for instance, by slashing downstream health care spending. But that wouldn't make anyone healthier.) Here's the point: If you think of spending on health as a giant pot of money, we are allocating that pot way differently than other countries. And if we want to improve health, we'd be wise to either *add* upstream spending or shift it from downstream to upstream.

My goal in this book is to convince you that we should shift more of our energies upstream: personally, organizationally, nationally, and globally. We can—and we should—stop dealing with the symptoms of problems, again and again, and start fixing them.

At the same time, we should be open-eyed about the challenges we'll face as we make that shift. Take this example from Mexico City: City officials in 1989 banned the general public from driving one weekday per week, based on the last digit of their license plates. The intent was to encourage use of mass transit options and thereby improve air quality. It was a noble upstream effort to *prevent* air pollution.

It didn't work. Many Mexicans bought a second car—often an old clunker, to keep costs down—so they could drive every day. Air quality did not improve.

Good intentions guarantee nothing.

What I find fascinating about upstream efforts is the way they reflect humanity at its best and worst. To go upstream is a declaration of agency: *I don't have to be at the mercy of these forces—I can control them. I can shape my world.* And in that declaration are the seeds of both heroism and hubris.

Sometimes that desire for control leads to astonishing success—think of the eradication of smallpox, a virus that had killed an estimated 300 million people in the 20th century alone, across every corner of the planet. Thanks to a massive worldwide effort, smallpox was systematically stamped out of existence. The last human being to be naturally infected with smallpox was a hospital cook named Ali Maow Maalin in Merca, Somalia. After he was found to be infected in 1977, a frantic two-week effort led to the vaccination of 54,777 people in the surrounding community, just to make sure the disease couldn't spread further.* And that was the end of smallpox. We didn't treat it; we vanquished it. That's upstream work at its best.

But that desire for control—*I can mold this situation to my desires*—can also tempt us to act in situations that we don't fully grasp. We tinker with systems we barely understand, stumbling into a maze of unintended consequences. There's no doubt that our noble efforts to make the world better can very easily make the world worse.

There are knotty problems that upstream leaders must untangle. How can you detect problems before they occur? How can you measure success when success is defined as things *not happening*? (Remember the scenario of the police officer who used her presence to prevent crashes, rather than filling her ticket book.) And, by the way, who should we expect to pay for those things that do not happen?

Ahead, we will dive into this complexity and meet people who have thrived in spite of it. We'll visit the first city in the US to eliminate chronic homelessness. We'll study a major urban school district that increased its graduation rate by 25 percentage points by focusing intensely on a single year of high school. And we'll encounter an internet company, offering a subscription service, that discovered it could predict

---

* An amazing postscript: Maalin lived and later devoted himself to eradicating polio in Somalia, using his experience with smallpox to highlight the importance of vaccines. By the way, there was another person *unnaturally* infected with smallpox in 1978 under tragic circumstances: Janet Parker, a medical photographer in the UK, whose darkroom was directly above Professor Henry Bedson's lab. Bedson had been working with the smallpox virus, and in a rush to complete some research, he had cut corners on safety, allowing the virus to travel up to Parker through an air duct. Parker died, and, shamed by what he had done, Bedson committed suicide.

which customers would cancel their annual subscriptions *within 4 weeks of their initial sign-up.*

Our exploration will come in three stages. First, we'll grapple with the three forces that push us downstream, impeding our ability to prevent problems. Then, in the heart of the book, we'll study the seven fundamental questions that upstream leaders must answer. We'll study both successful and unsuccessful prevention efforts, uncovering strategies that succeeded and obstacles to beware. Finally, we will consider "far upstream" thinking: What do you do when you're facing a problem that has never happened before (and may never happen at all)?

Most of us would agree that "an ounce of prevention is better than a pound of cure," but our actions don't match those words. In most of our efforts in society, we've optimized ourselves to deliver pounds of cure. Speedy, efficient pounds of cure. We celebrate the response, the recovery, the rescue. But we're capable of greater things: less Undo and more Outdo. What the world needs now is a quieter breed of hero, one actively fighting for a world in which rescues are no longer required. How many problems in our lives and in society are we tolerating simply because we've forgotten that we can fix them?

THE THREE BARRIERS TO UPSTREAM THINKING

~~~~~~~~

CHAPTER 2

Problem Blindness

In 1999, the doctor and sports trainer Marcus Elliott joined the staff of the New England Patriots, whose players had been plagued by hamstring injuries. At the time, there was a kind of fatalistic mind-set about injuries. People thought that injuries were "just a part of the sport," said Elliott. "It's just the nature of the sport and they're just freak injuries." Football is a tough game; players will get hurt. It's inevitable.

Elliott's philosophy was different. He thought that most injuries were simply the result of bad training. In most NFL training environments, the focus was on getting bigger and stronger. Even though players' bodies—and the positions they played—differed greatly, the training was mostly the same. "It's almost like walking into a doctor's office and—without interviewing you, without conducting any tests on you—he gives you a prescription," he said. "It makes no sense. But that's how the training of professional athletes was conducted. . . . It was a one-size-fits-all program."

Elliott brought a new, individualized approach. Players who were more at risk of hamstring injuries, such as wide receivers, got more attention. Elliott studied each player, testing their strength and watching their sprint mechanics and hunting for muscle imbalances (say, if one hamstring was stronger than the other). Based on those assessments, the players were put into groups by their risk of injury: high, moderate, and low. The high-risk players went through aggressive off-season training to correct the muscular warning signs that Elliott found.

The prior season, the Patriots players had suffered 22 hamstring injuries. After Elliott's program, the number plunged to 3. The success—and others like it—made believers out of skeptics. Twenty years later, the data-driven, player-tailored approaches, of the kind used by Elliott, have become much more prevalent.

Elliott later founded a sports science firm called P3, which assesses and trains elite athletes. The firm uses 3-D motion capture technology to micro-analyze athletes while they run, jump, and pivot. The results can be astonishingly precise: kind of like an MRI for elite athletes. Elliott can sit with an athlete and narrate: *See, when you land after a jump, you've got 25% more force coming through one side of your body, and we're noticing that your femur is rotating internally, and your tibia is rotating externally. That puts your relative rotation at the 96th percentile of the athletes we've examined, and every single athlete we've seen above the 95th percentile has suffered a knee injury within two years. So we should work on that, and after we train it, we are going to reassess it to see how much it has changed.* More than half of the current players in the NBA have been analyzed by P3.

"You don't wait for these bad things to happen," said Elliott. "Instead, you look for the signal that there's a risk there, and then you act on it. Because if you wait for the bad things to happen, you can never quite put things back together the way they were before." Elliott—and his peers with a similar philosophy—have made the science of injury prevention increasingly prevalent in pro sports.

Pro athletes play hard. Injuries are gonna happen. You

can't change that. That mind-set is an example of what I'll call "problem blindness"—the belief that negative outcomes are natural or inevitable. Out of our control. When we're blind to a problem, we treat it like the weather. We may know it's bad, but ultimately, we just shrug our shoulders. *What am I supposed to do about it? It's the weather.*

Problem blindness is the first of three barriers to upstream thinking that we'll study in this section. When we don't *see* a problem, we can't solve it. And that blindness can create passivity even in the face of enormous harm. To move upstream, we must first overcome problem blindness.

In 1998, the graduation rate in the Chicago Public Schools (CPS) was 52.4%. A public-school student in Chicago had a coin flip's chance of getting a high school degree. "Every system is perfectly designed to get the results it gets," wrote the health care expert Paul Batalden. And CPS was a system designed to fail half its kids.

Imagine that you were a teacher or an administrator inside this system, a good-hearted person eager to change those intolerable odds. Where would you start, exactly? Your noble aspirations would soon smack into the sprawling mass of CPS, with its 642 schools, 360,000+ students, and 36,000+ employees. For a sense of scale: the school district in Green Bay, Wisconsin, has 21,000 students. CPS has that many *teachers.* CPS's $6 billion budget is about the same as the entire city of Seattle's.

This is the story of how a group of believers tried to change a massive, broken system from inside—how they went upstream in hopes of stopping students from dropping out. To spark change, they first had to contend with a flawed mind-set. "For a long time, people had this notion—they think when you come to high school, you're gonna make it or break it," said Elizabeth Kirby, who as principal

23

of Kenwood Academy High School was one of the change leaders. "For these kids, this is where we'll decide who's going to be successful and who's not. And if they're not successful, it's their fault. And that's just how it is—so no one questions it."

That's just how it is—so no one questions it. That's problem blindness. Within CPS, many people had come to accept the high dropout rate. When students failed, they believed, it was because of root causes that were impossible to fix: poor families, inadequate K-8 education, traumatic emotional experiences, lack of nutrition, and more. On top of all that, the kids just didn't put forth the *effort*: They missed class; they didn't turn in assignments. They didn't seem to care. What could a high school teacher or principal do to affect any of that? The whole situation seemed intractable, and when another year went by, and the graduation rate continued to hover around 50%, it reinforced their helplessness. *It's a tough world, but that's the way it is, and I can't do anything about it.*

The first ray of hope—that school leaders could make a meaningful difference in the graduation rate—came from some academic research conducted by Elaine Allensworth and John Easton at the University of Chicago Consortium on School Research (CCSR). In 2005, CCSR published its findings that you could predict, with 80% accuracy, which freshmen would graduate and which would drop out.

The prediction was based on two surprisingly simple factors: (1) a student's completion of five full-year course credits; and (2) that student's not failing more than one semester of a core course, such as math or English. Those two factors, combined, became known as Freshman On-Track (FOT) metric. Freshmen who were on-track by this measurement were 3.5 times more likely to graduate than students who were off-track.

"Freshman On-Track matters more than *everything else put together*," said Paige Ponder, who was hired by CPS in 2007 to manage the FOT efforts. Conspicuously absent from the calculation were: income, race, gender, and—perhaps most incredibly—the student's own academic performance through eighth grade.

On that last point: Students in the *bottom* quartile of eighth-grade achievement who stayed on-track as freshmen had a 68% chance of graduating—far above the district average. What the researchers had discovered was that there is something peculiar about a *student's achievement specifically in the ninth grade* that predisposes them to succeed or fail in high school.

Why? What's so special about ninth grade? Part of the answer was that, in Chicago, there's no junior high: Elementary schools run from grades K to 8, and high schools start in 9th grade. So the pivot from eighth to ninth grade was a whopper of a transition: essentially a sudden graduation from childhood to adulthood.

"People are vulnerable during transitions," said Sarah Duncan, whose nonprofit the Network for College Success played a critical role in the CPS work. She said that students will often get their first taste of failure in the ninth grade, and that teachers almost seemed to relish delivering it, in a tough-love kind of way. "Teachers thought that the kids [who failed] would think, 'I need to work harder,' " Duncan said. "Sometimes that happens. But the majority of fourteen-year-olds, if they fail, interpret that as: 'I don't belong, I'm not good enough.' They withdraw."

But how do you keep students on track? Keep in mind: the FOT metric is just a prediction—it doesn't solve anything, just as your smoke detector doesn't put out fires. And like a smoke detector, if the alarm goes off, it means the bad thing has already happened; you've missed your chance to *prevent* the problem. (If a student finishes the freshman year off-track, the harm has already been done.)

Unlike a smoke detector, though, the FOT metric suggested a potential recipe for prevention: Make sure at-risk students can sustain a full course load and give them extra support in their core courses.* The quest to accomplish that mission upended CPS's practices in countless ways.

For one thing, if ninth grade is the critical transition point, then you'll want your best teachers teaching freshmen. That reversed the pecking order—usually the best teachers wanted to work with more mature juniors and seniors. But now you know that ninth graders deserve the A-team.

Also, seen through the lens of the FOT metric, certain discipline policies began to look self-destructive. "When we started this work, kids got suspended for two weeks all the time," said Sarah Duncan. "Not for bringing a gun to school. For a scuffle in the hallway where no punches were thrown." This was the "zero tolerance" era.

But what happens when at-risk students—those already struggling to hang on—are kicked out of school for two weeks? They fall behind in their coursework, fail classes, fall off-track, and don't graduate. It's unlikely any administrator realized that their get-tough policies might literally ruin a student's career prospects.

Every system is perfectly designed to get the results it gets.

The most profound change, though, was to the mindset of teachers. The Freshman On-Track work "changes the

---

* The old warnings about correlation not equaling causation apply here. There was no guarantee that improving freshmen's FOT scores would boost the graduation rates. But there were good reasons to believe the two were linked causally, and of course they were tracking their efforts so that they could prove it.

nature of how teachers see their jobs. It changes relation-ships between teachers and students," said researcher Elaine Allensworth. "It's the difference from 'I put the work out there and I assign the grades' to 'My job is to make sure all students are succeeding in my class. So I need to find out why they're struggling if they're struggling.'"

As a teacher, if you accept that your job is to support stu-dents, not appraise them, it changes everything. It changes the way you collaborate. For one thing, you can't adequately support a struggling student by yourself. You might see her for only an hour a day. Is she struggling only in your class or in several? How often is she missing school? Have other teachers found better ways to reach her? In short, you need to know more about her, and you need collaborators.

Traditionally, teachers would meet by department—the social studies teachers would meet together, and the English teachers, and so on. But now teachers began to meet across disciplines in what were called Freshman Success Teams. They'd meet regularly to scrutinize data reports provided by the district that provided real-time information on a student-by-student basis. For the first time they could share a 360-degree view of each student's progress.

"The beautiful thing about teachers—you can have what-ever philosophy you want, but if you're engaged in a conver-sation about Michael, you care about Michael," said Paige Ponder, conjuring a hypothetical student. "It all boils down to something real that people actually care about. . . . 'What are we going to do about Michael next week?'"

Every student needs something different. Aliyah needs extra help in math, but she won't ask for it—if you offer it, though, she'll accept it. Malik has to walk his sister to ele-mentary school every morning, so he will always be late—he needs an elective as his first period, so that if his tardiness causes him to fail, it won't be a core course. Kevin is a slacker and will dodge work when he can—but his mother will stay on him if you reach out to her. Jordan needs someone calling her house every single time she misses class. (Managing attendance is one of the most important parts of the FOT effort—as Ponder put it, "It's so obvious that if you get through school, you will *get through school*.")

Student by student, meeting by meeting, school by school, semester by semester, the numbers began to budge. Students' attendance improved, their grades improved, and their on-track measures improved. And four years later, they graduated in greater numbers than anyone thought possible. By 2018, the graduation rate had vaulted to 78%—up more than 25 percentage points in 20 years—on the strength of the upstream efforts of hundreds of teachers, administrators, and academics.

A ballpark estimate is that between 2008 and 2018 an additional 30,000 students earned a diploma who, in the absence of the CPS effort, would likely have dropped out. Those graduates will never know that, in a slightly different reality where the FOT work was delayed or never started, they would have dropped out, and their lives would have been immeasurably harder.

Because they graduated, though, those students will see their lifetime wages increase on average by $300,000 to $400,000. The leaders at CPS won an upstream victory worth $10 BILLION and counting—and that's tabulating just the extra income students will receive, not including the countless other positive ripple effects that come from higher incomes, from better health to greater happiness.

The story of CPS's success foreshadows many of the themes we'll explore in the book. To succeed upstream, leaders must: detect problems early, target leverage points in complex systems, find reliable ways to measure success, pioneer new ways of working together, and embed their successes into systems to give them permanence. Remember, though, that for anything to happen at CPS, leaders first had to awaken from problem blindness. You can't solve a problem that you can't see, or one that you perceive as a regrettable but inevitable condition of life. (*Football is a tough game—of course, people are gonna get hurt.*)

Why do we fall prey to problem blindness? For a clue, take a look at the image below, which shows several slides of a chest CT scan. It's the kind of visual sequence that radiologists might analyze while hunting for lung cancer. Notice anything odd?

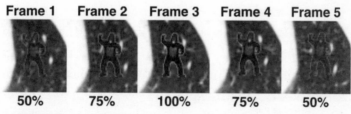

© [9/30/19] Trafton Drew. Image used with permission.

Yes, that's a tiny gorilla, and no, this patient did not inhale it. The gorilla was inserted into the images by some researchers, led by Trafton Drew, who were playing a trick on a group of radiologists. How many of the radiologists—focused on a search for potentially cancerous nodules—would notice the gorilla?

Not many: 20 out of 24 missed it entirely. They had fallen

prey to a phenomenon called "inattentional blindness," a phenomenon in which our careful attention to one task leads us to miss important information that's unrelated to that task.

Inattentional blindness leads to a lack of peripheral vision. When it's coupled with time pressure, it can create a lack of curiosity. *I've got to stay focused on what I'm doing.* When teachers and principals are hounded to boost students' test scores, year after year, and denied the resources they need to succeed, and buffeted by a never-ending series of regulatory and curricular changes, they lose their peripheral vision. They're like radiologists scouring a scan so intently for nodules that they miss the gorilla. So, with time, they stop worrying about the graduation rate, because they've got more than enough on their plates already, and anyway, what could they do about it?

And, by the way, if you're tempted to think less of these radiologists for their gorilla blindness, did you happen to notice that, for the last several pages, the page number below has been replaced with a leprechaun?

My early testing with readers suggested that about half noticed it and half didn't. If you *did* notice it, I suspect that the repetition caused your interest to fade. The first time you see it, you think, *What the hell? A leprechaun?* The second time, it's *Oh, there's another one.* The fourth time, it has vanished from your consciousness. That's habituation. We grow accustomed to stimuli that are consistent. You walk into a room, immediately notice the loud drone of an air conditioner, and five minutes later, the hum has receded into normalcy.

To reinforce that last point about attaining "normalcy," consider that habituation is frequently used as a therapy for people's phobias. People with a fear of needles, for instance, might be asked to look at images of needles, or to handle needles, so many times that eventually their irrational fear yields. The needle has been destigmatized. Normalized. In a therapeutic context, that normalization is desirable. But habituation cuts both ways: Imagine instead that what's being normalized is corruption or abuse.

In the 1960s and 1970s, sexual harassment had been normalized in the workplace to the extent that women were actually encouraged to embrace it. Here's Helen Gurley Brown, the longtime editor of *Cosmopolitan*, from her 1964 book *Sex and the Office*: "A married man usually likes attractive, approving females around him whom he may or may not think of as sex objects. (You'll never get *me* to say this is wrong!) He may not be planning to bag you for his collection but only trying to ascertain your basic attitude toward men. One Little Miss Priss who thinks hemlock is preferable to sin, even when it isn't *her* sin, can spoil a man's pleasure in his work. An attractive girl textile executive says, 'I'd rather have a man making a good healthy pass at me any time than have him cutting my work to ribbons.'" That is a real quote. It's like she's contracted sexual Stockholm syndrome.

A 1960 study by the National Office Management Association found that 30% of 2,000 companies surveyed agreed that they gave "serious consideration" to sex appeal in hiring receptionists, switchboard operators, and secretaries.

The term *sexual harassment* was coined in 1975 by the journalist Lin Forley, who'd been teaching a course at Cornell University about women and work. She invited female students to a "consciousness raising" session and asked about their experience in the workplace. "Every single one of these kids had already had an experience of having either been forced to quit a job or been fired because they had rejected the sexual overtures of a boss," she said in a 2017 interview with *On the Media* host Brooke Gladstone.

Forley cast about intentionally for a term—a label—that would capture these shared experiences, and she settled on *sexual harassment*. She later wrote in the *New York Times*, "Working women immediately took up the phrase, which finally captured the sexual coercion they were experiencing daily. No longer did they have to explain to their friends and family that 'he hit on me and wouldn't take no for an answer, so I had to quit.' What he did had a name."

Above we talked about how habituation can help with phobias by normalizing the problematic. What Lin was doing, with the term *sexual harassment*, was the opposite: She wanted to problematize the normal. To reclassify the coercive treatment of women as something abnormal—to attach a stigma to it. She helped society awaken from problem blindness by giving the problem a name.

~~~~~~

Problem blindness is as much a political phenomenon as a scientific one. We all participate in a perpetual negotiation about what we will sanction as a "problem" in our lives and in our world. These debates carry weight because once something is coded as a "problem," it demands a solution. It creates an implied obligation. Sometimes these negotiations are with ourselves, as with the drinker who denies she has a "problem," and sometimes with others close to us, as with a marital negotiation over whether to go to therapy. In society, there is a crowded marketplace of problems, all vying for a greater share of our resources and attention.

Sometimes we convince ourselves to address the wrong problems. In 1894, when more than 60,000 horses were transporting people daily around London, the *Times* predicted that, "In 50 years, every street in London will be buried under nine feet of manure." Let's leave aside for a moment the logistical implausibility of that particular nightmare. (How exactly would the 9th foot of manure have been added to the top of the pile?) Still, it was not a totally unreasonable fear: those 60,000 horses had an average daily "output" of 15 to 35 pounds of manure. At the first international urban planning meeting in New York City in 1898, the horse manure crisis was the talk of the conference. Fortunately, as we all know, the crisis never came. It was relieved by the advent of the automobile. (And, in turn, it's now the car's excretions— CO_2 and particulates—that have caused us big problems.)

To see what it's like to be on the inside of a present-day fight against problem blindness—a fight to awaken and mobilize the public against a problem—let's trace the work of a Brazilian activist named Deborah Delage, whose awakening came when she gave birth to her daughter.

In August 2003, Delage, who was 37 weeks pregnant, came to see her obstetrician in the city of Santo André, São Paulo, for a routine checkup. When she arrived, her doctor said she was already in labor—she'd been having contractions so mild that she hadn't taken them seriously. She was given a dose of oxytocin (often called Pitocin in the US), a drug that causes the muscles of the uterus to contract in order to speed up delivery. Twelve hours later, the doctor decided to perform a C-section, and Sofia was born. Both Deborah and Sofia were healthy and recovered well.

Delage was grateful for their health, but as she reflected on the experience, she grew increasingly unsettled. Why had they needed to accelerate the delivery? Why had her doctor seemed so eager to perform a C-section?

She found a discussion forum on the internet where mothers shared their experiences in childbirth, and many of their experiences mirrored hers: Despite wanting a natural childbirth, they had ended up receiving C-sections. Many of them, in fact, reported that their doctors had *discouraged* natural childbirth. "I realized that what had happened to me was also happening to other women across the country. It was happening to everybody," she said.

She soon discovered statistics that backed up her intuition. C-section rates vary quite a bit around the world: 18% in Sweden, 25% in Spain, 26% in Canada, 30% in Germany, and 32% in the US for live births in 2016. In Brazil in 2014, the rate was 57%, one of the highest in the world. And in the country's private health system, favored by wealthier Brazilians, a mind-boggling 84% of children were delivered via C-section.

A C-section is major surgery, of course—it has risks for both mother and child. It can be a lifesaver in certain situations. But at the rate of 84%, it's clear that C-sections weren't being used to escape risk or danger. They were being used to escape inconvenience. What caused the shift away from natural childbirth? It's a much-debated topic both in Brazil and worldwide. For some women, a C-section is a matter of preference—you can plan for them. Some argue that the C-sections in Brazil's private health system are a kind of status symbol. There are even stories about high-end private clinics in Brazil offering manicures and massages to go with the C-sections.

But the more convincing case is that *doctors* prefer C-sections. After all, C-sections can be scheduled in an orderly fashion, one after another. No need to work late hours or weekends or holidays. And the financial incentives strongly favored C-sections: Obstetricians could make much more money performing C-sections—which require maybe an hour or two of work—than they could delivering babies naturally, which might involve intermittent work over a 24-hour period.

Along with these structural explanations were cultural ones. "Childbirth is something that is primitive, ugly, nasty, inconvenient," said Simone Diniz, commenting on doctors' perceptions of natural birth, to the *Atlantic*. Diniz is a public health professor at the University of São Paulo. "There's the idea that the experience of childbirth should be humiliating. When women are in labor, some doctors say, 'When you were doing it, you didn't complain, but now that you're here, you cry.'"

That verbal abuse sounds like an extreme case—but according to Brazilian women, it's not. In a survey of 1,626 women who'd given birth in Brazil, about a quarter of them said that the doctor made fun of their behavior or criticized them for their cries of pain. Over half of them said that, during the childbirth, they felt "inferior, vulnerable, or insecure."

This was the reality Deborah Delage—who had felt misgivings about her own C-section—was discovering as she researched childbirth in Brazil. On the online forum she'd found, the mothers' overlapping experiences reinforced their belief that something needed to change. Delage joined a new group called Parto do Princípio (roughly, "Principled Childbirth"), which had been founded to advocate for mothers.

In 2006, Parto do Princípio submitted a 35-page document—half research paper, half manifesto—to the Federal Public Prosecutor, arguing that something had gone wrong with childbirth in Brazil. Women overwhelmingly reported that they wanted natural childbirth, the research showed, but they didn't get it. They got C-sections instead. And as a result, the health of both mothers and babies suffered. The paper explained both the systemic causes of the problem and offered a set of recommendations for the health system.

Parto do Princípio won converts within the government,

including Jacqueline Torres, an obstetric nurse and maternal health expert who worked at the ANS, Brazil's regulator for private health insurance. Torres searched the country for people who had shifted the odds back in favor of natural childbirth, and eventually she came across Dr. Paulo Borem.

Borem was working on a pilot project in Jaboticabal—a town about 200 miles north of São Paulo—to increase the rate of natural birth using continuous improvement methods. It had been hard to find a partner for the project. At the first place he'd visited with his idea, he said, "They laughed at me. They said, 'This is ridiculous. The women want C-sections. The doctors want them. There's nothing wrong.'" (This is a perfect articulation of problem blindness.)

But he found a local hospital that was receptive to change. "The doctors told me they want to change," he said. "They thought they were sending too many newborns to the NICU. It was disturbing for them." Babies delivered via C-section are more frequently sent to the neonatal intensive care unit (NICU) after birth, often due to breathing problems that come from being born before full term.

When Dr. Borem started the project, the rate of natural childbirth at the hospital was 3%. "The system was designed to produce C-sections," he said. So he and his collaborators started tweaking the system. Doctors were forbidden to schedule an elective C-section before 40 weeks; the norm had been 37 weeks. They were put into shifts; if a baby was delivered during a doctor's shift, she would handle it—otherwise, another doctor would take care of it. (This was a break from the tradition of a doctor always delivering her patient's baby, which the use of C-sections made easier.) Obstetric nurses were matched with patients to provide continuity through the delivery. And incentives were adjusted to make sure doctors' incomes did not suffer.

Nine months later, the rate of natural childbirth had shot up to 40%.

When Torres from the ANS discovered Dr. Borem's work, she knew she'd found a formula that might work nationwide. In 2015, the ANS launched a major project—Project Parto Adequado (the Adequate Birth Project)—to scale the work of Dr. Borem and his team in Jaboticabal. During the first 18-month phase of the project, which included 35 hospitals, the rate of vaginal delivery increased from 20% to 37.5%. Twelve of the hospitals showed a significant decrease in NICU admissions. In sum, at least 10,000 C-sections were avoided. The next phase of the project, with over three times as many hospitals, began in 2017. Pedro Delgado, a leader at one of the project's partner organizations, the Institute for Healthcare Improvement, said, "The results of phase 1 offer hope for what is possible in Brazil, and as importantly, in several other countries with similar rates across the globe such as Egypt, Dominican Republic, and Turkey."

There is still a long way to go—the work to date is covering only a tiny fraction of Brazil's 6,000+ hospitals. Nevertheless, there are signs that the health system is ready to change. Where initially Dr. Borem's idea was met with mockery, there is now a waiting list of hospitals ready to embrace the project. Dr. Rita Sanchez, an obstetrician and the coordinator of Project Parto Adequado in a participating hospital, said that the campaign struck a chord with her: "We stopped and realized that the number of C-sections was too high," she said. "Much higher than 20, 30 years ago. So we started questioning why and how we got to that point. And I realized that I wasn't even informing my own patients about the risks of a C-section and the benefits of vaginal labor. We, the doctors, didn't see the system changing."

The escape from problem blindness begins with the shock

of awareness that you've come to treat the abnormal as normal. *Wait, why did I feel pressured to get a C-section? Wait, why have we come to accept a 52% high school graduation rate?* The seed of improvement is dissatisfaction.

Next comes a search for community: Do other people feel this way? (Delage: *I realized that what had happened to me was also happening to other women across the country.* Forley on "sexual harassment": *Working women immediately took up the phrase, which finally captured the sexual coercion they were experiencing daily*.) And with that recognition—that this phenomenon is a *problem* and *we see it the same way*—comes strength.

Something remarkable often happens next: People voluntarily hold themselves responsible for fixing problems they did not create. A journalist makes the choice to fight on behalf of the millions of women enduring sexual harassment. A woman pressured into a C-section becomes a champion for thousands of other mothers she'll never meet.

The upstream advocate concludes: *I was not the one who created this problem. But I will be the one to fix it.* That shift in ownership—and its consequences—is what we will analyze next.

CHAPTER 3

A Lack of Ownership

Until 1994, Ray Anderson, the founder of the industrial carpet firm Interface, had lived every entrepreneur's dream. He'd
grown his company from nothing to roughly $800 million in
annual revenue. He'd taken it public. Then came a moment
that gave him grave doubts about what he'd accomplished.

Raised in a small town in Georgia, Anderson attended
Georgia Tech on a football scholarship and spent his early
career in the carpet industry. In 1969, on a trip to Kidderminster, England, he saw modular carpet tiles for the first time,
and it was love at first sight.

Traditional broadloom carpet came in bulky rolls that
might be 12 feet wide or more, which meant that any alter-
ation in an office—say, rearranging the floorplan, or replac-
ing a stained area—required a huge stretch of carpet to be
ripped up and replaced. But 18-inch-square modular carpet
tiles made changes easy. The tiles could be pulled up and reas-
sembled painlessly. They didn't even require glue.

Anderson founded Interface in 1973, at age 38, to bring
carpet tiles to the US on a broad scale. By 1994, after two
decades of extraordinary growth, Interface was one of the largest carpet companies in the world. That year, he was invited
to speak to an internal group that was working to define the
company's stance on "environmental sustainability," a rela-

tively new term at that time. Customers were starting to ask about the issue. Anderson wasn't sure what he would say—his environmental vision up to that point had been nothing more ambitious than staying compliant with the law.

Shortly after receiving the invitation, serendipitously, Anderson received a copy of Paul Hawken's book *The Ecology of Commerce*. In the book, Hawken assailed corporate leaders for their environmentally destructive practices. Hawken was an entrepreneur himself—the cofounder of the retail garden chain Smith & Hawken—and he insisted that business leaders had an obligation to reverse course and steer the global economy away from the brink of man-made environmental collapse.

Another corporate leader might have scoffed at the sentiment. Anderson wept.

He was 60 years old. Retirement was in sight. Interface's success was his greatest professional achievement, but now he wondered whether that success had come at too great a cost. He considered his legacy: *Ray Anderson, the man who plundered the earth's resources in order to make himself and his investors wealthy.* "Hawken's message was a spear in my chest that is still there," he wrote in his memoir.

But, realistically, what could he do? Interface's core business was to sell carpet tile, made from nylon yarn—and nylon is a plastic made from chemicals found in coal or petroleum. In short, Interface burned fossil fuel to make products out of fossil fuel. A double whammy of unsustainability.

Anderson was devastated. What do you do when you realize that the cause of an enormous problem is . . . your own actions?

Jeannie Forrest, an associate dean at Yale Law School, was sitting in the back row of a faculty meeting. There was a guy with a big head in the front row who was blocking her view of the presenter.

"The big head was one of those friendly ones," she said. "You know the kind, tilting first to one side and then another in an attentive way. Driving me nuts. I kept tilting in the reverse to accommodate: He'd tilt left and I'd tilt right. Then he'd tilt right, and I would swivel left. I could feel myself getting aggravated . . . Suddenly it occurred to me that I was completely capable of moving my chair instead of getting further annoyed. I did," she said. Problem solved.

It frustrated her that it had taken so long to figure out what should have been obvious: that she had full control over the "problem." Her memory of the chair-moving moment became a kind of instructional metaphor: "Whenever I start to get aggravated about some inane problem, I think, 'Hey, move your chair, why don't you?' and it's an internal code for trying a new approach," she said.

At first, Forrest had perceived the problem—i.e., the presenter-blocked-by-big-head problem—as outside her control. External to her. But then, in a quick mental shift, she claimed ownership of the situation. *Move your chair, why don't you?* This shift mirrors what happens in preventive work.

What's odd about upstream work is that, despite the enormous stakes, it's often *optional*. With downstream activity—the rescues and responses and reactions—the work is demanded of us. A doctor can't opt out of a heart surgery; a day care worker can't opt out of a diaper change. By contrast, upstream work is chosen, not demanded.

A corollary of that insight is that if the work is *not* chosen by someone, the underlying problem won't get solved. This lack of ownership is the second force that keeps us downstream. The first force, problem blindness, means: *I don't see the problem*. (Or, *This problem is inevitable*.) A lack of ownership, though, means that the parties who are capable of addressing a problem are saying, *That's not mine to fix*.

These two forces often go together. Consider the leaders at Chicago Public Schools. In the beginning, what held back work on the graduation rate was problem blindness: *Yes, a lot of students drop out—that's just the way it is*. On top of that, though, was the sense among some teachers and administrators that, even if the poor graduation rate *was* a problem, it wasn't theirs to fix: It's the kids' problem to fix. Or their parents'. Or society's.

And, in a way, those skeptics were right! Dropping out of school is certainly going to hurt the student and her parents more than anyone. But the question is not: Who suffers most from the problem? The question is: Who's best positioned to fix it, and will they step up? The leaders at CPS made the graduation rate *their problem*. They took ownership.

Why do some problems lack "owners"? Sometimes self-interest is to blame: Tobacco companies are in the best position to prevent the millions of deaths caused by their products, but of course doing so would interfere with their ability to make money. Other times the lack of ownership is more innocent, the result of fragmented responsibilities: At Expedia, remember, many groups were *involved* in the issue of customer support calls, but no single group owned the problem of reducing call volume.

In some cases, people may resist acting on a perceived problem because they feel as though it's not their place to do so. Think of a young man in college who is appalled by the incidence of date rape on campus but wonders if it's appropriate for him to join protests led by women. The Stanford researchers Dale Miller, Daniel Effron, and Sonya Zak, in a paper exploring this sense of reluctance, wrote "what often prevents people from protesting is not a lack of motivation to protest, but rather their feeling that they lack the legitimacy to do so."

They call this sense of legitimacy "psychological standing," inspired by the concept of legal standing. You can't bring a suit in the justice system simply because something offended your sensibilities—you've got to show that it affected you. The evidence that you were harmed gives you standing to bring a case. The young man who's reluctant to join a protest against date rape may feel he lacks psychological standing, since he hasn't been affected personally by the issue.

How could the college women leading the protest extend psychological standing to the young man, assuming they wanted to? It might be surprisingly simple. In a study by Miller and Rebecca Ratner, Princeton students were presented with a proposal—called Proposition 174—that was designed to "offend their sense of justice." It proposed reallocating government funds from a worthy cause to an unworthy one. Some students were told the shift would hurt women in particular; others were told it would hurt men.

Both men and women shared the same opinions on the proposition—they both strongly opposed it. But the researchers were interested in whether their opinions would lead to action. So the students were given the opportunity to assist a group called Princeton Opponents of Proposition 174. When students had a vested interest in the outcome (that is, when male students were told it would hurt men and women were told it would hurt women), 94% agreed to sign a petition against the proposition, and 50% agreed to write a statement opposing it. When students lacked a vested interest, those numbers declined to 78% and 22%, respectively. The researchers attributed this drop-off not to selfishness—

remember, both sexes opposed the measure equally—but to a lack of psychological standing. The men didn't feel quite right fighting for a "woman's cause," and vice versa.

To confirm this intuition, the researchers changed the name of the organization, in another condition of the study, to Princeton Men and Women Opposed to Proposition 174. The addition of the words *Men and Women* was a simple way to extend psychological standing to both genders, and it was effective. As a result, students with a vested interest *and* those without one agreed to sign the petition and write statements in equivalent numbers.

Granted, this is Princeton we're talking about, an academic oasis where student life affords plenty of time to sign hypothetical petitions and be opposed to things. Could this idea of extending psychological standing work outside academia? In 1975—long before the term *psychological standing* had been coined—the auto safety advocate Annemarie Shelness and the pediatrician Seymour Charles wrote an article in *Pediatrics* that was intended to motivate pediatricians to take ownership of a problem that they hadn't seen as theirs to fix: the deaths and injuries caused by automobile accidents. The number one killer of kids (older than newborns) was the automobile, and the epidemic was being ignored. More young children, the authors wrote, were killed and injured *inside* vehicles than outside.

At the time of the *Pediatrics* article, all new cars were required to have seat belts for drivers and front passengers, but the great majority of people didn't use them. And car seats for children were available but not widely adopted. (Car seats had actually been in existence since the 1930s, but those early seats had been designed not to boost safety but to elevate kids so they could see out the windows, in hopes that they wouldn't pester the driver.) This may be hard for present-day parents to understand. In today's world, it is difficult to imagine what social and legal sanctions would befall a parent who drove around with a bunch of unsecured toddlers flopping around in the backseat. In the 1970s, that sight was commonplace. Our current obsessiveness about child safety in automobiles is a relatively new phenomenon—and due, in no small part, to the story that follows.

Shelness and Charles insisted that pediatricians were well positioned to be auto safety advocates: "The use of restraints is as much preventive medicine as immunization. . . . No one is in a better position to alert parents to the danger of allowing children to ride 'loose' than the child's doctor," they wrote. Note that the authors were trying to extend psychological standing to pediatricians: *You are the right people to lead action on this problem. It's yours to own.*

It was not an obvious role for pediatricians to play. Pediatricians were trained to diagnose and treat illness, not to lobby for public safety. But the call to take ownership of the issue was well received. One of the people who answered the call was Dr. Bob Sanders. "That article was a stunner to me and I think to other pediatricians across this country," said Sanders in an oral history taken in 2004. Sanders was a pediatrician and county health director who lived in Murfreesboro, Tennessee. He was passionate about prevention. While a medical student, he had delivered one of the first polio vaccine shots ever administered in Tennessee. Later, serving as a resident in an emergency room, he watched a baby die as a result of swallowing an open safety pin. He was devastated; it was a needless, preventable death. "The whole idea of prevention and care was just a big, big part of him," said his wife, Pat, in 2018.

Sanders had joined a statewide safety council, and in 1975, the council's members had begun discussing legislation to require the use of car seats in Tennessee. When the *Pediatrics* article was published, it sparked the council to move more quickly.

The council drew up legislation requiring car seat use for those under four. In 1976, the bill found a sponsor but never made it to the floor for a vote. Following the failure, Bob and Pat Sanders began to step up their lobbying efforts. They transformed their dining room into a war room, with the table covered with the names of the lawmakers and pediatricians they wanted to reach. On the weekends, Bob Sanders would call them in their home districts to make his case.

Opponents of Sanders's bill argued that it encroached on the freedom of parents. "This is a Ralph Nader kind of bill that would take the parents' rights away from them," said State Representative Roscoe Pickering. "I don't want poor people to have to buy these expensive seats." Looking back on the time, Pat Sanders remembers reading a letter written by a parent who complained, "I have the right to send my child in a rocket to the Moon."

In 1977, after intense lobbying, the Child Passenger Protection Act finally made it to the floor of the legislature for a vote, and it passed with about two-thirds support.* On January 1, 1978, Tennessee became the first state in the US to require car seats for children under the age of four.

But there was an unfortunate loophole. Representative Pickering—the parents' rights advocate—had attached to the bill a "Babes-in-Arms" amendment, which allowed parents to keep babies in their arms while driving. "One of the great-

---

*One clever bit of strategy: Bob Sanders recalled in his oral history a rumor that the Tennessee governor might not sign the bill. Sanders called on the pediatrician of the governor's grandchildren to press his case. (Source: AAP oral history of Bob Sanders.)

est thrills a young mother with a new baby can have is to hold and visit with it on the ride home from the hospital," Pickering said in a 1978 article in the *Tennessean*. "Now why go and strap it into a seat belt?"

Because of Pickering's amendment, Sanders knew he had won only a partial victory. Essentially, the law guaranteed safety for young children but made it optional for babies. Sanders started referring to the "Babes-in-Arms" amendment as the "Child Crusher" amendment. In the years that followed the bill's passage, Sanders kept fighting to overturn the amendment, but opponents weren't budging. Then, at a transportation committee hearing in 1981, two parents testified. One was a mother whose 11-week-old infant had survived a crash in a car seat. The other was a father whose month-old baby, unsecured, had died after colliding with the dash in an accident. "We were the unlucky ones who didn't have the seat," the father said. Sanders found that, in 1980, 11 children under the age of 3 died in car crashes. Nine of them were in their parents' arms at the time.

This evidence shifted opinion against the amendment, and in 1981, it was repealed. That same year, West Virginia became the third state to require car seats for young children. By 1985, all 50 states had passed child restraint laws.

The National Highway Traffic Safety Administration estimates that from 1975 to 2016, 11,274 children under the age of four had their lives saved by car seats. Think of the cascade of impact: Two automobile safety champions write a pediatric journal article about a problem. The article spurs a Tennessee pediatrician to take ownership of the problem. He motivates a state to act, and that state influences 49 other states, and four decades later, thousands of children are alive who otherwise would have met violent, preventable deaths.

Just as the *Pediatrics* article had spurred Sanders to act, Paul Hawken's book had shaken up Ray Anderson of the carpet-tile company Interface. "I read it, and it changed my life," he said in his memoir. "It hit me right between the eyes. . . . I wasn't halfway through it before I had the vision I was looking for, not only for that speech but for my company, *and* a powerful sense of urgency to do something."

Anderson had a disadvantage relative to Sanders: He wasn't just perceiving a problem that merited action. His company had *exacerbated* the environmental problems Hawken railed against. And at that moment, Anderson had no idea how to undo the harm. But he also had an advantage over Sanders: He could make things happen quickly. He was the boss.

When Anderson arrived to speak to his environmental task force leaders about sustainability in 1994, they had no idea what was coming. They expected to get a stock speech. What they got instead was a call to arms.

Anderson proposed a radical idea: to eliminate Interface's negative impact on the earth. *All those destructive things we're doing to the environment—we're going to prevent them. And we'll do that while still running a great carpet business.* "I gave that task force a kick-off speech that, frankly, surprised me, stunned them, and then galvanized all of us into action," said Anderson. "Unless somebody leads, nobody will. That's axiomatic. I asked, 'Why not us?'"

"When he first came up with this idea, I have to admit I thought he'd gone around the bend," Daniel Hendrix, then the company's chief financial officer, told the *New York Times.* Interface was still recovering from a recession that had battered the company for the previous three years. Was Interface really healthy enough, financially, to take on a new mission of uncertain promise?

But Anderson was relentless. In the short term, he challenged the company to focus on using less energy and consuming fewer resources. The mantra internally was: reduce, reuse, reclaim, and recycle. Some of the early victories came with astonishing quickness: In one division of Interface, simply adding new computer controls on the boilers in a fabric factory slashed carbon monoxide emissions—from two tons a week to a few hundred pounds per year.

Those victories added up. From 1995 to 1996, the company's revenue increased from $800 million to $1 billion *without increasing* the amount of raw materials consumed. The revolution was working. Anderson told *Fast Company*, "The world just saw the first $200 million of sustainable business."

In 1997, at a company meeting that would become famous in company lore, Anderson gave a speech that laid out what would eventually become known as Mission Zero: the quest to achieve an environmental footprint of zero by 2020.

Zero.

This was Interface's "move your chair" moment. *We must take responsibility for fixing this problem.* Anderson had a seven-part plan for achieving Mission Zero: Eliminating waste. Making emissions benign. Running on renewable energy. Using resource-efficient transportation. Closing the loop (by reclaiming anything they put out in the world and reconstituting it as an input). Sensitizing stakeholders (explaining to people why sustainability is important so they will value it). And redesigning commerce, by focusing on delivering value rather than material.

Anderson prodded his team to think in new ways. As one example, he noted that when customers buy new carpets, they're usually disposing of old ones. Could Interface reclaim the old carpets and recycle them into new products? It was an interesting idea with at least two key flaws. One: No one was aware of any technology that could recycle carpets. Two: Shipping recycled carpets to the home office in Georgia might run afoul of another Mission Zero principle, "using resource-efficient transportation." Here's why: A typical amount of carpet ripped up at a customer site, ready for disposal, might be 400 to 500 square yards. To recycle it, you'd have to ship it via truck to Interface's plants in Georgia. But it's horribly inefficient to send 400 square yards of carpet when a full trailer could hold 4,000 yards.

Given these obstacles, the carpet-recycling idea might have been abandoned at another manufacturer. But the team at Interface knew Anderson wanted them to figure it out. For the carpet-hauling problem, they organized a network of partners around the country that could store loads of carpet, 400 yards at a time, until they had a trailer's worth to send to Georgia. Meanwhile, a global search was underway for a technology that could recycle carpets. They found and acquired an expensive backing machine from Germany that could break down old carpet tiles, transforming them into vinyl crumb, which could be remelted into a new carpet backing. Old carpets became new carpets. They had closed the loop.

Anderson's new "save the world" mission had become intoxicating to employees. Somehow the employees found ways to maneuver around every roadblock. Even Daniel Hendrix, the CFO who'd been skeptical at first, became a convert: "We became a culture of dreamers and doers."

Suddenly people were seeking out work at the boring carpet manufacturer. David Gerson cold-called the company in 2000 after hearing about the company's work on sustainability. He'd grown up in New York City, and he said, "If you'd told me then that someday I'd be working for a carpet company in LaGrange, Georgia, I would have laughed. And been a little bit offended." What he found at Interface surprised him. "It was the perfect outlet to enable me to be a part of something much bigger than I could do on my own."

By 2007, Interface was well on the way to realizing Anderson's vision. Fossil fuel use was down 45% even as sales had grown 49%. Interface used only a third of the water it had used previously, and its use of landfills had been cut by 80%. Anderson scored Interface as having traveled about halfway to where it needed to be. No one had demanded that Interface become more sustainable—they demanded it of themselves. They took ownership of their environmental impact. And it was working.

Four years later, in 2011, Anderson passed away at the age of 77. At his funeral, he was eulogized by Paul Hawken, whose book had sparked Anderson's transformation. Hawken said that Anderson was "extraordinarily credible. He was also courageous. He stood up again and again in front of big audiences and told them that pretty much everything they knew, learned, and were doing was destroying the earth. He meant every word he spoke, and those words landed deeply in the hearts and minds of the hundreds of thousands of people he addressed. . . ."

~~~~~~~~~~

What should we make of the Interface story? There are some aspects that read like fantasy. In 2012, the company helped to run a project in which fishermen were paid to retrieve abandoned fishing nets from the ocean—nets that polluted the waters and endangered wildlife—and those nets were shipped to a plant in Slovenia, transformed into nylon fiber, and woven into Interface carpet tile, which was subsequently purchased and installed in an office somewhere in the US, and right now there's an employee walking across it to get a cup of coffee, and she has no idea that the supply chain for the carpet under her feet *actually made the earth's oceans cleaner*. That's magical.

On the other hand, Interface as a business enterprise has not been a roaring success for shareholders. If you'd invested your money in Interface at the beginning of 1994, the year of Ray Anderson's epiphany, through the end of 2018, your annual return would have been 3.6%, compared to the market's overall return of 9.06%. It's possible that the company's environmental work traded off directly with shareholders' returns. It's also possible, though, that without the product innovation and branding that came from the focus on sustainability, the company would have performed worse. It's hard to judge. But it's fair to say that this wasn't a fairy-tale story where everyone won.

Perhaps what the Interface story illustrates is not that efforts at preventing problems always pay for themselves, or that good intentions are always rewarded—neither is true— but that we should push against complacency. What harms do we accept that we're capable of changing?

It would have been effortless for Interface to assume that, as a carpet manufacturer, it would always be a polluter. And in Tennessee, Dr. Bob Sanders could have led a long, successful life as a pediatrician, never dipping his toe into politics, assuming it was beyond his influence.

The question they asked themselves was not: Can't someone fix this problem? It was: Can *we* fix this problem? They volunteered to take ownership. Notice, though, that it wasn't obvious to Ray Anderson or Bob Sanders that they should accept that burden. They were provoked. Challenged. Might the rest of us be unwittingly allowing problems to persist that we could help solve? How do we open our own eyes?

One idea comes from Jeannie Forrest, the "move your chair" woman. Before joining Yale, she was a clinical psychologist and executive coach, and that training in deciphering human motives has aided her work as a manager. In February 2019, for instance, she had to untangle a dispute between staff members. One woman—we'll call her "Dawn"—reported to another woman, "Ellen." Dawn had filed a complaint about Ellen, accusing her of constantly undermining and belittling her.

Forrest brought the two women together in her office. As she remembers the meeting, she started by stating, "I'm accountable for this. Let me tell you how I'm responsible. I've heard rumors that you weren't getting along, and I've heard from your boss that there was trouble. You know what I did? I looked the other way. I thought, *They'll work it out.* I ignored you and I'm sorry."

Then she said, "I'd like each of you to tell the story of this situation as though you're the only one in the world responsible for where we are." Both of the women had a hard time honoring this request. They lapsed quickly into finger-pointing. "Every time I try to give you instructions," said Ellen, "you shut me down. You ask a bunch of unnecessary questions." Forrest would redirect her: *No, that's blaming Dawn. Tell me the story as if YOU were responsible.*

Eventually, they got it. Ellen said, "Well, I assumed her questions were mean-spirited. I thought that, well, she should just take what I said without questioning me. But I could have explained what I wanted better."

Dawn said, "I accepted her huffing and eye-rolling and didn't address it immediately. I should have said, 'Look, you're huffing at me and I don't understand what you want. Help me understand it better.' "

(To be clear, there are limits to this "find your accountability" approach. Imagine if the situation had involved a supervisor who sexually harassed a female subordinate. It would have been outrageous to ask the woman to "tell the story as if you were the only one responsible." That's victim-blaming. The strength of this tool is in helping to identify possible "levers of action" in situations where many factors may contribute to a problem.)

All three women (including Forrest) had initially handled the situation as though they were trapped in it. But when Forrest prodded them to explain the situation as if they were the ones responsible, they uncovered their power. They went from feeling like victims of the problem to feeling like co-owners of the solution. Six weeks after this mediation, Forrest reported, they were "working together productively and cheerfully. It's a little insane."

This, in essence, was the same thing Ray Anderson had demanded of his staff: Let's tell our story as if we were 100% responsible for the environmental degradation we cause. And when you look at the world that way, you start to see angles of influence: computer controls on boilers, methods for melting down old carpet, incentives for dredging the seas of nylon nets. You start to surface strands of causation that were always there—but buried.

Forrest's question can help us filter out the noise in complex situations. What if you told the story of your relationship problems as if you were the only one responsible? What if employers told the story of their employees' health as if they were the only ones responsible? What if school districts told the story of high school dropouts as if they were the only ones responsible? Asking those questions might help us overcome indifference and complacency and see what's possible: *I choose to fix this problem, not because it's demanded of me, but because I can, and because it's worth fixing.*

CHAPTER 4

Tunneling

John Thompson, semi-retired and living in Goderich, Ontario, had been forgetting to use the twice-daily eye drops that were prescribed for his glaucoma. So he decided to put the drops on the windowsill above the kitchen sink—that way, he'd spot them every time he made coffee in the morning. "Also, I put the drops on the east side of the sill so I would know they were for the morning," he said. "After putting them in my eyes, I would move them to the west side of the sill. That would confirm that I had put drops in in the morning and cue me to put drops in at night. After I did that, I would put the drops back on the east side of the sill." Thompson's windowsill system eliminated the problem.

Rich Marisa had a similar upstream epiphany in his personal life. "My wife had been unhappy with my leaving on lights, particularly the one light in the hall when I go out or come in," said Marisa, an application programmer who lives near Ithaca, New York. The hallway lights were a minor source of marital friction—the kind of trivial thing that keeps people bickering for years. ("You left the toilet seat lid up again!")

But Marisa realized he could prevent these arguments from happening. By filing for divorce.

I'm kidding. Sorry. Here's what he actually did: "I took

ownership of the situation and got a timer light switch. Now I push the button and get five minutes of light. Then the light turns off, and what was an issue just isn't anymore," he said.

In my research, I sought out stories like these—people who stopped reacting to problems and started preventing them. I found them oddly inspirational. I started micro-analyzing my own life, looking for recurring irritants that I could vanish with a bit of upstream witchcraft.

I used to spend a lot of time shuffling my laptop power cord, for instance. Despite having a proper office with a proper desk, I seem to do my best work in coffee shops. I was always unplugging the cord, packing it, and plugging it in somewhere else. So—prepare to be astonished—I bought a second power cord. Now one stays on my desk permanently, and the other resides in my backpack.

These are easy victories. All they require is an awareness of the problem and a small measure of planning. Yet in my interviews, I found that it was difficult for most people to think of their own examples. (This is not my way of bragging, by the way: Remember, I shuffled power cords for years—and what finally sparked action was, um, *writing a book on upstream thinking*.) Which raises the question: If upstream thinking is so simple—and so effective in eliminating recurring problems—why is it so rare?

Consider how easy it would have been to derail my own upstream thinking. If anybody in my family had been sick, I wouldn't have been pondering small improvements. Or if I'd been stressed out over work or relationships. All of this is probably intuitive: We would expect big problems in life to crowd out little problems. We don't have the bandwidth to fix everything.

But this issue of "bandwidth" is actually more insidious than that: Researchers have found that when people experience *scarcity*—of money or time or mental bandwidth—the harm is not that the big problems crowd out the little ones. The harm is that the little ones crowd out the big ones. Imagine a single mother who can barely pay the bills each month and who has maxed out her credit card. Her kid needs $150 to play in a local basketball league. She can't bear to say no—it's one of the few healthy opportunities open to him in the neighborhood. But she doesn't have the money and is still 10 days from her next paycheck. So she takes out a payday loan from the lender down the street. She'll need to repay the loan in a month with 20% interest (the equivalent of a 240% APR). And if she doesn't, it will roll over, and the interest will mount. It's not a huge amount of money, but it might be enough extra debt to make her precarious finances topple.

A financial advisor would say the woman has made a bad financial decision. But her son got his opportunity, and she has bought herself a few days or a few weeks of crucial maneuvering room. The crisis may come, but not today. The psychologists Eldar Shafir and Sendhil Mullainathan, in their book *Scarcity*, call this "tunneling": When people are juggling a lot of problems, they give up trying to solve them all. They adopt tunnel vision. There's no long-term planning; there's no strategic prioritization of issues. And that's why tunneling is the third barrier to upstream thinking—because it confines us to short-term, reactive thinking. In the tunnel, there's only *forward*.

It's often said that a chain of bad decisions can lead people to be poor. That is undoubtedly true in some cases. (Think of the highly paid superstar athlete who later declares bankruptcy.) But Shafir and Mullainathan argue convincingly that we've got the causation backward: that in fact it's poverty that leads to short-sighted financial decisions. As the authors write, scarcity "makes us less insightful, less forward-thinking, less controlled. And the effects are large. Being poor, for example, reduces a person's cognitive capacity more than going one full night without sleep. It is not that the poor have less bandwidth as individuals. Rather, it is that the experience of poverty reduces anyone's bandwidth." When people's resources are scarce, every problem is a source of stress. There's no way to use money as a buffer—by keeping a car's maintenance up to date, by paying out of pocket for a dental visit, by taking a few days off work to stay with a sick parent. Life becomes a tightrope walk.

People who are tunneling can't engage in systems thinking. They can't prevent problems; they just react. And tunneling isn't just something that happens to poor people—it can also be caused by a scarcity of time.

"Scarcity, and tunneling in particular, leads you to put off important but not urgent things—cleaning your office, getting a colonoscopy, writing a will—that are easy to neglect," wrote Shafir and Mullainathan. "Their costs are immediate, loom large, and are easy to defer, and their benefits fall outside the tunnel. So they await a time when all urgent things are done."

But of course we never run out of urgent things to do, and all of the sudden, we're 70 years old without a will. This tunneling trap plagues organizations, too. Anita Tucker, an industrial engineer who once supported the operations of a General Mills frosting plant, did her dissertation at Harvard by shadowing 22 nurses in 8 hospitals for almost 200 hours in total. What she discovered was that the nurses were, in essence, professional problem solvers. An unexpected problem popped up every 90 minutes or so, on average. As a representative example, after one three-day weekend when some of the laundry staff had been off duty, a nurse noticed that her unit had run out of towels. So she nabbed some towels from a neighboring unit, then asked the secretary to call laundry for more.

The most common types of problems encountered by nurses, Tucker noted, included dealing with missing/incorrect information and contending with missing/broken equipment. In one case, Abby, a nurse on duty, was preparing to discharge a new mother from the hospital. Abby noticed that the woman's newborn wasn't wearing a security tag. The tags, worn around the ankle, are expensive (about $100 apiece) and important—they reduce the risk of abductions. After a quick search, Abby found the tag in the baby's bassinet. Then, three hours later, the same thing happened again: Another baby who was about to be discharged was missing a tag. This time, a hunt by multiple people came up empty, so Abby let her manager know that the tag was lost. Because of her quick actions, both mothers were discharged with only a brief delay.

To overcome problems like these required the nurses to be creative. Persistent. Resourceful. They didn't go running to the boss every time something went wrong. They worked around the problems, so they could keep serving their patients. That's what it meant to be a good nurse.

It's an inspiring portrait, isn't it? Until you realize something: What Tucker is describing is a system that *never learns*. Never improves. "I was really shocked, to be honest with you," Tucker said. Shocked because what Tucker had observed was the utter absence of upstream action.

Abby, who dealt with two missing security tags in three hours, didn't think to ask, *Why does this keep happening?* The nurse who nabbed extra towels didn't think, *Hey, we've got a process problem here—we need a plan for handling three-day weekends.*

The nurses were tunneling. Their time was scarce; their

attention was scarce. Grabbing towels from another department—which might cause *that* department to run out a few hours later—is roughly the equivalent of taking a payday loan. The bill will come due, but not right now. For the moment, the nurses can keep digging forward.

Is the intent of this story to throw stones at nurses? Hardly. My guess is that if Anita Tucker had picked another group of professionals to shadow—lawyers or flight attendants or teachers—the results would have been about the same. And, by the way, think of how unnatural it would have been for those nurses to escape the tunnel. Okay, so a nurse discovers that newborns' security tags are prone to falling off. She tells her supervisor. What else could she be expected to do? Conduct an on-the-spot root cause analysis, while she's got a dozen patients who need her attention right now? And, by the way, how are her colleagues going to feel about someone who is always yammering on about "fixing processes" rather than simply grabbing more towels from another unit? It's so much easier—and more natural—to stay in the tunnel and keep digging ahead.

It's a terrible trap: If you can't systematically solve problems, it dooms you to stay in an endless cycle of reaction. Tunneling begets more tunneling.

Tunneling is not only self-perpetuating, it can even be emotionally rewarding. There is a kind of glory that comes from stopping a big screw-up at the last second. Look at all the clichés we have at our disposal: "Team, we owe Steve a big round of applause for putting out that fire / saving the day / bailing us out / rescuing us from disaster. If it weren't for him, those inventory stock-out reports would have been a day late." Saving the day feels awfully good, and heroism is addictive. We all have colleagues who actually seem to relish those manic "stay up all night to meet the critical deadline" adventures. And it's not that the day doesn't need saving, sometimes, but we should be wary of this cycle of behavior. The need for heroism is usually evidence of systems failure.

How do you escape the tunnel? You need slack. Slack, in this context, means a reserve of time or resources that can be spent on problem solving. Some hospitals, for instance, create slack with a morning "safety huddle" where staffers meet to review any safety "near-misses" from the previous day—patients almost hurt, errors almost made—and preview any complexities in the day ahead. A forum like that would have been the perfect place for a nurse to mention, "The security ankle bands keep falling off the babies!"

The safety huddle isn't slack in the sense of idle time. Rather, it's a guaranteed block of time when staffers can emerge from the tunnel and think about systems-level issues. Think of it as structured slack: A space that has been created to cultivate upstream work. It's collaborative and it's disciplined. The same idea was used in the Chicago Public Schools effort to reduce the dropout rate: The Freshman Success Teams had a standing meeting where they reviewed progress on a student-by-student basis. This kind of forum will never happen "naturally": It's no trivial feat to carve out time from teachers' already crazy schedules.

Escaping the tunnel can be difficult, because organizational structure resists it. Remember the quote from Mark Okerstrom, the CEO of Expedia: "When we create organizations, we're doing it to give people focus. We're essentially giving them a license to be myopic." Focus is both an enemy and an ally. It can accelerate work and make it more efficient, but it puts blinders on people. (Racehorses wear blinders so they'll ignore distractions and run faster.) When your emphasis is always *forward, forward, forward*, you never stop to ask whether you're going in the right direction.

It's even fair to say that our own brains are designed for tunneling. Harvard psychologist Daniel Gilbert argues that a focus on the immediate and the urgent is a default feature of our thinking. In an article for the *Los Angeles Times*, he wrote:

> Like all animals, people are quick to respond to clear and present danger, which is why it takes us just a few milliseconds to duck when a wayward baseball comes speeding toward our eyes. The brain is a beautifully engineered get-out-of-the-way machine that constantly scans the environment for things out of whose way it should right now get. That's what brains did for several hundred million years— and then, just a few million years ago, the mammalian brain learned a new trick: to predict the timing and location of dangers before they actually happened.
>
> Our ability to duck that which is not yet coming is one of the brain's most stunning innovations, and we wouldn't have dental floss or 401(k) plans without it. But this innovation is in the early stages of development. The application that allows us to respond to visible baseballs is ancient and reliable, but the add-on utility that allows us to respond to threats that loom in an unseen future is still in beta testing.

Upstream thinking, in Gilbert's telling, is a new feature of our brains.

There are only two areas of concern that seem to reliably trigger our upstream instincts: our kids and our teeth. When it comes to our children, we're capable of thinking *years* down the road: Are they getting too much screen time? Are they eating healthy diets? Will they be able to get into a good college?

Somewhat more puzzling is the regard we show for our

teeth, the most coddled organ in our body. Even as our skin is shorted sunscreen and our hearts denied a brisk jog and our immune systems refused an annual flu shot, we make it a priority on every single day of our lives, even the busiest ones, to perform a twice-daily regimen of preventive scrubbing. And then we report to a dentist regularly for a more rigorous appraisal. We might even cap or fill a particular tooth, even if it's not causing us any discomfort at the time. Ponder this fact for a moment: The most successful preventive habit we have developed as a species is for the preservation of our . . . ~~lungs brains hearts~~ teeth.

Could we someday learn to pamper and preserve the planet half as much as we do our teeth? The ongoing international failure to slow down climate change meaningfully would suggest not. For years we've been laughing at those dumb metaphorical frogs that won't jump out of the boiling pot until it's too late. Turns out we're the frogs.

Climate change is like a product designed by an evil mastermind to exploit every weakness in the human psyche: It changes too slowly to spark urgency. It lacks a human face: As Dan Gilbert wrote in the piece cited above, "If climate change had been visited on us by a brutal dictator or an evil empire, the war on warming would be this nation's top priority." To address climate change successfully would require people to collaborate across nations and parties and organizations in tribe-defying ways. Finally, climate change features a mismatch of acts and consequences: The people who are causing most of the harm are not the ones who will suffer the most as a result.

That portrayal appears bleak, but here's one hopeful counterpoint: In the recent past, humanity rallied to solve a major global environmental threat that shared all of the traits described above: the depletion of the ozone layer. Let's go back to 1974, when the scientists Mario Molina and F. Sherwood (Sherry) Rowland published a paper in *Nature* titled "Stratospheric Sink for Chlorofluoromethanes: Chlorine Atom-Catalysed Destruction of Ozone." It was a sober title for a frankly apocalyptic finding.

The scientists had discovered something about chlorofluorocarbons (CFCs), chemicals used as propellants in spray deodorants and coolants in air conditioners, among other applications. CFCs were a dream to work with, because they were both nonflammable and nontoxic. Extremely stable, too—they hung around in the atmosphere for a long time, and nobody had thought very much about where they ended up after they escaped from your fridge or armpit. What Molina and Rowland figured out is that the CFCs would rise in the atmosphere higher and higher until, eventually, they'd be broken down by the sun's rays, releasing chlorine, which would eat up the world's ozone layer, a critical shield against ultraviolet radiation. The potential result: disruption of the world's food supply and skin cancer in epidemic proportions.

So what happened after their bombshell findings were released? Not much. "It didn't make any noise because we were talking about invisible gases reaching an invisible layer [that protected us from] invisible rays," said Molina in the excellent PBS documentary *Ozone Hole: How We Saved the Planet*. "They said, 'Oh, you must be exaggerating.'"

They weren't exaggerating. Fortunately, the world didn't end, because an international coalition came together to restrict CFCs in a series of agreements, including the Montreal Protocol in 1987, which was described by one climate scientist as "a tap on the brakes," and progressing to the Copenhagen amendment in 1992, which was more like a screeching deceleration. (There have been several more agreements since.) As a result, humanity has stopped making the problem worse. The ozone layer is not "fixed" by any stretch—it won't return to its 1980 level of health until 2050, if present trends continue. But we have stopped digging our own grave, and our willingness to set aside that shovel seems worth celebrating.

There's a paradox inherent in preventive efforts: We've got to create an urgent demand to fix a problem that may not happen for a while. We've got to make the upstream feel downstream, in other words. Think about the situation in 1974, when Molina and Rowland released their paper. There were a few dozen people in the world, maybe, who felt the hair-on-fire urgency needed to address ozone depletion. Imagine a global heat map depicting "passion for fixing the ozone layer," with a blazing red speck marking the location of Molina and Rowland's academic departments and the rest of the planet covered in an indifferent blue. By 10 years later, red had spread like wildfire—we were on the cusp of a global agreement. How did that happen?

The first thing to realize is that "creating urgency" is basically coopting the power of tunneling for good. Rather than try to escape the tunnel—as with the discussion on slack—we can try to use the extreme focus it provides to our advantage. Who hasn't been at their most productive—and most motivated—when staring down a deadline? A deadline supplies artificial urgency to a task. Consider the April 15 tax deadline in the US. It's an arbitrary date, but it has real power over behavior. About 21.5 million Americans file their taxes in the last week before the deadline. As the deadline looms, you eventually drop everything else and get it done.* It's not that you've

---

* Imagine if we didn't face a tax deadline, and instead, we could submit our taxes for the previous year any time we liked. After January, though, each month we waited would add an additional 2% interest to the amount owed, like a credit card balance that keeps rolling over. One suspects that this would be a terrific moneymaker for the federal government—if we didn't eventually run out of cash as a nation as the IOUs mounted.

stopped tunneling. It's more like the government has jammed the task into the tunnel, ensuring that you'd get it done.

We'd all love for our pet issues to be "in the tunnel," but it's crowded in there. Our demands have to compete with many other pressing and emotional concerns: getting the kids to soccer practice and crunching the data for the boss and visiting grandma at the nursing home. If you don't do these things, they don't get done. Meanwhile, the ozone layer stuff sounds important but ultimately outside of your daily concerns. Out of your tunnel. To combat that indifference, many of the scientists involved, including Sherry Rowland, became vocal advocates for action—against their own training and instincts—stressing the human consequences of ozone depletion, even to audiences who were hostile to their findings.

Their advocacy created converts in unexpected places. In 1975, the TV show *All in the Family*—the most popular show in America—ran an episode in which Mike (aka "Meathead"), a liberal college student, chastises his wife, Gloria, for using hair spray with CFCs, saying the chemicals will destroy the ozone layer and "kill us all." The sale of aerosol sprays dropped noticeably after the episode aired.

What also helped spread urgency was the term *ozone hole*, which is familiar today but actually was not embraced until the mid-1980s—a decade after the *Nature* publication. Some scientists objected to the term as inaccurate, but it caught on immediately with the public. The research scientist Richard Stolarski said on a podcast that "it certainly made it easier to reach a greater part of the public by having a simple key word that you could describe it by." The notion of a "hole" made the problem easier to visualize and invoked an action mind-set. When there's a hole in something important—a roof or a boat or a sweater—you fix it. Holes are urgent; slow depletion of the ozone layer isn't.

There was also another side of the campaign: handling potential opponents to international action. Companies like DuPont, a top producer of CFCs, had fought the bans for years, but by the time of the Montreal Protocol, DuPont had become a supporter. Two researchers who later studied DuPont's role in the issue concluded that "DuPont's support for the protocol had also depended on US officials' ability to assure that the European-based producers could not gain a competitive advantage through any provisions of the international treaty." In other words, DuPont likely would have resisted a US-only ban. But if all its global competitors faced the same ban, it wouldn't feel disadvantaged.

Other opponents included the leaders of developing nations, who complained about bearing high costs for a problem that was largely not of their making. Margaret Thatcher, then prime minister of the UK, led the charge to ask industrialized countries to contribute most of the necessary resources. (The "Iron Lady" might seem an unlikely champion of the ozone work, but her background provides one clue: She studied chemistry in college and was briefly a research chemist.)

Before these compromises, international action on the ozone layer would have been a *threat* to DuPont and to the developing nations. Threats are urgent, by definition. So what international negotiators were accomplishing was a kind of orchestration of urgency: Supporters needed to feel more urgency and opponents needed to feel less.

Success stories like this one can acquire inevitability in retrospect. *Of course we fixed the ozone layer—we had to!* But there were countless ways for the whole effort to have blown up. To cite just one example: In May 1987—just a few months before the Montreal Protocol was signed—the US Interior Secretary Donald Hodel was quoted as speaking critically in internal debates about the proposals, suggesting that instead of a CFC ban, people could start wearing hats, suntan lotion, and sunglasses. A media firestorm followed. (You almost wish Twitter could be beamed back in time to react to that comment.) Hodel backpedaled, and the Reagan administration remained a critical player in the accords.

President Reagan, initially a skeptic, eventually became a believer in the work. As Secretary of State George Schultz said of Reagan's attitude in the PBS documentary: *Maybe you're right that nothing is going to happen, but you must agree that if this does happen, it's going to be a catastrophe, so let's take out an insurance policy.*

Climate scientists use the phrase "the world avoided" to discuss the problems that were prevented by the ozone layer agreements. "I think it helps us to contemplate the world we've avoided," said Sean Davis, a researcher at the National Oceanic and Atmospheric Administration (NOAA), in a TEDx talk. "The world we've avoided by enacting the Montreal Protocol is one of catastrophic changes to our environment and to human well-being. By the 2030s, we'll be avoiding millions of new skin cancer cases per year, with a number that would only grow."

"The world avoided" is an evocative phrase. In some ways it's the goal of every upstream effort: To avoid a world where certain kinds of harm, injustice, disease, or hardship persist. The path to "the world avoided" is a difficult one because of the barriers we've seen: problem blindness (*I don't see the problem*), lack of ownership (*That problem is not mine to fix*), and tunneling (*I can't deal with that right now*).

As we move into the next section of the book, we will study leaders who've fought for "the world avoided." The problems they're seeking to avoid are wide ranging in both domain and significance: from domestic violence to elevator breakdowns to invasive species to broken sidewalks to lost customers to school shootings. But despite the great difference in focus, the strategies they've embraced share critical similarities. They've each, in their own way, had to address seven key questions, ranging from: "How will we unite the right people?" to "Who will pay for what does not happen?"

Just ahead we will encounter a nation that has accomplished the unthinkable: almost eliminating the problem of teenage substance abuse. If you think a generation of happily sober teenagers is a fantasy, turn the page.

SEVEN QUESTIONS FOR UPSTREAM LEADERS

~~~~~~~~

CHAPTER 5

How Will You Unite the Right People?

In 1997, a photograph was taken in downtown Reykjavík, Iceland, that would later become emblematic of a major national problem. It shows a city block jammed thick with people—the heads are mostly blond, with a few brunettes sprinkled in. It's summertime in Iceland, when the sun doesn't really set so much as take a breather for a few hours. So even though the photo was shot at 3:00 a.m., all those faces are pretty easy to see, and almost every last person in the picture is a drunk teenager.

The teens have taken over the city.

In 1998, 42% of Icelandic 15- and 16-year-olds reported having been drunk in the previous 30 days. Almost a quarter smoked cigarettes daily, and 17% had already tried cannabis. "I remember having helped a friend of mine to puke in an alley," said Dagur Eggertsson, a physician who became mayor of Reykjavík in 2014. "And another friend actually fell into the sea—he was trying to balance on an oil pipe in the harbor area. . . . These were normal stories. This was part of growing up. This was part of getting your first paycheck, when you were working during the summer, when you were 14."

This behavior went beyond normal teenage hijinks. Among 22 European countries, Icelandic tenth-graders had the second-highest rate of accidents or injuries related to alcohol use. They were near the top, too, in other disturbing categories: the percentage who'd been drunk at the age of 13 or younger and the percentage who'd been drunk 10 or more times during the previous year. To the Icelandic teenagers, this was all normal—it was the world they knew. But as the rate of substance abuse crept up almost every year during the 1990s, a group of leaders grew concerned.

The leaders had awoken from problem blindness—they were no longer willing to write off this teenage behavior as natural or inevitable. They resolved to move upstream. So, now what?

To succeed, leaders of upstream interventions need to address seven key questions, and in this section of the book, we'll devote a chapter to each one. We'll explore both the reasons why each question can be difficult to answer *and* the strategies smart leaders have used to overcome those obstacles. The first of those seven questions is: How will you unite the right people?

Recall that many upstream efforts are a kind of volunteer work. Chosen, not obligated. That was true in Iceland: Many people and government agencies had to cope with the consequences of teenage substance abuse, but it was no one person's or agency's job to prevent it (at least at the beginning). But many people cared enough to try. So the first step, as in many upstream efforts, was to *surround the problem*—to recruit a multifaceted group of people and organizations united by a common aim.

In 1997, a handful of those people—primarily academic researchers and politicians—launched an anti-substance-abuse movement called Drug-free Iceland. The campaign team eagerly courted help from anyone who was willing to assist: researchers, policymakers, schools, police, parents, teenagers, singers/musicians, NGOs, government agencies, municipalities around Iceland, private companies, churches, health care centers, sports clubs, athletes, media members, and the State Alcohol and Tobacco monopoly. This may sound like a sprawling set of collaborators, but keep in mind that most Icelanders live in or around the capital city of Reykjavík, which has a population of less than 250,000. In land area, the whole nation is about the size of Kentucky (the key distinguishing features from Kentucky being its active volcanoes, massive glaciers, and Björk). The point being, in Iceland a few hundred leaders from different domains could be connected together relatively quickly.

What attracted these parties was a brand-new vision for combatting drugs and alcohol. Traditionally, the work had focused on individual behavior change: getting teenagers to abstain from alcohol or drugs. But the campaign leaders in Iceland believed that the historical focus on "saying no" missed the big picture: What if the drugs were never offered at all? Or what if the teens enjoyed some other activity—soccer or theater or hiking—so much that they didn't feel like getting drunk? In short, what if drug and alcohol use came to feel *abnormal* in their world rather than normal? "We wanted to change communities in order to change behavior among the kids," said Inga Dóra Sigfúsdóttir, a social scientist and one of the campaign's key leaders.

Academic research has identified a number of risk factors for teenage substance abuse: Having friends who drink or smoke is an obvious risk. Another is having lots of unstructured time available to hang out with those friends—at parties or, say, in downtown streets at 3:00 a.m. There are also *protective* factors that reduce the risk of substance abuse.

Most of them boil down to having better ways for teens to spend their time: by participating in sports and extracurricular activities, or simply by hanging out more with their parents. (Interestingly, research suggests the quantity of time spent matters more than quality—which was not altogether welcome news for many Icelandic parents, Sigfúsdóttir reported.) In short, a teenager's discretionary hours are finite, so a well-behaved hour can crowd out a badly behaved one.

The campaign's guiding philosophy, then, was simple: Change the culture surrounding teenagers by reducing the risk factors for substance use and boosting the protective ones. The people involved—from parents to politicians to sports club leaders—had different resources at their disposal, but what they shared was an ability to influence one or more of those factors.

Communities and parents worked to change the culture around popular festivals, where many teens had hung out unsupervised, to encourage families to attend together. Teenagers were recruited to script and shoot anti-drinking television commercials.

Most of the efforts relied on cooperation by multiple players. One example: Iceland had long prescribed certain hours when kids could be outside, depending on their age. This "outside hours" policy was basically a friendlier version of a curfew, with no legal penalties for kids caught in violation. And the policy was frequently ignored. All those kids jamming the streets of Reykjavík in that memorable photograph, for instance—they were all breaking the rules.

To combat this nonchalance, the campaign sent a letter from Reykjavík's mayor and police chief to all parents of young people, encouraging them to honor the outside hours. The letter also included a refrigerator magnet, which showed the specific times when young people were allowed outside.

Previously, said Sigfúsdóttir, enforcement of the outside-hours laws was largely left to parents, which made a villain of the lonely parents trying to stick to the policy. Teens would predictably protest, "Nobody else's parents care about the curfew!" The magnets made the curfews seem more "official" somehow, and compliance increased significantly. (Parents in some communities also took organized walks at night, nudging any teens found outside to go home.)

One of the most creative aspects of the campaign arose from the research of Harvey Milkman, an American clinical psychologist who specializes in addiction. "I had the realization that people were not getting addicted to drugs so much as changing the chemistry of their brains," said Milkman. "So the corollary to that was natural highs." In other words, we shouldn't fight teenagers' instinct to "get high." Instead, we should give them safer ways to get high. The campaign leaders had already known that kids needed better ways to spend their time—that was a classic protective factor—but Milkman's insight added some nuance. Teens don't just need more activities of any kind, they need activities with natural highs: games, performances, workouts, exhibitions. Activities that compel them to take physical or emotional risks.

After the school day ends, Icelandic kids often go to "sports clubs": facilities where students can play a variety of different sports, ranging from soccer to golf to gymnastics. Many communities invested in better coaching in the clubs, so that the soccer coach was no longer a volunteer parent but a paid, experienced veteran. This "professionalization" of the sports was critical: The Iceland team's work on substance abuse draws a distinction between informal and formal sports participation, and it's the latter that counts. If you play pickup basketball down the block with your friends, you're likely to drink just as much (or more) than another teenager who doesn't. But if you play in a basketball league, it's different. You've made a commitment. You're on a team. Your social network orbits a healthy activity. To support participation in sports clubs and other recreational activities, the City of Reykjavík—and later other cities—gave every family what amounted to a gift card, worth hundreds of dollars, to spend on membership fees or lessons.

All these efforts made a difference. An annual survey, "Youth in Iceland," was conducted to measure the alcohol and drug habits of the country's teenagers—and it also tracked the risk and protective factors the campaign had identified (e.g., time spent with parents). The survey served as a kind of scoreboard for the campaign. To review these results, and to plan each successive wave of action, there were meetings. Always meetings. Doctors prescribe, miners dig, teachers teach, and upstreamers *meet*. The steering committee alone met 101 times during the first five years of the campaign. But these meetings are not the same glazed-eye snooze fests that you suffer through at work. When they're done right, upstream meetings can be energizing: creative and honest and improvisational, with the kind of camaraderie that emerges from the shared struggle to achieve something meaningful.

Even in the first few years, the movement saw progress: Participation in formal sports was up. Time spent with parents was up. Compliance with outside hours was up. And that feeling of success—that's the emotional payoff that keeps people engaged in the work and attracts new collaborators to the mission. In 2018, twenty years after the campaign began, teenage culture had been transformed. To make the results tangible, imagine a high school class with 40 students. In 1998, 17 of those students would have been drunk in the last 30 days; in 2018, only 3 had been. Before, 9 students would have smoked every day; after, only 2. Before,

7 would have tried cannabis; after, only 1. The plummeting lines in the graph below tell the story:

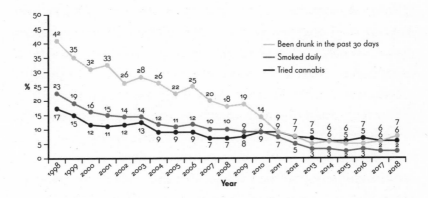

Perhaps the most astonishing part of the story in Iceland is that its success has been so complete as to be invisible. Most teenagers today aren't really aware of it. They've simply grown up in a world where substance abuse is largely absent.

Iceland's campaign became the envy of the world, and teams from cities in other countries—including Spain, Chile, Estonia, and Romania—have been quick to adopt the approach. "There's this one element of this model that is the most important, and it's empowerment," said Sigfúsdóttir. "It's giving communities, giving parents, giving kids a voice. For all of the players in the system, each one of them gets a role. I think that's the driving force behind it."

How will you unite the right people? Start with Sigfúsdóttir's insight: *Each one of them gets a role.* Given that your progress may hinge on people's voluntary effort, it's smart to maintain a big tent.

But a philosophy of "the more, the merrier" is not sufficient. The core team should be selected more strategically. Preventive interventions often require a new kind of integration among splintered components. To succeed in upstream efforts, you need to surround the problem. Meaning you need to attract people who can address all the key dimensions of the issue. In Iceland, the campaign leaders engaged the teenagers *and* almost all the major influences on them: parents, teachers, coaches, and others. Each one had something critical to contribute. By contrast, downstream action is often much narrower. Think of the Expedia example that opened the book: To react to a customer's call required the effort of just one call-center representative. But to prevent that customer from calling *at all* required integration among multiple teams of people.

Once you've surrounded the problem, then you need to organize all those people's efforts. And you need an aim that's compelling and important—a shared goal that keeps them contributing even in stressful situations where, as in the next story, people's lives may depend on your work.

~~~~~~~~~

In 1997, Kelly Dunne, a recent college graduate, had just arrived in the quaint town of Newburyport, Massachusetts, about an hour's drive north of Boston. Shortly after arriving, she responded to a flyer requesting volunteers to help victims in court who had filed restraining orders. After completing some training, she showed up one Monday at the local district court for her first official volunteer shift. She brought a book to read, figuring that not much would have happened over the weekend.

But there were three women already waiting to talk with her. One had spent the weekend locked in her basement. Another had a bruise on her arm, where her child had gripped her frantically while the woman's husband was beating her.

"I was just horrified," said Dunne. She thought, *Holy shit, I can't believe what's going on in this sleepy little New England town over the weekend.* She grew more and more devoted to the work—helping the victims of domestic abuse—and soon she was working full-time for the organization where she'd volunteered, now called the Jeanne Geiger Crisis Center.

Five years later, one of the women she was assisting—Dorothy Giunta-Cotter, a longtime victim of abuse who had tried to exit her marriage while keeping her daughters safe—was murdered by her estranged husband, as reported in the *New Yorker*. He had pushed past one of their daughters at the front door, broken down the door to Dorothy's bedroom, and dragged her out. When the police arrived, he shot Dorothy and then himself. Their two daughters were orphaned.

The murder caused a crisis of faith for Dunne. "I either had to leave the work or really think about what are we doing: How have we set up these systems? And are they really set up in a way that helps people?" Dunne said about her reaction to Dorothy's murder. "Her case showed us where all the gaps in the system were."

The system was splintered into specialized functions: police officers to respond to 911 calls; health care providers to mend wounds; advocates to help victims; district attorneys to prosecute cases; and parole officers to monitor abusers after they served sentences. Women like Dorothy were essentially falling in the cracks between these roles. None of the groups that performed these functions had both the mission and the wherewithal to prevent homicide. Dunne saw that the only way to prevent murder was to unite these groups and to direct their focus toward the women at greatest risk.*

But how can you know, in advance, which women are at the greatest risk of becoming victims of homicide? The question led Dunne to the work of Jacquelyn Campbell, a nurse and a leading domestic violence researcher at Johns Hopkins University. Earlier in her career, Campbell had had her own awakening to the epidemic of domestic violence. While seeking a master's in nursing, she worked with the local police department in Dayton, Ohio, to review all the cases in which a woman had been murdered by a husband, boyfriend, or ex. (If a woman is murdered, there's a nearly 50% chance that the perpetrator fits one of those descriptions.)

Many of the files she reviewed contained crime-scene photographs, and one of those scenes is chiseled into her memory. It showed a woman handcuffed to a chair, dead from a gunshot wound. Her husband had shot her in the temple. It was a gruesome scene, but there was another detail that drew Campbell's attention. The woman had a cast on her arm. The file showed that she'd broken her ulna—one of two parallel bones in the forearm—along with the radius. When people have accidents, they typically break both bones or just the radius. To break the ulna only is unusual and suggests a defensive injury. The woman had been holding up her arm to protect herself when she was hit with something hard enough to break her bone.

But it wasn't the injury that surprised Campbell—every file she reviewed included physical brutality. It was the cast. Because the cast meant that the woman had sought help in

---

* Rachel Louise Snyder in the *New Yorker* tells the story of Dorothy Giunta-Cotter—and the Jeanne Geiger Crisis Center—at greater length. Snyder's moving and insightful article is how I learned about the center's work.

the health care system, and no one had been willing or able to protect her against further harm. "That's why I became convinced that I needed to work with abused women," said Campbell.

Campbell began to study the patterns in cases where domestic abuse escalated to homicide. Some risk factors were foreseeable, such as the abuser having access to guns or being an alcoholic. Others were less obvious: If an abusive partner became unemployed, that put the victim at greater risk. Based on the patterns in the data, Campbell developed a "Danger Assessment" tool, which has been validated multiple times as an accurate predictor of intimate partner homicide. The current version of the tool asks female victims of abuse to mark on a calendar the approximate dates, over the previous year, when they were abused. Then they are asked to answer 20 yes/no questions about the abuser, including:

- Is he unemployed?
- Does he threaten to harm your children?
- Does he control most or all of your daily activities? For instance: Does he tell you who you can be friends with, when you can see your family, how much money you can use, or when you can take the car?

Years later, Kelly Dunne, who had become one of the top leaders at the Geiger Center, realized Campbell's Danger Assessment tool represented an early-warning system that might have prevented Dorothy's homicide. Had Dorothy filled out the questionnaire, she would have scored an 18 out of 20: Extreme danger. Campbell's tool offered advocates something new: the time to intervene before the worst happened. Now Dunne had to figure out how to use that time.

In 2005, she organized the Domestic Violence High Risk Team, composed of all the people who had regular interaction with abuse cases: police officers, parole and probation officers, staff from a local hospital, advocates for victims, someone from the DA's office, and even a group that offered an intervention for batterers. She was surrounding the problem. The high-risk team of 13 to 15 people met once a month to review the cases of women who had scored the highest on Campbell's Danger Assessment.

It's hard to overstate how uncommon—and unlikely—this collaboration was. In many communities there was outright hostility between victims' advocates and police officers, for instance. What all these people had done up to that point, primarily, was pass the baton to each other in the course of their work: The hospital would refer a victim to the advocates; the advocates would tell the police about a violent abuser; the police would refer a case to the DA; and so on. But they'd never sat at the same table to work together—and certainly not with an eye toward *prevention* rather than reaction.

In their meetings, the high-risk team would review cases, one by one. Often the first step was to create an emergency plan for a woman: Where would she go if she needed to escape? Who would pay for a hotel or taxi? Who would be notified? Another frequent conversation concerned the need for "drive-bys": Police officers would start driving by a victim's house during their rounds, in order to send a signal to the abuser: *We're watching.*

The drive-bys sent a signal to the victims, too. Bobby Wile, a now-retired detective in nearby Amesbury, mentioned an officer who was doing a drive-by of one woman's house and noticed something that made him stop. "So he parked and knocks on the door and he asks the lady, 'Is everything okay?' And she said, 'Yeah, why? What's up?' And he goes: 'Well, that light is on in the attic and that light hasn't been on. I just want to make sure everything is okay.' She was ecstatic." Ecstatic because a police officer was paying close enough attention to notice that a new light was on. She invited the officer in and gave him cookies.

As the team worked together, they began to identify flaws in the system that could be exploited by abusers. When offenders were required to wear GPS bracelets as a condition of release, for instance, there was often a gap of a few days between their release and their first parole appointment, at which point they'd receive the bracelet. "Well, for two days, where are they?" said Detective Wile. "Now it's protocol: You get released. We bring you up to probation, and the bracelet is put on immediately. That way, [the offender] is not going to get those two days."

"Twenty years ago, if you told me police officers would be sitting in the same room with domestic violence advocates, sharing coffee and a laugh and socializing together, I would have told you that you were delusional," said Doug Gaudette, an advocate from another organization that's part of the high-risk team. "But now that's happening."

Since 2005, the team has accepted over 172 high-risk cases. Ninety percent of those victims reported no subsequent re-assault. In the 10 years prior to the formation of the high-risk team, there were 8 domestic violence–related deaths in the area, according to Dunne. And in the 14 years since the high-risk team began to serve those communities, with a mission to protect the women at greatest risk of violence, not one woman has been killed in a domestic violence–related homicide. Not one.

The lesson of the high-risk team's success seems to be: Surround the problem with the right people; give them early notice of that problem; and align their efforts toward preventing *specific instances* of that problem. To clarify that last point, this was not a group that was organized to discuss "policy issues around domestic violence." This was a group assembled to stop particular women from being killed.

Note the similarity to the Chicago Public Schools story earlier in the book. Remember this quote from Paige Ponder, who led the district's Freshman On-Track efforts: "The beautiful thing about teachers—you can have whatever philosophy you want, but if you're engaged in a conversation about Michael, you care about Michael. It all boils down to something real that people actually care about. . . . 'What are we going to do about Michael next week?' "

That same motivation led the work in Newburyport. The cops and DAs and advocates and health workers all had different institutional priorities. But what they shared was a desire not to see one of their neighbors murdered by her abusive husband. And that shared aim became the fuel for their coordination.

The other point of connection between the two stories is the primacy of data, which was a theme I observed repeatedly in my research, and one that surprised me. I knew data would be important for generating insights and measuring progress, but I didn't anticipate that it would be the *centerpiece* of many upstream efforts. I mean this even in a literal sense— what the teachers and counselors in Chicago were doing, and what the high-risk team members in Newburyport were doing, was sitting around a table together and looking at data. Discussing how the fresh data in front of them would inform the next week's work.

In Chicago, the data was: Has Michael been coming to

school since we last met? How are his grades in all of his courses? How can we help him this week? In Newburyport, the data was: Where was Nicole's abuser? What has he been doing? How can we help her this week?

This kind of system is what Joe McCannon calls "data for the purpose of learning." McCannon is an expert in scaling up efforts in the social sector—a former nonprofit and government leader, he has advised movements in many countries. McCannon distinguishes "data for the purpose of learning" from "data for the purpose of inspection." When data is used for inspection, it sounds like this: *Smith, you didn't meet your sales targets last quarter—what happened? Williams, your customer satisfaction numbers are going down—that's unacceptable.*

Using data for inspection is so common that leaders are sometimes oblivious to any other model. McCannon said that when he consults with social sector leaders, he'll ask them, *What are your priorities when it comes to data and measurement?* "And I never hear back 'It's important to set up data systems that are useful for people on the front lines.' Never," he said. "But that's the first principle! When you design the system, you should be thinking: How will this data be used by teachers to improve their classrooms? How will this data be used by doctors and nurses to improve patient care? How can the local community use the information? But that's rarely how the systems are designed."

McCannon believes that groups do their best work when they are given a clear, compelling aim and a useful, real-time stream of data to measure their progress, and then . . . left alone. The situation at Expedia, with its millions of unnecessary calls, provides a model. A cross-functional group is presented with a goal: Help millions of our customers avoid the nuisance of calling us. That's a valuable and challenging target. And then the group is basically locked in a room together, armed with regularly updated data to see if the number of calls is going up or down. The team members come up with theories and then they test them. They watch what works. That's the "data for learning" part. They don't need a boss standing over them, hollering out specific targets: "We need to cut four percent call volume by tomorrow!"

The team members hold each other accountable, and the data keeps them honest and keeps them pushing. Making data useful for the front lines can be a daunting task. But sometimes grounding an effort in concrete data is the only way to unlock the solution to a major problem.

In 2014, Larry Morrissey, the then-mayor of Rockford, Illinois, was challenged by a colleague to take the Mayor's Challenge, a campaign promoted by the federal government with the goal of ending veteran homelessness in communities around the nation. Morrissey was approaching the midpoint of his third term as mayor, and he'd been working on the issue of homelessness since he first took office, nine years prior.

Homelessness was partly a by-product of the hard times Rockford was enduring. In 2013, an article in the *Wall Street Journal* painted a bleak picture about the city, which is about 90 miles northwest of Chicago: "Once a prosperous manufacturing hub that created the airbrush and electric garage-door opener, Rockford is now the nation's underwater capital. In about 32% of the metro area's mortgages, the homes are worth less than the money owed." Morrissey felt the pain; his mortgage was underwater, too.

Rockford's population (about 150,000 in 2018) had been shrinking since the great recession as people fled for better opportunities. "The entire town had a form of codependency," said Morrissey. "We were addicted to mediocrity. We were accustomed to failure. We resembled as a community a lot of the characters you would see in a family bound by addiction. A lot of finger pointing, a lot of blame." To Morrissey, homelessness was a symbol of this defeatism: It was "ground zero for encompassing so much of what was wrong."

Even though Morrissey knew homelessness was important, when he was challenged to take the pledge, he was skeptical. "For a decade, I'd been working on homelessness," he said. "In my first term, we developed this ten-year plan to end homelessness, and we hadn't done it. If anything, maybe things had gotten worse. . . . What's gonna change?"

He reluctantly took the pledge and agreed to attend a training session in Chicago along with some social services colleagues in early 2015. The training was led by the federal Department of Housing and Urban Development (HUD). He was the only mayor in a room filled with housing people.

Morrissey and his colleagues weren't expecting a transformational experience—it was a workshop run by a federal agency, after all. Yet the session became a turning point in Rockford's work on homelessness, for the simple reason that Morrissey finally understood why they'd failed. "The lightbulb went off," he said. "I realized what the missing ingredients were."

Less than a year later—on December 15, 2015—Rockford became the first city in the United States to have effectively ended homelessness among local veterans. How could the city spin its wheels on homelessness for nine years and then achieve dramatic success in less than one?

The first change was mental. Jennifer Jaeger, Rockford's community services director, and one of the key leaders in the work on homelessness, called it her "'I believe in fairies' moment." "The very first step is to believe you can actually do it," said Jaeger. "It's hard. It's a big mind shift. It's no longer just taking care of the problem, which is what we were doing historically, but *ending* the problem."

I met with Jaeger in the fall of 2018 in the city's human services department building in Rockford. Her drab, windowless office was large and peculiarly shaped, like a jigsaw puzzle piece, and in the tab of that puzzle piece was a towering stack of small white boxes—hundreds of low-flow showerheads. They were to be part of some energy-efficiency kits being distributed to low-income people; there was apparently nowhere else to store them. If there were a recruitment poster for upstream work, it would feature Jaeger's office, with its mountain of showerheads, along with the slogan: IF IT'S GLAMOUR YOU'RE AFTER, GET BACK DOWNSTREAM.

In the aftermath of the HUD training, the team in Rockford made three critical shifts en route to ending veteran homelessness: a shift in strategy, a shift in collaboration, and a shift in data. The strategic shift was to embrace what's called "housing first." In the past, the opportunity to receive housing was like a carrot dangled in front of homeless people to encourage them to fix themselves: to receive substance abuse treatment, or treatment for mental illness, or job training. The idea was that homeless people needed to earn their way into housing.

"Housing first" flips that sequence. It says that the *first* step in helping the homeless—not the last—is to get them into housing as soon as possible. "I stopped thinking of people as 'homeless' and started thinking of them as people without houses," said Jaeger. "All a homeless person is, is somebody without a house. The same issues homeless people have, people who are housed have. . . . People who are housed can start working on those other issues."

Along with the "housing first" strategy came a shift in collaboration, involving what's known as "coordinated entry."

Cities have many different housing options for homeless people—supportive housing, transitional housing, shelters, and more—and there are many different agencies that interact with the homeless. Imagine a hotel with seven different front desks, each with its own set of policies for who can book a room and how long they can stay, and so on. It was a "willy-nilly" system, said Angie Walker, a colleague of Jaeger's. "Everybody just took whomever they wanted, whenever they wanted," she said.

Now, Walker said, "Our office here, we're the single point of entry. If you're homeless and you need a place to live, you need to come in here." The advantage of coordinated entry is that you can be thoughtful about who receives housing. You can prioritize. In the willy-nilly system, the people who received housing were often the people who asked for it first—or worse, the people who were *easiest* to house. Since organizations were often rewarded for how many people they had housed, they had an incentive to cherry-pick the ones who could be housed with the fewest headaches.

The new mandate was: House the most vulnerable people, the people who most desperately need housing. And that's where the final shift—the shift in data—fits in. Previously, Rockford's housing team conducted an annual "point in time" census of the homeless population. It was required by HUD. And its method was to visit all the homeless shelters in the area during a particular day and count the number of people there. "Nobody even went out to the streets to actually count unsheltered people," said Walker. When she took over the count, she fixed that. The census evolved from a "point in time" count, conducted once a year, to something that's called a "by-name list."

The by-name list is a real-time census of all the homeless people in Rockford, listed by name in a Google Doc. It includes notes on their history and their health and their last-seen location. And the use of the by-name list is uncannily similar to the high-risk team's work in Newburyport. Once or twice per month, a group of collaborators in Rockford—representatives of the VA, the fire department, the health and mental health systems, and social service agencies—meet to discuss homelessness. And when they meet, they talk about the specific people on the by-name list.

Angie Walker described how she might kick off a typical meeting: "I would say, 'John Smith, he is thirty-two. He stated he was fleeing domestic violence. He last said he's with friends. Who here has seen John Smith?'" And the fire department might say, *Oh, we took him to the hospital last week—he might still be there.* Then someone from the mental health team might say, *No, I was under the bridge two days ago and I saw John.* A worker at the local homeless shelter, the Carpenter's Place, might add, *John has come for lunch quite a bit recently.* And then the group would make a plan. *Okay, Carpenter's Place, it seems like you see him the most. Could you check with him and find out where he's staying and what he needs? And let him know that when he's ready, we have housing available for him.*

These meetings had happened in the past, but the use of the by-name list transformed them. Mayor Morrissey said that, previously, the meetings had been "bitch sessions." "We'd sit around and we'd talk about what's broken," he said. Jennifer Jaeger said the meetings "feel alive now. The data itself feels like it's sort of a living creature. Because it talks. It talks to us. . . . It tells us, 'You need to look at this, you need to think about this.'"

Beth Sandor, the head of Built for Zero, a national effort to help communities end homelessness, said that when communities begin to use data in this way, it's transformational.

"Data takes you away from philosophical insights. You move away from anecdotal fights about what people *think* is happening to what *is* happening," she said. "You can't solve a dynamic problem with static data." (Rockford is one of more than 60 communities that have joined the Built for Zero movement.)

Using the process outlined above, Rockford housed 156 veterans in 2015 before they achieved what's called "functional zero."* In 2017, they achieved functional zero on the chronic (long-term) homeless population, and they hoped to reach that milestone with youth homelessness by the end of 2019. It's remarkable, really, how much changed in Rockford—given how little had changed. What hadn't changed: the people involved with homelessness, the resources they had at their disposal, and the city's macro conditions. Simply by changing the way they collaborated, and the goals that guided their collaboration, their efforts became dramatically more effective.

"Every day is hard," said Walker. "Getting people housed is hard. Dealing with landlords is hard. I fight with my clients. I fight with agencies. It's an uphill battle, it really is—you know the picture they always show of the guy pushing the rock up the hill? I mean, it's like that every day. But if the outcome is to end homelessness, it seems to be worth it."

Walker and Jaeger have begun to work on the problem of

---

*Functional zero means that the number of homeless people on the street is lower than the city's monthly housing placement rate. E.g., say that the city has proven that it can move five people per month from the street into housing. If there are only four homeless people in the community, then the city still maintains its "functional zero" status. This is not some kind of loophole—it's just an acknowledgment that "real zero" is impossible, for the time being, because new people will unfortunately become homeless. The point is that even if new people become homeless, they can quickly be housed because the system is working.

"inflow"—reducing the number of new people who become homeless. It's a thorny problem, for all the reasons you'd expect, but they've already identified one leverage point: evictions. In some neighborhoods in Rockford, the eviction rates are as high as 24%. In early 2019, the city conducted a pilot program in which it acted as an intermediary between tenants and landlords in situations where eviction was imminent. In some cases, the city negotiated a new payment plan for the landlord and tenant; sometimes, the city also contributed money on behalf of the tenant. A month or two of rent payments was far more cost-effective than re-housing people if they became homeless. Jaeger reported that the pilot had decreased the number of people who became homeless due to eviction by 30%.

They're moving further upstream: Rather than acting quickly to serve people who are homeless, they're trying to keep people in their homes to begin with. That's an example of systems change, which is the topic we'll explore next. Can we learn to reengineer the machinery that *creates* problems? And, in the process, can we improve the odds that the problems will not arise in the first place?

CHAPTER 6

How Will You Change the System?

Raised in Montreal, Anthony Iton moved to Baltimore in 1985 to go to medical school at Johns Hopkins University, intending to become a surgeon. But when he first arrived in Baltimore, he saw a sight that would change his life: the blighted neighborhoods of East Baltimore.

"I thought somebody had dropped bombs on the place," he said. "People sitting with these dazed looks on their stairs and I was like, 'What the hell is this?'" Iton, who is African Canadian, had never seen black people in conditions like what he saw in Baltimore. There's no real equivalent in Canadian cities.

"I was being toured around by a black upperclassman, and I looked shocked, and he asked me what was wrong," said Iton. "I said, 'When was there a war here?' He said to me, looking at me disdainfully, 'What did you expect? It's the inner city.'"

Iton couldn't believe the way Americans just shrugged their shoulders about urban poverty. "How is this possible in this first world country?" he said. "This country that describes itself as number one in everything and the greatest place on earth? What is this? It just didn't make any sense to me. It was a shock to my conscience."

Years later, in 2003, this sense of injustice would return to him. In the interim, Iton had completed his medical degree and added a law degree from the University of California at Berkeley as well as a public health master's, also from Berkeley. He'd taken a role as the director of the Alameda County Public Health Department, and he'd grown interested in the life expectancy of the people he served. While many public health departments published data on life expectancy, it was often aggregated into a regional summary—the average life expectancy of everybody in Alameda County. But Iton and his colleagues were interested in something more precise: tracing life expectancy *by neighborhood*. His inspiration? "East Baltimore," he said. "Having been there, I thought, *You can't tell me that this doesn't have an impact on people's health*."

None of his predecessors had ever done this analysis, but Iton realized that he had all the data he'd need at his fingertips. It was all there on the county's death certificates: race, age at death, cause of death, place of residence. As part of his job, Iton signed or robo-signed every one of those certificates. ("No one dies until I sign off on it," he joked.)

The results of this analysis were shocking. In 2009, the writers Suzanne Bohan and Sandy Kleffman, assisted by Iton's colleague Matt Beyers, chronicled the results in a series for the *East Bay Times* called "Shortened Lives." In the 94597 ZIP code in Contra Costa County (Walnut Creek), life expectancy was 87.4 years. In the 94603 ZIP code in nearby Alameda County (Oakland neighborhood Sobrante Park), it plummeted to 71.2 years. Iton's team had uncovered a 16-year gap in life expectancy in two areas that were 22 miles apart.

The same pattern was unearthed in other cities where the data was compiled: Baltimore, Minneapolis, Los Angeles, and others. In Cleveland, a 4-mile walk from the Shaker Heights neighborhood to the Baldwin Water Treatment Plant took about 80 minutes, and over the span of that walk, 23 years of life expectancy vanished. "It's like having Sweden and Afghanistan in the same city," Iton said.

What was fascinating to Iton was that no one could seem to explain these gaps. Many believed that the key issue must be health care access—perhaps the people with shorter life expectancies were uninsured or had poor medical-care options. But analysis of the data showed that access accounted for only a small part of the variance. Maybe people in poorer areas of town died more often from AIDS or homicide? Maybe the infant mortality rates were higher? All three theories were accurate, unfortunately—but, again, they made up only a small part of the variance. Even larger factors, such as unhealthy behaviors (in particular a higher incidence of smoking), failed to explain a big part of the gap.

As the analogy to Sweden and Afghanistan suggests, a 15- to 20-year gap in life expectancy is *massive*. You can't account for it with a few incremental factors. It takes huge, systemic forces to produce a disparity like that.

What Iton realized was that it wasn't a particular thing that was causing the life expectancy gap. It was everything. "Fundamentally, what causes people to get sick and feel sick is a sense of a lack of control over what's happening to them," he said in a radio interview. "They're literally under siege. They're struggling to find housing, they're struggling to find good education, to avoid crime, to find jobs, to find healthy food, in some cases even potable drinking water. So low-income people in this country are basically juggling a whole bunch of balls simultaneously."

The result of that constant juggling is stress. These communities were "incubators of chronic stress," he said in a TEDx talk. "Low-income people are physiologically different than high-income people. Not because they were born that way, but because we made them that way." There's a well-established link between chronic stress and a variety of health problems, among them cardiovascular disease, diabetes, and inflammation.

And that's why the health care system was so poorly positioned to close the gap. The problem was not the lack of treatment. It was the lack of health. Remember: "Every system is perfectly designed to get the results it gets." These neighborhoods were systems designed to produce premature deaths.

For Iton, this was a tough realization: The tools he had been trained to use, as a doctor and a public-health official, were inadequate to address the problem. How do you remake a system that's hopelessly broken?

~~~~~

In 1962, the San Francisco Giants were preparing to host the LA Dodgers for a crucial three-game series, late in the season. The Dodgers, led by master base stealer Maury Wills, were five and a half games ahead of the Giants. Before the series began, the Giants manager approached Matty Schwab, the team's head groundskeeper, and asked if anything could be done—wink wink—to slow down Wills.

"Dad and I were out at Candlestick before dawn the day the series was to begin," said Jerry Schwab, Matty's son, as quoted by Noel Hynd in *Sports Illustrated*. "We were installing a speed trap." Hynd continues:

> Working by torchlight, the Schwabs dug up and removed the topsoil where Wills would take his lead off first base. Down in its place went a squishy swamp of sand, peat

moss and water. Then they covered their chicanery with an inch of normal infield soil, making the 5- by 15-foot quagmire visually indistinguishable from the rest of the base path.

The Dodgers were not fooled. When the team began batting practice, the players and coaches noticed the quicksand, and so did the umpire, who ordered it removed. Schwab and the grounds crew came out with wheelbarrows, shoveled up the mixture, and returned soon after with reloaded wheelbarrows.

It was the same bog. They'd just mixed in some new dirt, which made it even looser.

Somehow the umpires were satisfied. Then Matty Schwab ordered his son to water the infield. Generously. By the time the game started, there was basically a swamp between first and second base. ("They found two abalone under second base," wrote an irritated Los Angeles sports columnist.) Maury Wills, en route to an MVP season, stole no bases, and neither did his teammates, and the Giants won, 11–2. Pleased, the Schwab father-son team continued to conjure more marshy conditions, and the Giants swept the Dodgers—and went on to leapfrog them to win the National League pennant.

There's something admirably mischievous about this story. I mean, it's cheating, let's be clear, but it's *cheeky* cheating. It's fun to think that the father-son groundskeeping team pulled one over on the National League's MVP. The underdogs won one—they tilted the odds in favor of their home team.

Now, imagine a black-mirror version of this story, outside the world of sports, where it's the underdogs who lose, again and again, because the game has been rigged against them. Their bats are heavier, their gloves are smaller, the fences are pushed back, and in every direction, they must run through a bog. That's in essence what Tony Iton had found in his ZIP code work. The odds were tilted so far against the people in certain neighborhoods that they couldn't win.

There are always exceptions, of course: There are healthy people in low-life-expectancy areas and sick people in healthy neighborhoods. With tremendous effort and support, individuals can transcend bad neighborhoods. Every year, we read about a kid with every strike against her who is admitted to Harvard. We rejoice for her. But should we?

"Every year I read that story, I get irritated," said Iton. "Of course, there are smart kids of color in the inner city! There are millions of them. We're celebrating this one kid— who deserves to be celebrated—but we're not asking the real question: Why is this such a rare story?"

Systems are machines that determine probabilities. In the most well-designed systems—like the neighborhoods with the highest life expectancies—the probabilities are overwhelmingly in your favor. It's like playing a game of roulette where you win if you hit red—and you win if you hit black. In badly flawed systems, like the worst neighborhoods, you still get to play roulette. There's still an element of choice and chance. But the only way you can win is by hitting one of those green pockets, 0 and 00.

When we marvel at the inner-city kid who gets into Harvard, we're marveling at the odds she defied. But what we don't appreciate is that our celebration of her carries an implicit indictment of the environment we put her in. *We forced you to climb Everest to get ahead in life—and you did it! Congratulations!* (No one gets misty-eyed reading the story about the Greenwich, Connecticut, hedge funder's kid who makes it into Harvard.)

Upstream work is about reducing the probability that problems will happen, and for that reason, the work must culminate in systems change. Because systems are the source of those probabilities. To change the system is to change the rules that govern us or the culture that influences us.

The writer David Foster Wallace once told a story: "There are these two young fish swimming along and they happen to meet an older fish swimming the other way, who nods at them and says 'Morning, boys. How's the water?' And the two young fish swim on for a bit, and then eventually one of them looks over at the other and goes, 'What the hell is water?'"

The system is the water. Sometimes, it's literally the water. For decades, tiny amounts of fluoride have been added to community water supplies as a way to protect people's teeth against cavities. It's an invisible program—when's the last time you thought about fluoride in your water?—yet its impact has been enormous. More than 200 million people in the US have access to fluoridated water, and the program has been so successful that the CDC named it 1 of the 10 greatest public health achievements in the twentieth century. One study estimated that for every $1 spent on water fluoridation, society saves $20 in avoided dental costs.*

A well-designed system is the best upstream intervention. Take auto safety: In 1967, about 5 people died for every 100 million miles driven. Fifty years later—thanks to fewer drunk drivers and better roadways and seat belts and airbags and better braking technologies—that number has declined to about 1 death per 100 million miles driven. That's a vastly improved system, and there was no central planner. No single "system architect." Rather, thousands of people—auto safety experts and transportation engineers and Mothers Against

---

*And that's not counting the anxiety avoided by fewer dentist visits. In the spirit of upstream thinking, I'd like to propose "preemptive laughing gas" treatment, to commence 24 hours before visiting the dentist. . . .

Drunk Driving volunteers—tweaked the system so that millions of other people could be safer. They shaped the water.

And they shape it still: Despite the success, there are still more than 37,000 people who die annually from car crashes in the US. Someday, self-driving cars might come close to eliminating those fatalities. In the meantime, there are countless tweaks being made every week to help fallible human drivers. On sharp curves where accidents tend to happen, transportation departments have begun to install high friction surface treatments (HFSTs)—overlays of ultra-rough material superglued to existing roads. In Kentucky, where the treatments have been used widely, crashes have been reduced almost 80%. None of those drivers, who avoided crashes they would have suffered in an alternate world, will ever know that they may owe their lives to some construction workers who installed a super-gritty road. When the water changed, the outcomes changed.

The same logic can be applied to business, of course—problems can sometimes be solved with minor changes to the environment. In some fast-food restaurants, customers were throwing away the plastic trays their food was served on. So the restaurants responded by using trash cans with smaller circular holes that do not accommodate trays. Problem solved, forever.

The Dutch bicycle company VanMoof received complaints that many of its bikes were damaged during shipping. Bex Rad, the creative director, wrote on Medium that "too many of our bikes arrived looking like they'd been through a metal-munching combine harvester. It was getting expensive for us, and bloody annoying for our customers." Their solution? They started printing images of flat-screen televisions on the side of their shipping boxes, which are very similar in shape to flat-screen TV boxes. "Our team sat together and we imagined that couriers would be more careful with packages if they knew even more precious goods were in them," the cofounder Taco Carlier told a journalist. Damaged goods were reduced by 70% to 80%.

What's the "water" you're not seeing in your home life or at work? What's interesting is that our kids can often see the water. They pick up on things we're not even aware of. My friend told me about watching his baby daughter hunched over a pack of playing cards, running her index finger back and forth and poking it. He was confused until he realized: *She's mimicking me on my phone.* "That's when I realized maybe I was spending a bit too much time on my iPhone," he said. Another father reported online that, while driving on the interstate, his two-and-a-half-year-old asked from the backseat: "Any idiots out today, Dad?" Our kids see the real us.

They don't see everything, of course. For our children, we're the system architects. We are the justice system, the housing department, social services, and (for a while at least) the education system. As mentioned a few chapters back, parenting is a rare exception where upstream thinking comes naturally. Almost everything we do as parents is with an eye toward our kids' future happiness and health: the childproofing and the "say please" hectoring and the books and the rules and the lessons and the vain attempts to get them interested in things without glowing screens. It's all upstream.

What would the world look like if we extended half of the same concern to our neighbors' kids and their futures?

No child should have to hit the green zeroes on a roulette wheel to succeed in life. A fair and just society is built on fair and just systems. And as obvious as that may seem, even the people who strive for fairness and justice sometimes forget it. The tragedy of so much work in the social sector is that leaders tacitly accept the flawed system that begets their work. Years ago, I worked with the leaders of a foundation whose goal was to boost the financial security of low-income people. One of the programs supported by the foundation offered financial coaching to low-income people. But, let's be clear, the people they served were not poor because they lacked financial know-how; they were poor because they lacked money. They were the products of a system that offered inadequate opportunities. Had they been born inside a better system—say, a neighborhood six miles away—they likely would have earned income sufficient to survive subpar budgeting skills.

Meanwhile, if you followed the flow of the foundation's cash—as it passed through the investment managers who likely skimmed a percent or two every year to watch the foundation's portfolio, through the six-figured top executives, through the grant managers, through the people who managed the facilities where the coaching happened, and the coaches themselves, and the academic evaluators who assessed whether the whole thing was working—you'd eventually realize something shocking: Everyone in this whole ecosystem got paid—except for the low-income people. They got coached.

Think about this program through the lens of systems change. In some ways, the program actually entrenched the very inequalities that spawned it, by creating wonderful job opportunities for well-intentioned and well-educated leaders, but none for the people it was meant to serve. I often wondered whether it wouldn't have been simpler and dramatically more effective to shut down the foundation and walk around the lowest-income neighborhoods handing out cash. That's not systems change, certainly, but at least it would have demonstrably affected the "financial security of low-income people."

DonorsChoose is a website that allows teachers to seek crowdfunding for supplies, computers, books, or other classroom materials. It's a well-run, effective organization, founded by a teacher, that in just under 20 years has allowed over 500,000 teachers to raise upward of $875 million for supplies that otherwise they would have lacked.* Imagine that its rapid growth continues and that 20 years from now, it's serving vastly more teachers—say, a substantial proportion of all classrooms. How is it possible to escape the conclusion that this work would have excused school districts from funding the kinds of supplies that teachers desperately need; trained already overworked teachers to add fundraising to their job descriptions; and empowered private donors to be the gatekeepers who determine which resources can be used in the classroom, granting or withholding funding as they see fit. There is no true equivalent of DonorsChoose in other countries, perhaps because their schools pay for the supplies that students need.

Should DonorsChoose shut itself down for fear of enabling an unjust system? By the same logic, should we criticize food pantries because they make it easier to sustain an inadequate social safety net? It does not seem fair to withhold food from today's needy families—or supplies from today's students—while we wait for reforms that may never come.

DonorsChoose is a crutch for a broken and underfunded education system. And crutches are vital. They are also supposed to be temporary. The DonorsChoose team should aspire to live in a world where DonorsChoose need not exist.

---

* I have donated repeatedly to teachers' projects on DonorsChoose; I gave a keynote at one of the organization's events, and I even wrote about the group glowingly in a past book for its extraordinary practice of sending thank-you notes, hand-drawn by students, to donors. I love this group. I root for them even as I worry about their long-term systemic effects.

The food pantry volunteers, too, should be impatient for a world without food pantries. But they shouldn't just wish for that future, they should push for it. DonorsChoose's website reports roughly 4 million supporters, 500,000 teachers, and 36 million students in their orbit. What if those constituents could be mobilized as a political force? Couldn't they help change the system rather than work around it?

I asked Charles Best, the founder of DonorsChoose, about these issues, and he pointed out that about half of the project requests on the site "go beyond what you'd expect the system to fund: a field trip to see the Supreme Court consider a case, butterfly cocoons to experience the circle of life, therapeutic horseback riding for a disabled student, etc." He also acknowledged that, when it comes to the more basic requests (books, supplies, equipment), "we'd love to be put out of business." Godspeed.

Part of *every* social-sector organization's mission should be to push upstream. To prevent wounds as well as bandage them; to eliminate injustices as well as assisting those who suffered them. That's why the team in Rockford, Illinois—having just made history as the first city to eliminate veteran and chronic homelessness—immediately started pushing upstream. *Can we prevent homelessness by interrupting evictions?*

Systems change is important *within* organizations as well as outside them. Consider, for instance, the efforts of many organizations to hire a more diverse workforce. The first thing to realize is that if you have a large organization filled with a relatively homogenous population of employees, then that composition did not happen by chance. Remember the quote: "Every system is perfectly designed to get the results it gets."

I'm not implying that these hiring systems were engineered

consciously to discriminate. In this age, not many organizational leaders are *opposed* to diversity. But good intentions can't overcome bad systems. (Just as, in the Chicago Public Schools, no teachers or administrators were *opposed* to a higher graduation rate. Quite the opposite. Still, for many years they unwittingly served a system that failed half its students.)

The mystery to be solved is: Why, if most people in this organization want to hire more diverse employees, are we failing to do so? The answer will likely be complex: We're casting our net for employees in a pond that's shallower than we think. Or we're valuing certain kinds of credentials that limit our pool of applicants while not contributing much to job performance. Or we're filtering out candidates because of biases that we're not even aware of.

The solutions to these problems are systemic, not personal. The advocates for change inside the organization should rethink every part of the mis-engineered system. *Maybe we shouldn't recruit only at those same 10 college campuses. Maybe we should disguise the names and genders on the resumes we consider. Maybe we should train our leaders how to conduct better interviews, so that the conversations don't degenerate into small talk.* (Small talk leads us to favor "likable" candidates—in other words, candidates who are just like us.)

Systems change starts with a spark of courage. A group of people unite around a common cause and they demand change. But a spark can't last forever. The endgame is to *eliminate* the need for courage, to render it unnecessary, because it has forced change within the system. Success comes when the right things happen *by default*—not because of individual passion or heroism.

Success comes when the odds have shifted.

And this was the calculus of change that Tony Iton considered as he weighed what could be done about the injustice his team had discovered in its analysis of neighborhoods—the shocking finding that, when it comes to your health, your ZIP code matters more than your genetic code. In 2009, the same year that the newspaper series revealing the discrepancies was published, Iton was offered the opportunity to help undo those injustices. He joined the California Endowment, the largest private health foundation in the state, and helped to create and subsequently lead an ambitious program called Building Healthy Communities (BHC). Launched in 2010, BHC was a 10-year, $1 billion program to address health inequities in 14 of California's most challenged communities.

How did Iton and his team propose to reverse the odds in these fraught communities? Would they start with a focus on chronic diseases such as diabetes or asthma? By building visible symbols of health such as community gardens? By attracting grocery stores to fill food deserts?

No, their vision was to start with *power*: showing the citizens in these neighborhoods how to fight for themselves and to reshape their environments.

"The idea of this work is that you are part of something bigger than yourself," said Iton. "You're not helpless. You have an enormous amount of individual power and collective power. . . . Meaningful participation in democratic processes allows you to express agency, and agency is good for your health."

BHC's theory of change is that, if you empower people to fight for their interests, they will win policy victories—they will change the system—which will allow them to transform their environment, piece by piece, shifting the odds back in their favor. One of the 14 communities funded by BHC was Fresno, where some of its early work focused on the lack of parks in south Fresno. In 2015, BHC paid to put this ad on the city's buses:

Thank you to Fresno Building Healthy Communities for sharing your work and continuing to work to create #OneHealthyFresno for everyone.

The city manager vetoed the ad, saying it was too political, which created a flurry of media and public interest—precisely the point. At a press conference, Fresno BHC activist Sandra Celedon posed in front of a blown-up version of the ad. "The City of Fresno decided that the sign behind me, this beautiful sign with this lovely young girl is too controversial and too political for all of you to see," she said.

The political organizing led by Fresno BHC slowly began to bear fruit. In 2015, the city council agreed to develop a new Parks Master Plan, the first step toward allocating resources more equitably. In 2016, BHC helped to build a new skateboard park, and the Fresno school district agreed to open up 16 school playgrounds for public use outside school hours. In 2018, the Fresno City Council approved a measure that opens the door for an 18-acre property to be converted into a giant soccer park.

Another change won by Fresno BHC arose from a state program called Transformative Climate Communities (TCC). In California, a state greenhouse gas reduction program enables companies to buy air-pollution credits as part of a cap-and-trade law, and that money is then redistributed via TCC grants to the communities most impacted by pollution. The state had agreed to allocate $70 million to Fresno. But there was controversy about how it would be spent. "The city wanted all that money to go to the high-speed rail being developed in the state, which starts in Central Valley," said Sarah Reyes, a former state legislator and a director of communications at the California Endowment. "The community said, 'No, that money is supposed to go to the most polluted and disenfranchised communities. You can't take all that money.'"

Fresno BHC led a series of public meetings to create an alternate proposal. Eventually, after a long political struggle, more than half the money was reallocated to southwest Fresno and Chinatown, including $16.5 million for a Fresno City College satellite campus, and $5.4 million for an MLK Magnet Core Park.

Greater power leads to policy victories, which leads to a better environment. In Fresno, the system is changing.

In April 2019, I spent a day with Sandra Celedon, the activist who'd led the press conference in front of the banned poster. Celedon introduced me to a variety of local leaders who are fighting to transform their community: The lawyer who helped secure the relocation of the noxious Darling rendering plant, located less than a mile away from public schools. The teenagers who collected survey data to help redraw the route map for city buses, a crucial source of transportation in low-income communities. The advocates pushing for code enforcement in pest- and mold-infested properties run by slumlords, who know that that their legal and illegal immigrant renters will not complain to authorities.

I also met Kieshaun White, a student at Cambridge High School, who is installing air quality monitors in schools across his district. He's developing an app that would display in real time the air quality in each location. "I'm letting my community know about the air quality they live in and the long-term health effects of living in bad air," said White to a *Fresno Bee* reporter. White has asthma, a common health problem in communities like southwest Fresno with poor air quality.

BHC has shown it can secure policy wins and environmental improvements in places like Fresno. Across its network of 14 communities, from 2010 to 2018, BHC logged 321 policy wins and 451 systems changes. Power works.

"The law is just a set of rules based on inputs from power sources," said Iton. "If you want to change the rules, you've got to change the power inputs so that the outcome will be different."

Will all of this be enough to improve health? That's the ultimate goal, let's not forget: to start chipping away at those horrific gaps in life expectancy. We don't know the answer yet. It took many decades—centuries, really—to create these broken systems. It will require decades to fix them. Most institutions do not have patience denominated in decades. Foundations give grants for a few years; nonprofits see about a fifth of their employees turn over every year, on average.

But people like the activist Sandra Celedon are playing the long game. "It took 50 years for us to get Medicare," said Celedon, "and it wasn't the same people at the finish line who were at the start. Many of us are not going to see the outcome of this work." She knows it will be her children—and more likely, her grandchildren—who will reap the benefits of the changes.

On whatever scale we work—in organizations or across communities—systems change takes time. But those changes are our best hope for improving people's odds in life. Celedon, and hundreds of other leaders like her, are helping to uproot a system that tends to produce early death, and to plant in its place a new one that radically improves the probabilities for finding opportunity and health.

CHAPTER 7

Where Can You Find a Point of Leverage?

The Greek polymath Archimedes said, "Give me a lever long enough and a fulcrum on which to place it, and I shall move the world." It's an inspiring quote for change leaders.

Actually, though, if you give the quote a second reading, you'll notice that there's an awful lot riding on that request for a lever and fulcrum. What he's really saying is: *If you rig up a system that makes it easy for me to move the world, then I shall move the world!* Nobody's gonna put that one on a coffee mug.*

Because when it comes to preventing problems in complex systems, finding the right lever and fulcrum is precisely the hard part. In the last chapter, we saw that systems have great power and permanence; that's why upstream efforts must culminate in systems change. At the same time, that power and permanence is exactly what makes systems change so difficult. So in the pursuit of systems change, where do you start? What do you do in, say, the first month of what might

---

* I'm being unfair to Archimedes. It's a great quote when applied to physics. It's really the Uplifting Quote Mafia we're concerned with here.

be a decades-long effort? You look for a point of leverage. This chapter is about that hunt.

In 2008, in the midst of a crime wave in Chicago, the University of Chicago (UC) Crime Lab was cofounded by three colleagues: Jens Ludwig, a UC economist who studies crime and gun violence, UC public policy professor Harold Pollack, and public health expert Roseanna Ander. Their goal was to build an evidence base that policymakers could rely on to reduce crime—to bridge the gap between academic research and public policy. They were looking, in short, for leverage points.

Ludwig was frustrated by the city's lack of progress in combatting crime. Everyone had "answers." The schools had answers, local nonprofits had answers, and policymakers had answers. The problem was that no one knew whose answers were right—or even if *anyone's* answers were right. There was little evidence about what worked in preventing violence.

At the time, Ludwig said, when he talked with city leaders and academics about violence in Chicago, they tended to focus on gang activity. People imagined scenes from *The Wire*, with feuding gangs gunning down each other's leaders. Through that lens, the violence seemed intentional, even strategic—the by-product of gangs jockeying for money and power. The three Crime Lab founders wanted to test that "common sense." (Upstream leaders should be wary of common sense, which can be a poor substitute for evidence.)

Pollack, Ludwig, and Ander pored over medical examiner reports for 200 consecutive homicides in which the victim was a young man. As they studied the files, they did find a number of "strategic" gang hits, but more common was a pattern they didn't expect. Here was a typical case: Two groups of teenagers were arguing in the middle of the afternoon about whether a kid from one of the groups had stolen a bike. The argument got heated. The kid being accused turned his back and started walking away. Another kid felt disrespected by that move and pulled out a gun and shot the kid in the back. In another case, a couple of guys were playing basketball and they argued about a call. One of them ran off, got a weapon, and somebody ended up dead.

These cases were not gang related. There was no strategy to this violence. The deaths were needless. And the circumstances were so ordinary. Anywhere there are teenage boys in the world, there will be fights over trivial stakes—bikes and basketball games. But in Chicago, those boys had access to guns, and they used them.

"Very often you read these reports and you think, 'I just cannot believe that someone is dead because of this,'" said Pollack, the public policy professor. Pollack emerged from his research with a new mental model of what was causing violent deaths. "We're the University of Chicago, so we have to have equations," he said. "My fundamental equation is a couple of young guys plus impulsivity, maybe plus alcohol, plus a gun, equals a dead body."

All of those are potential leverage points: moderating impulsivity or reducing alcohol consumption or restricting access to guns. The next question becomes: Can you identify an intervention that could plausibly accomplish one of those goals?

The Crime Lab launched an "innovation challenge" that invited organizations to submit their best proposals for reducing youth violence. A nonprofit called Youth Guidance submitted a proposal that described a curious program, one that had little to do with violence, at least on the surface. It was called Becoming a Man (BAM).

BAM, at that time, was indistinguishable from its charismatic creator, Anthony Ramirez–Di Vittorio, better known as

Tony D. He grew up on the southwest side of Chicago. "I was a good kid in an at-risk environment," he told *Forbes*. "My mom raised me after my parents' divorce; she was on welfare and had five kids. I saw lots of violence in my neighborhood and house—my brother high on cocaine and kicking in windows, mom yelling at him, his arrest. My saving grace was my mom, who raised me with beautiful values—to respect people, be nice."

Tony D, the first person in his family to go to college, discovered a love of psychology, earning an undergraduate degree in the subject and later a master's. But his most important learning was personal. At age 23, he met his first male mentor, a martial arts instructor who challenged him and affirmed him. "I thought I was a man because I could bench 275 pounds, smoke three joints, and stay up all night. He taught me to push and focus and concentrate," he said.

Having a male role model filled a hole that Tony D had felt in his life, and it sparked a search for meaning and identity. He joined men's groups who weren't afraid to struggle with big questions: What does it mean to be a man? How do you overcome childhood wounds? What does it mean to live with integrity?

He emerged from this period of self-discovery with a clear sense of purpose: He would support young men, as he had been supported, and help to break the cycle of fatherlessness in Chicago's most challenged communities. He was hired by Youth Guidance to serve as, essentially, a career counselor in Chicago high schools.

He was supposed to be helping kids craft resumes and develop job readiness skills, but he couldn't help pushing beyond career guidance. He started inviting young men to join small-group sessions with him. The lure? They could skip class once a week. In the early sessions, Tony D would lead icebreaker activities to get them laughing, to get them comfortable with each other. One was called The Fist. Students were paired up, and one member of each pair was given a ball. The other was told that he had 30 seconds to get the ball from his partner. Pandemonium ensued, with each pair wrestling for control of the ball. After the 30 seconds, the partners would switch roles and a second round of chaos would begin.

Afterward, Tony D would point out that no one had thought to simply ask his partner for the ball. At first, the young men would scoff: "He wouldn't have given it!" "He would have thought I was a punk!" But Tony D would ask, "How would *you* have reacted if your partner asked you nicely for the ball?" Many would admit something to the effect of "I probably would have given it. It's just a stupid ball."

Tony D introduced a tradition called the "check-in" at the beginning of each session. He'd arrange the young men in a circle—there were usually 8 to 10 in each class—and ask each to reflect briefly on how he was doing that day: physically, emotionally, intellectually, and spiritually. At first, the young men were reluctant. Skeptical. Tony D would goad them for a one-word answer, at least: mad, sad, or glad. With time, they began to open up. They saw it was safe to share problems, to talk about their pain or their anger. By the end of the semester, it had become one of their favorite activities— the one time in the school day when they could lower their guards and just be themselves. As one young man said to researchers who were studying BAM, "I like how we can just sit down and just talk to each other . . . it's calming."

Managing anger became a recurring theme in the sessions. You can let your anger overwhelm you so that you act like a "savage," Tony D taught them, or you can channel it to become a "warrior." Anger could be a destructive force or a constructive one, he stressed, and we're free to choose.

The moral guidance seemed to sink in. One young man recalled to a researcher how he had used the BAM training: "One of my teachers did not want to accept one of my projects, because it was late by maybe one or two days, but instead of freaking out and maybe just calling attention at his desk, I accepted it." He continued to talk with the teacher, asking if there was any other work he could do to boost his grade. Eventually, the teacher agreed to accept the paper with a penalty. The teen said, "If I would have [gotten upset], I would have probably, maybe gotten expelled or my grade would have dropped even more."

For years, Tony D continued to shape the BAM sessions. They evolved into a fascinating hybrid, blending the confessional aspect of support groups with the tough love of male mentoring and elements of cognitive behavioral therapy (CBT), a technique that helps people learn to change their patterns of thought and, as a result, their behavior. Beyond that, it had to be fun. It had to be *cool*. What teenage male would voluntarily sign up for therapy or a "support group"? Balancing these demands was a tightrope act, but it seemed to work. There was never a shortage of young men who wanted to join BAM.

Tony D and his colleagues at Youth Guidance sent a proposal to the Crime Lab, describing the BAM program. And when the Crime Lab's leaders read about the program, they saw a connection to their own discovery from the medical examiner's reports. What if BAM, with its focus on CBT and anger management, could be a leverage point to reduce impulsivity? (Recall Harold Pollack's "equation" for violence: a couple of young guys plus impulsivity plus alcohol plus a gun.) What if the program could slow down or interrupt a young man's rage, so that a dispute over a basketball game wouldn't end in a murder?

In May 2009, Youth Guidance won the Crime Lab's "innovation challenge" and received funding to scale up its work to 18 schools. One condition of the funding was that the work would be studied via a randomized control trial (RCT).* The key question that would be studied was: Would BAM reduce arrests—especially for violent acts?

Youth Guidance was taking a risk in agreeing to this. The probability, in general, of finding a large, significant result in a social-science RCT is pretty low—which is not hard to understand when you realize that interventions might act upon only one or two variables within the overwhelmingly complex and interconnected system that is the human life. Worse, if the research established that BAM did not work, it could dry up the funding stream for Youth Guidance. No donor would support an intervention that was proven not to work. On the other hand, many funders will support an untested intervention, based on the strength of anecdotal feedback. In the social sector, this dynamic creates an incentive to embrace the ostrich strategy: Stick your head in the sand and avoid knowing.

---

* RCTs are the kind of gold-standard research that pharmaceutical companies must follow when seeking approval for a new drug. In an RCT, you start with a population of people—in this case, hundreds of young men in high school—and then assign people randomly to either the intervention group (which receives the intervention, such as BAM) or the control group (which does not receive it). Then you watch the outcomes of both groups and, if there are significant differences between them, you can reasonably say that the intervention caused those differences. In the absence of a control group, it's trickier to pin down causation.

What made the decision even more risky was that, before they could test the program at scale, they had to . . . scale it. Until that point, BAM had been Tony D's show. Youth Guidance had run the program at a few schools, but in the study, there would be 18. What if Tony D was the only person who could handle the requisite juggling act of therapy, fun, self-control, and tough love?

In a few months, the team recruited 13 other facilitators while Tony D frantically tried to convert his home-brewed course notes into a formal "curriculum" suitable for train-ing others. He was not able to finish the curriculum before the semester started, so the facilitators started receiving their instructions on a rolling basis. (*Here's what you'll be doing in class next week.*)

During the 2009–10 school year, Youth Guidance's coun-selors in each participating school led 27 one-hour, weekly BAM sessions. The anecdotal feedback was positive: Kids were coming, they were engaged, they seemed to be benefit-ting. Amazingly, there were no major hiccups in the scale-up of the work. On a week-by-week basis, the staff's impressions were generally positive. But as to the main question—would BAM reduce arrests?—they were almost completely in the dark. They didn't have access to that data. The only visible evidence tended to be negative, as when facilitators would learn that one of their students had been arrested.

After the school year ended, there was an agonizing nine-month wait while the Crime Lab team analyzed the data.*

---

* The study could not have happened, by the way, without the Illinois State Police's agreement to allow the team access to the rap sheets of the teenagers involved. It's amazing how often upstream efforts live or die based on mundane, does-the-plumbing-work matters such as database access.

Finally, in the spring of 2011, Harold Pollack from the Crime Lab gathered the Youth Guidance team to share the results.

Among the students who participated in BAM, arrests were down 28% versus the control group. Violent-crime arrests were cut practically in half (down 45%). In the room, jaws dropped. Pollack said it was "one of the greatest moments of my entire career. They had no idea what the results were going to be. Because they see—in the kids that they work with—they see a lot of tragedy. A kid is shot. People fail. People get arrested. What they never got to see is what would have happened if they hadn't been there."

~~~~~~~

The Crime Lab researchers concluded that the BAM program had been successful in getting teenage males to slow down their thinking in fraught situations. A shouting match over a call in basketball could remain a shouting match, rather than escalating to a gunfight. The Crime Lab had found a leverage point in the impulsivity part of Pollack's crime "equation." (See the footnote for a note about subsequent testing of BAM.*)

While every domain of upstream work will have its own unique equation—and thus its own leverage points—the strategy used by the Crime Lab's leaders to *find* those leverage points is closer to universal: Immerse yourself in the problem.

---

* The second study of BAM replicated its positive effects, and the third study (which covered a much larger group of teens) had more mixed results. This phenomenon happens a lot: Early successful pilots prove difficult to scale. This is a critical issue in the social sector, but it's somewhat tangential to our work in this chapter. So I've added an appendix on the subject if you're interested.

Recall that the Crime Lab's leaders had started by poring over 200 medical examiner reports. They weren't satisfied with common-sense explanations for violence—they went back to the source. A similar strategy was used by the Permanente Medical Group in Northern California. In 2008, Alan Whippy, the medical director of quality and safety, was pushing hospital leaders to reduce preventable errors and infections, a major cause of patient death. She challenged those leaders to do detailed case studies of the last 50 patients who had died at each of their hospitals. To their astonishment, about a third of those deaths were due to sepsis, a problem that was barely on their radar at that time. By 2011, those leaders had reduced mortality for patients with sepsis by 60%. By getting close to the problem, they found leverage points to prevent unnecessary patient deaths. The postmortem for a problem can be the preamble to a solution.

If you work on a non-deadly problem, you'll have other strategies for getting closer to the problem. Two architects from the international design firm Corgan, which plans public buildings such as airports and schools, were trying to anticipate the problems that elderly people might face in navigating their buildings. How could you get closer to that problem? Interviewing elderly people about their experiences, maybe? Walking alongside them, so their impressions would be fresher? Or you could consult incident reports—the details and locations of accidents and falls. The architects Mike Steiner and Samantha Flores went a step further, though. They donned an "age simulation suit," which is designed to make you *feel what it's like to be old.*

"It's a series of straps that reduce your mobility, and it's a series of weights that simulate what happens when you age," said Steiner, describing his suit to the host of the radio show *Here & Now.* "These are elbow braces that mimic reduced movement in my elbow joint. As you age, you lose dexterity in your fingers. So those gloves simulate the loss of dexterity." Weights at the extremities make your limbs feel heavier. Goggles simulate vision loss and headphones, hearing loss. So-called overshoes simulate nerve loss in your feet, which makes it harder to perceive where the ground is.

Steiner and Flores wore the suits through Dallas/Fort Worth International Airport (which business travelers will know is a place that can age you all by itself). "The first thing that I noticed," said Flores on the show, "is that it takes a longer time to get to different places, and so the need to rest and to sit is very impactful: have more benches, have more places for someone to grab on to. Typically we design these concourses to be wide-open spaces so that multiple people can move. But there's not really a place to grab on to if you've lost your balance, or if you just need a moment to rest." They noticed that ramps could be disorienting—design cues were needed to signal that the floor would slope. And getting onto escalators was difficult when there were only two flat steps before the rise or fall. Corgan now recommends three-step escalators in the airport's public spaces.

When you get close to a problem, what exactly are you looking for? How do you know a promising lever and fulcrum when you spot it? In searching for a viable leverage point, your first pass might be to consider, as the leaders in Iceland did, the risk and protective factors for the problem you're trying to prevent. For teenage alcohol abuse, a protective factor is being involved in formal sports—it eats up a teen's time and provides a source of natural highs. A risk factor is parental inattention—if her parents are always gone, she'll be more likely to act out. Every problem will have its own array of factors that increase risk for or protect against it, and each of those factors is a potential leverage point.

As an alternative to the focus on risk and protective factors, consider whether your leverage point might be a specific subpopulation of people. Many successful upstream interventions are actually very expensive programs targeted at small groups of people. At first glance this may seem like an inherently undesirable combination: Why would we ever want to spend a lot on a few people? Because in many domains, a very small set of people can create an inordinate burden on the system. The Crime Lab developed a model to predict the 5,000 people in the city at the highest risk for "gun violence involvement," which means either being arrested for a violent crime with a gun, or being the victim of one.* Five thousand people is about 0.2% of Chicago's population. A year later, when the Crime Lab team studied the city's homicide victims, 17% of them came from their list of 5,000. The pool of people who are riskiest—and most at risk—is small. Meanwhile, some other research by the Crime Lab has estimated that the social cost of a single gunshot injury is $1.5 million. What these figures suggest is that society could afford to spend a massive amount of money trying to change the bleak prospects of this group of people. In keeping with that spirit, the Crime Lab is currently testing a program in which convicted violent criminals, who otherwise would be likely to re-offend, are given a fresh start, placed in a paying job, and given CBT therapy. The program's cost is about $22,000 to $23,000 per person per year.

In health care, a small number of patients can be heavy utilizers of emergency medicine, sometimes visiting emer-

---

* Why focus on victims *and* perpetrators rather than on the perpetrators only? Because they tend to be the same people—many people who commit violent crimes end up being victimized by violent crimes. And many violent crimes go unsolved, which means that (sadly) the victims end up being easier to measure.

gency rooms over 100 times per year. Often these are people with very complicated personal and health histories. A sample profile might be a morbidly obese man with diabetes, asthma, chronic pain, and unreliable housing. The cost of treating them can be extraordinary. Because of that, health systems can afford to create what are, in essence, bespoke individualized health plans for these people, including housing assistance, home health care, concierge-type staffers who look after them, and more. When you can precisely target a group of people who are causing big problems on an ongoing basis, you can afford to spend a small fortune trying to help them.*

A necessary part of finding a viable leverage point is to consider costs and benefits. We'll always want the biggest bang for our buck. But I want to draw a sharp line between "bang for the buck," which is critical, and another, more pernicious idea. One of the most baffling and destructive ideas about preventive efforts is that they must *save us money*. Discussions of upstream interventions always seem to circle back to ROI: Will a dollar invested today yield us more in the long run? If we provide housing to the homeless, will it pay for itself in the form of fewer social service needs? If we provide air conditioners to asthmatic kids, will the units pay for themselves via fewer ER visits?

These aren't irrelevant questions—but they aren't necessary ones, either. *Nothing else in health care*, other than prevention, is viewed through this lens of saving money. Your

---

* Notice there's a comparable phenomenon on the other end of the spectrum: customers who generate enormous and disproportionate profit. Think of high rollers in Vegas, whose mega-losses are so valuable that casinos can afford to lavish them with attention and amazing perks. What could be more precious, indeed, than a guest who enjoys leaving behind millions of dollars?

neighbor with the heroic all-bacon diet—when he finally ends up needing heart bypass surgery, there's literally no one who is going to ask whether he "deserves" the surgery or whether the surgery is going to save the system money in the long haul. When he needs the procedure, he'll get it. But when we start talking about preventing children from going hungry, suddenly the work has to pay for itself. This is madness. The reason to house the homeless or prevent disease or feed the hungry is not because of the financial returns but because of the moral returns. Let's not sabotage upstream efforts by subjecting them to a test we never impose on downstream interventions.

~~~~~~

In health care circles, discussions of the conditions in the environment that affect people's health, ranging from housing to public safety to air quality—the so-called social determinants of health—have spread widely. You would struggle to find an industry conference without sessions on the topic. This is good news on the merits, because it reflects a shift in interest toward upstream health. The only drawback, really, is linguistic. "Social determinants of health" is one of those ostentatiously bland phrases that seem engineered to deter interest in the topics they name. Kind of like if dating were rebranded "aspirational interpersonal exchange."

It's an exciting time in health care, because you can feel the problem blindness lifting. "Doctors historically have been trained to focus on clinical interventions and counseling," said Carmela Rocchetti, a primary care doctor who practices at Hackensack Meridian Health in New Jersey. "You come to me, in the four walls of my office, and I try to change your health. I'm going to write a prescription on my pad, and it's going to improve your health. But that is the tiniest part of the health equation. In order to move the needle on someone's health, you need to open up their refrigerator. You need to ask how they're sleeping. You need to understand the chronic stress they're under and address those issues."

That's the kind of perspective that is spreading quickly—a growing appreciation for the importance of the upstream factors that influence health. Yet there are also daunting barriers to action. What exactly can a doctor do to help a patient who lacks healthy food? Or is profoundly stressed? Never mind that in most health systems, doctors would actually lose income by trying, because they're paid on a fee-for-service model. The more acts of maintenance they can cram in a day, the better, and talking for an extra 15 minutes to a stressed or lonely patient doesn't count as maintenance. (In chapter 11, we'll study some new payment models that make it easier to fund prevention.)

I've read and heard countless discussions of these dilemmas by leaders in health care, and you can feel the tension. On one hand, there is palpable enthusiasm for moving upstream. I believe that many, if not most, leaders genuinely believe it's the right thing to do. On the other hand, there is an understandable reluctance to "own" patients' upstream health needs, simply because so many of those factors are outside the purview of the health system. So what those leaders have done so far is look for leverage points, small in the scheme of the health care system but symbolically meaningful. Many primary care doctors, for instance, will now ask their patients if they often go hungry, and if so, they can be matched with community partners such as local food banks. The benefit to patients comes from reaching outside the health system, aligning efforts with other players who can help.

What if the change could come from within the health system, though? What if those upstream efforts that seem unnatural to doctors—because their training and incentives usually push them downstream—could be made to seem *natural*? One new medical school, the Hackensack Meridian School of Medicine at Seton Hall University in New Jersey, is pursuing that vision, reinventing the way doctors are trained. The social determinants of health are at the core of the curriculum.

At the beginning of the school year, students are matched with an individual or a family from a nearby community. Over the course of the first year, the students will meet every month or two with that family in their home, learning about their lives and their health. The students can't *treat* them, of course—they're just first-year med students—but they are assigned to help the families realize a goal related to their health. *My son has autism—I need some help getting him resources.* Or, *I'm home alone in a wheelchair, and I'm feeling depressed—I need some social outlets.*

"We can tell the students about this, we can lecture them, but until they meet a real person and feel connected to that person, they're not really going to internalize how important this is," said Dr. Rocchetti, the primary care doctor quoted above, who is also director of this program, called the Human Dimension.

Aamirah McCutchen and a classmate, both first-year students in the first-ever class for the med school, were matched with a 91-year-old man in a nursing home. McCutchen was nervous going to see him for the first time. She is soft-spoken; when she talked at a level he could hear, she felt like she was yelling. The students asked him what goals they could help him with. He said, "I'm ninety-one. I don't really have a goal." But then he came up with two things: learning to use a computer and fighting his short-term memory loss. So the next time McCutchen came back, she and her classmate taught him how to play memory games on the computer in the nursing home.

Another pair of students were matched with a man who had uncontrolled diabetes. (That means his blood sugar levels were unhealthy, something which can usually be avoided with regular monitoring, the right foods, and the appropriate doses of insulin.) The students couldn't figure out why the man was having trouble—he seemed knowledgeable and engaged. Then, during one of their visits, a neighbor knocked on the door and said, "I'm going to the store—do you have your list ready?" And it dawned on the students: The man can't go to the grocery store on his own. He's dependent on a neighbor for his food. So it was harder for him to ask for the specific foods (often perishables) that would have helped him manage his condition.

Another part of the medical students' work is to engage with the community, not just particular people. They meet with leaders in local nonprofits and attend public meetings and do service work. "When we first started planning the course, people would say to me, 'Well, what are you creating? Is this a school of social work or a school of medicine?'" said Rocchetti.

The first class of students began in the summer of 2018. At first, the students were enthusiastic about this work. Maybe overenthusiastic. In the first few weeks of school, they'd show up at Rocchetti's office with plans for solving various community problems. Then, in the middle of the year, the reality of exams and board preparation started to intrude on their idealism. These were high achievers—stars of the meritocracy. They knew how to ace tests and submit brilliant papers. But how do you "ace" an assignment to help a lonely elderly woman?

At one point, some students seemed near revolt. A few had been assigned to attend a board of education meeting. The first 45 minutes of the meeting were unexpectedly closed to the public, so they waited. Then the public part of the meeting was dominated by a contractual dispute between a teacher and the board. The students were furious, emailing Rocchetti to ask, "Why did you waste our time by sending us to this?" It wasn't why they came to med school.

Except that, in a weird way, it was exactly why they came to med school. Because, in Rocchetti's mind, a doctor's calling is to make people healthy, which involves knowing not only the technical side of medicine but also the social side. Learning to appreciate the full complexity of people's lives as well as the complexity of the systems in which they operate. You start to realize that even something as simple as *showing up on time at the doctor's office* can be derailed by countless different factors: the city buses ran late, or bad weather prevented the patient from walking to the bus stop, or she couldn't afford the parking fee outside the clinic, or the directions were sent online and she didn't have a computer, or she just felt so bad that morning that all the hassle didn't seem worth it. And when you're tempted to fall back on easy black-and-white judgments—*Yeah sure all that's hard but, still, if she cared about her health, she should've been here on time, and she should've taken her insulin, and she should've refilled her prescriptions*—then you flash back to that two-hour school board meeting where nothing seemed to happen, and you recall the elderly man's neighbor who brought his groceries, and you take a deep breath and say, *Nothing is easy. The world is complex and there are no quick fixes. But if I can learn to uncross my arms and extend my hands, I can be someone who eases suffering rather than ignores it.*

By late spring 2019—the end of the first year of the first

class in the med school—the students' enthusiasm had been restored. They reported, unanimously, that they had valued the time spent with their families and in the community. Over the final two years of their med school experience, they will continue to be involved with communities and people, and when they graduate, they'll have a perspective far different from that of most doctors. Many of them will stay in New Jersey and practice at Meridian Health, and Rocchetti believes they will transform the health system from the inside: "Our students are going to grow up and be the force that changes the culture."

The school is betting that by drawing future doctors closer to the sources of disease and despair, they will be quicker to identify the leverage points that lead to health. Bryan Stevenson, a law professor at NYU, author, and the founder of the Equal Justice Initiative, calls this the "power of proximity."

"I believe that to make a difference in creating a healthier community, a healthier society, a healthier nation, and thus a healthier economy, we've got to find ways to get proximate to the poor and the vulnerable," said Stevenson in a speech to *Fortune*'s CEO Initiative conference in 2018. "I absolutely believe that when we isolate ourselves—when we allow ourselves to be shielded and disconnected from those who are vulnerable and disfavored, we sustain and contribute to these problems. I am persuaded that in proximity there is something we can learn about how we change the world. . . ."

Getting proximate is not a guarantee of progress. It's a start, not a finish. Upstream change often means fumbling our way forward, figuring out what works and what doesn't, and under what conditions. But in this context, even a defeat is effectively a victory. Because every time we learn something, we fill in one more piece of the map as we hunt for the levers that can move the world.

CHAPTER 8

How Will You Get Early
Warning of the Problem?

In late 2010, Roli Saxena was hired to run the customer success group for LinkedIn's flagship product for recruiters. ("Customer success" is like an upstream version of "customer service"—the mission is to keep customers happy with the products/services they've bought.) The recruiting product, offered on a subscription basis, was designed to help companies find and attract new hires. It was selling incredibly well, but the "churn" was high. The churn rate is the percentage of customers who don't renew their subscriptions, and it's a critical diagnostic of health for any subscription business, from Netflix to *People* magazine. When Saxena joined the company, the churn rate was roughly 30%, meaning that 3 out of 10 customers stopped using the recruiting product every year.

The company's traditional approach to managing churn was to assign people to work closely with customers—especially those feared to be at risk of leaving—around the time of renewal. The emphasis was on "saving" accounts. But then, said Dan Shapero, the head of sales and Saxena's boss, they asked themselves a new question: How early can we predict whether someone's going to churn? The hope was that if they could detect the risk early, they could intervene to get a better result.

When they crunched the numbers, they realized that they could reasonably predict who would churn and who wouldn't as early as 30 days after someone bought a subscription. How could you possibly predict someone's churn so early? Saxena found that there was a strong negative correlation between product usage and churn. That is, if recruiters used their LinkedIn subscription a lot, they tended to renew it. This surprised no one. (The people most likely to cancel *People* are, after all, the people who aren't reading it.) What was new was the insight that it was critical to get customers using the product *early*: "We found that customers who engaged [with the product] in the first 30 days were four times more likely to continue using LinkedIn," said Saxena.

"We were floored," said Shapero. "We said, 'Let's take all these resources that we've been using to "save" customers and apply them to onboarding clients properly.'" They created a new role called an "onboarding specialist," who would call customers to show them how to use the product. But it wasn't just the usual soporific software feature training. These onboarding specialists would actually do some of the clients' work for them.

A typical call might go like this: "I know you were looking to hire a software engineer in Atlanta. I've taken the liberty of designing a search to help you find people who fit that profile. I'll walk you through how to adjust the search parameters as you see fit. And then, after you identify a bunch of good candidates, the next step will be to reach out to them using our InMail service. So I've drafted a sample email for you, using the lessons we've learned about the kinds of messages that tend to get a response from candidates."

Within two years, the churn rate was cut roughly in half, even as the company's revenue exploded, and one of the critical drivers of that success was the onboarding work. The improvement in churn was worth tens of millions of dollars annually.

When we can foresee a problem, we have more maneuvering room to fix it. That's why a key question bearing on upstream efforts is: How can you get early warning of the problem you're trying to solve? Imagine a smoke detector that's custom-tailored to your work. At LinkedIn, the smoke that activated the alarm was a customer's inactivity in her first month as a subscriber. In Chicago Public Schools, the smoke was being off-track as a freshman.

There's no *inherent* advantage to early warning signals. Their value hinges on the severity of the problem. You may not need or want an early-warning signal that the bulb in your bedside lamp is about to burn out. (Versus it might be incredibly valuable to have an early-warning signal for the bulb at the top of a lighthouse.) The value also depends on whether the warning provides sufficient time to respond. A car tire that gave you a 30-second advance warning of a blowout might save your life. A half-second warning might be worthless.

Sometimes, as with LinkedIn, we can use historical patterns to inform predictions. That approach was followed by Northwell Health, a network of hospitals and health care facilities that operates in New York City and the surrounding area. Its EMS (Emergency Medical Services) leaders face a life-or-death operations challenge: They want their ambulances to arrive as quickly as possible when people call 911. So they've created elaborate models, using historical data, to anticipate where and when 911 calls will come from.

"We're not actually taking a crystal ball out and predicting emergencies, but what we're predicting is: What is the behavior of the population going to be, based on history?" said Jonathan Washko, assistant vice president for Northwell's Center for Emergency Medical Services.

It turns out that emergencies follow predictable patterns. There are patterns in time (more 911 calls during the day than at night) and patterns in geography (more calls from areas with older citizens than younger ones). On July 4th and New Year's Eve, volume is up (drunken idiocy), whereas on Christmas and Thanksgiving, volume is down. (The love factor? Or just quieter drinking patterns?) Friday and Saturday nights are busy, and Sundays are slow. Flu season is nuts.

And then there are the nuances: Curiously, mealtimes at nursing homes create a spike. You might wonder, Is the food *that bad?* No, those are the times when a caregiver is guaranteed to check on a patient and discover that something bad has happened. For the same reason, there's a spike when nursing home workers change shifts. And the patterns vary by weather, too: Washko knows that during heavy snows there's often an uptick in heart attacks—sometimes caused by people shoveling snow a little too vigorously.

How does Northwell use this predictive modeling to accelerate ambulance response time? By forward-deploying ambulances around the city, based on the model. Picture paramedics sitting in an ambulance in the parking lot of a McDonald's, a quick drive away from a few nursing homes. No one has called yet, but chances are that someone will. And they'll be right there.

This is very different from the norm. Most Americans reading this book live in a community where the EMS is run by the fire department. The ambulances are parked at the local fire stations, and when a 911 call comes in, EMTs or paramedics will drive out to help the person. It's a reactive system. And there's a strange consequence: If you suffer a cardiac arrest in one of these communities, your life may literally depend on how close you live to the fire station. (This could become a selling point for real estate agents: *First floor master—AND just a three-minute drive from the fire station!*)

By contrast, Northwell—and some other EMS systems in large cities—spread their ambulances strategically around the city to ensure that the entire population they cover is only a short drive away. At the EMS command center in Syosset, New York, there's a room that looks a bit like NASA's Mission Control Center. Large screen monitors cover the walls, featuring maps of the areas covered by Northwell EMS. The real-time location of all the ambulances is pinpointed on the maps, and each one is surrounded by a halo that shows the area it could reach within 10 minutes. When a 911 call comes in, the closest ambulance to the emergency is deployed. Then all the other nearby ambulances shift their locations dynamically in order to fill the hole left by the deployed ambulance.

It's an incredibly sophisticated system, and it makes a difference. Northwell's average response time is about 6.5 minutes, compared with a national average of 8 minutes. Partly because of that speed, Northwell has superior results on a metric called the ROSC (return of spontaneous circulation) rate, which measures what percentage of people experiencing cardiac arrest have their circulation restored by effective treatment. And patients apparently appreciate the care they're given: 94% say they would recommend Northwell to others.

This is the model of an early-warning story: Data warns us of a problem we wouldn't have seen otherwise—say, needing ambulances deployed closer to nursing homes at mealtimes. And that predictive capacity gives us the time to act to prevent problems. Northwell paramedics can't stop people from suffering cardiac arrest, but they *can* stop some of those people from dying.

At Northwell, minutes matter. There are other cases where even seconds of warning can be precious. Japan has one of the world's best early-detection systems for earthquakes, including an observation center that collects information from more than 3,200 seismographs and seismic intensity meters around the country, according to a 2012 article by Alex Greer, a professor who specializes in emergency preparedness. The center can detect so-called primary waves—the first warning signals that an earthquake has been triggered—which are mostly imperceptible to humans.

This system paid off for Japanese citizens in 2011: "When the primary waves arrived from the Great East Japan earthquake of 2011 at 2:46:45 p.m. local time," wrote Greer, "the closest inland sensor interpreted the waves, and the system issued a warning to major businesses, railway operators, factories, hospitals, schools, nuclear plants, and the general public's cell phones in a mere 3 seconds (2:46:48 p.m. local time)."

Three seconds! The earth began to shake in Sendai about 30 seconds after the warning was issued—and then in Tokyo about 60 seconds after Sendai. "This may not seem like much time," Greer wrote, "but it is enough of a window for businesses to shut down production lines, doctors to stop medical procedures, schools to get children under desks, motorists to pull off to the side of the road, backup generators to be turned on, and trains to stop."

Similar early-detection systems are also a source of business advantage. In a TV commercial for IBM, a maintenance guy approaches a security guard in the lobby of an office building.

MAINTENANCE GUY: Hey.
SECURITY GUARD: Pass, please.
M: I'm here to fix the elevator.
S: Nothing's wrong with the elevator.
M: Right.
S: But you wanna fix it?
M: Right.
S: So who sent you?
M: New guy.
S: What new guy?
M: Watson.

The maintenance guy looks over at a black computer box sitting on a table, and the security guard follows his glance.

WATSON [speaking in a goober-ish voice]: My analysis of sensor and maintenance data indicates elevator three will malfunction in two days.
M: There ya go.
S: Still need a pass.

This is not fantasy.* Many major elevator companies today offer "smart" elevators, which send a smorgasbord of diagnostic data to the cloud—including lighting, noise, speed, temperature, and much more—that can be scoured for early signs of problems.

"One of the most important things that an online connection to the cloud gives you is the ability to spot trends in advance before they start creating problems," John Macleod,

---

*Although it's striking how far Watson has slipped: from "the computer who won *Jeopardy!*" to a black box sitting in a random office building, making predictions out loud to no one.

an IBM Watson IoT technical specialist, told *Computerworld.* "Take the time it takes a door to close; normally 5 seconds, but it may gradually extend to 5.1, then 5.2. Nobody's really noticing it as you get in and out of the lift, but the gradual change in time might well indicate something's becoming sticky and needs lubrication. . . . And then you can act in advance to deal with them rather than waiting for the doors to stick shut and catch people inside the lift."

With the rise of the Internet of Things, this kind of advance-warning solution will become more and more common. Our world will be stocked with sensors: Smart watches that detect atrial fibrillation. Smart devices (called "smart pigs," weirdly) that warn about leaks in oil pipelines. Smart video cameras that can alert when a bus driver is falling asleep. But while technology can aid our early-detection efforts, sometimes the best sensors are not devices, but people.

Every year, the American Heart Association trains 16 million people to perform CPR—that's the equivalent of 16 million human sensors, deployed around the world, who can detect a cardiac emergency. Even better, those CPR-trained people can act on the problem, not simply detect it. (And they may keep the victim alive long enough for the ambulance to arrive with a full suite of life-saving tools.)

The anti-terrorism "If You See Something, Say Something" campaign is another example of early-detection work that hinges on human beings. The slogan was created by adman Allen Kay on the day after the 9/11 attacks. "The model that I had in my head was 'Loose Lips Sink Ships,'" Kay told the *New York Times.* "In this case, I thought it was ironic because we want just the opposite. We want people to talk. I wanted to come up with something that would carry like that. That would be infectious." In a sense, we have all become sensors deployed to provide early warning of potential terrorist acts.

To anticipate problems, we need eyes and ears in the environment. But we need to be cautious about what we learn: Sometimes we may detect things that are not as they seem.

~~~~~~~~

In the 2000s, the number of South Koreans diagnosed with cancer of the thyroid—the butterfly-shaped gland at the base of the neck—was rising precipitously. By 2011, the rate of thyroid cancer cases had increased *15-fold* since 1993. As a public health problem, this was terrifying. Cancers are not infectious diseases—they shouldn't spread so rapidly. Something odd was going on.

The one bright spot in the epidemic was the South Korean health system's sterling record of managing these cases. The nation's five-year survival rate for thyroid cancer was 99.7%, the best in the world. These numbers were so impressive that South Korea actually promoted "medical tourism"—i.e., the idea that patients from around the world with thyroid cancer should consider flying for treatment to the country with the best record of keeping patients alive.

The twin mysteries of the thyroid cancer epidemic were: What had caused such an explosion of cancer? And how had South Korea managed to fight it so successfully?

Gil Welch, a physician and cancer researcher, saw the South Korean story in a radically different light. "When I was in medical school, I was taught that anything labeled 'cancer' would inexorably progress," he wrote in his eye-opening book *Less Medicine, More Health*. "Once a cell had the DNA derangement of cancer, it was only a matter of time until the cancer spread throughout the body. And it was only a matter of time until it killed the patient."

But in recent years, doctors' ideas about cancer have changed. No one thinks anymore that "it's only a matter of time" before cancer kills a patient. To explain the way medical thinking has evolved, Welch uses the analogy of a barnyard pen of cancers, containing turtles, rabbits, and birds. The health system's goal is to keep the animals from escaping the pen—that's the equivalent of a cancer that becomes deadly—and the pen represents our system of early detection and treatment.

The turtles are incredibly slow, so the pen is kind of pointless. They never would have escaped anyway. Turtles represent sluggish, nonlethal cancers, of which there are many. Meanwhile, the birds will fly out at will; we can't stop them. These are the most aggressive forms of cancer. Even if we detect these cancers in patients, we can't stop them. They're deadly. From the perspective of public health, then, the only animal that matters is the rabbit. It represents a potentially lethal form of cancer. It can hop out of the pen at any time, but if we act quickly, we can stop it before it escapes.

So when Welch looked at the epidemic of thyroid cancer in South Korea, he realized it was actually an epidemic of nonthreatening turtles. Let's review the history: Before mass screening for thyroid cancer began in South Korea, patients would only be tested for it if they were symptomatic, meaning something was wrong that brought them to the doctor. (Just as a woman might seek a mammogram if she felt a lump in her breast, or a man might seek a prostate exam if there was blood in his urine.) Those cases were relatively rare, and they were more likely to be rabbits. But then the health community in South Korea began encouraging more people to get screened, and as it turns out, huge numbers of people have quiet little turtles living in their thyroids, which were discovered by the screening tests. So the incidence of thyroid cancer skyrocketed (even though nothing had really changed in health terms), and patients received invasive treatments—typically, a surgery to remove the thyroid gland. Five years later, 99.7% of them were still alive!

But they weren't alive because of medical wizardry. They were alive because they never had a problem. The South Korean patients probably thought their doctors had saved their lives, and the doctors thought so, too, but in reality, a lot of them were harmed (from the side effects of surgery) with no compensating health benefit.

So where does this leave us? Some early-warning systems work wonders: They can keep elevators from failing and customers from churning. Other times, they may cause more harm than benefit, as in the thyroid cancer "epidemic" in South Korea. How do we distinguish between the two? One key factor is the prevalence of false positives: warnings that incorrectly signal trouble.

Have you ever rolled your eyes when you heard a fire alarm? That's alarm fatigue, and it's a critical problem. A group of researchers studied five ICUs (intensive care units), treating 461 patients, for a month in 2013. Over that period, there were more than *2.5 million alarms* triggered on the bedside monitors: automated alerts about changes in heart rates, respiratory intake, blood pressure levels, and more. Granted, many of those alarms were just text messages flashing on a screen for nurses and clinicians to observe. The hospital had restricted the audible alarms to those considered clinically important. Nevertheless, there were almost 400,000 audible alarms logged in a month, which broke down to 187 audible alarms per bed per day. When everything is cause for alarm, nothing is cause for alarm.

As we design early-warning systems, we should keep these questions in mind: Will the warning give us enough time to act effectively? (If not, why bother?) What rate of false positives can we expect? Our comfort with that level of false positives may, in turn, hinge on the relative cost of handling false positives versus the possibility of missing a real problem.

In circumstances where the consequences of missing a problem are devastating, we might be willing to endure a very high rate of false positives. And that brings us to the organization Sandy Hook Promise, founded in the aftermath of the massacre at Sandy Hook Elementary School in 2012, when a young man shot and killed 20 children and 6 adult staff members. The founders, who had loved ones killed in the incident, were tired of the numbness and resignation that many Americans felt about school shootings. They wanted action.

It struck Nicole Hockley, one of the group's cofounders, as wrongheaded that many schools had reacted to the threat of shootings by retreating into a defensive crouch. "There's been so much focus in schools around: You have an active shooter—what are you going to do?" said Hockley. "How do we teach the kids to hide? To run? To in some cases *attack back*, which I think is ludicrous. . . . Why are we focusing everything on the point of no return, when it would be so much more effective to look backward and say, 'How can we help this person before it ever gets to that point?'"

Hockley's decision to target a potential shooter's mental health is clearly upstream—trying to intervene before disaster happens—and probably wise politically, given our partisan warfare. ("We've tried [gun] policy for a few decades now," she told the *Guardian*. "Try something else. Why keep banging yourself against the wall, doing the same thing and expecting different results?") But it would be authorial malpractice to write about how to prevent school shootings without addressing the "shooting" part. "There is one developed country—and only one—in which it is not only legal, but easy and convenient, to amass a private arsenal of mass slaughter," wrote David Frum in the *Atlantic*. "That country also happens to be the one—and the only one—regularly afflicted by mass slaughters perpetrated by aggrieved individuals." Frum, a former speechwriter for George W. Bush, is not exactly a liberal. Talk about national problem blindness.

Ultimately, Hockley and her cofounders didn't think they could wake up the country from this blindness, so they looked for another way to save lives. As they researched other school shootings, they learned that in almost all cases, there were early-warning signs that were missed. Most mass shootings are planned at least six months in advance. Typically, 8 in 10 shooters tell at least one other person of their plans. Many actually post threats on social media. Their actions could have been prevented if the right people had been paying attention or had taken them seriously.

Sandy Hook Promise launched a training program to educate students on the warning signs, which include: a strong fascination with firearms, acting aggressively for seemingly minor reasons, extreme feelings of social isolation, and bragging about access to guns. And of course explicit threats of violence—which had often been overlooked in past shootings. The students were taught that, if they observed other students acting in these ways, they should share their concerns with a trusted adult.

To spread this message—about paying attention to warning signs—Sandy Hook Promise released a video in 2016 called *Evan*. In the video, a cute high school kid named Evan starts exchanging flirty notes with a mystery girl. They scrawl their messages on the top of a table in the school library. A jaunty tune plays in the background as Evan tries to figure out who his correspondent is. At the end of the video, there's a meet-cute moment in the gym as the girl identifies herself. Then, just as we're enjoying the sweet scene, the gym door suddenly slams open and a boy enters bearing a rifle. He cocks it. The kids scream, and the video fades to black.

It's a shocking moment, but not as shocking as what comes next: The video is replayed, quickly, to show us that the shooter was in the background of almost every scene: flipping off another student, being bullied at his locker, sitting alone at lunch, surfing gun videos on the web, and posting on social media a picture of himself with a gun. The signs were right in front of us, but we didn't see them. Our attention was elsewhere. The *Evan* video was a sensation—it has since racked up over 100 million views. (And if there has been a more jarringly effective PSA in the last decade, I haven't seen it.)

Sandy Hook's Know the Signs program was well-received among school leaders who wanted some way to reduce the likelihood of shootings. The training spread to hundreds of schools. (Notice this is another example of deploying "human sensors.") Early on in their work, the Sandy Hook team realized that they needed to broaden their focus to include students vulnerable to bullying and self-harm (especially suicidal tendencies and cutting). Some of the warning signs for those behaviors were similar to those for school shooters—social withdrawal, an attraction to violence, and more—and these kinds of incidents were far more common than school shootings. It became routine, in the aftermath of a Know the Signs training, for a student to alert school leaders about a classmate who had talked seriously of suicide.

But not all students were comfortable taking their concerns to adults. Sometimes they didn't feel they had anyone they could trust; sometimes they were afraid of being seen as a snitch, or even, in the case of school shooters, of being retaliated against. So in 2018, Sandy Hook Promise launched the Say Something Anonymous Reporting System, a tip line on which students could submit their concerns (via phone or an app) anonymously. "Most of these threats don't happen 8:00 a.m. to 3:00 p.m., Monday through Friday, September through June," said Paula Fynboh, Sandy Hook Promise's vice president for field operations. "It gives them an easy way to report the threats without some of the stigma."

When the reporting system was adopted by public schools in Pennsylvania in 2019, over 178,000 students were trained. The results were immediate: 615 tips and calls were received in the first week alone. There were 46 suicide interventions, 3 major drug busts, 2 father/stepfather sexual assault interventions, and dozens of self-harm interventions.

Another tip led to police action. On January 24, 2019, at 2:30 a.m., the police received a referral from the tip line. An anonymous source had reported a shooting threat made against the Hazleton Middle School by a 14-year-old student on Snapchat. After some investigation revealed that the tip was credible, the police visited the student's home at 4:30 a.m., meeting with the kid's mother and uncle. (The gender of the student was not released.)

The officers learned there was a Glock handgun in the home. They were assured that it was locked in a safe place that the juvenile could not access. But a cursory search revealed that the Glock was not secured at all. It was lying on the top of a nightstand. Fully loaded.

This is the power of early detection: The Safe2Say Something program identified a potential shooter with the means and apparent intent to carry out a massacre *before* any harm was done. Other credible school-shooting threats have also been averted thanks to Sandy Hook Promise.

In the aftermath of cases like these, there will be a strong incentive for many of those involved to claim it was a false positive. The teen will say, "I didn't really mean that stuff!" The parents will agree: *He's troubled, but he's not violent!* And the school administrators would likely prefer to dodge the media storm themselves. To be fair, they might all be telling the truth! The Safe2Say system will no doubt be prone to overreactions and even cruel pranks. It will almost certainly surface many false positives for every genuine threat avoided. To make matters worse, it's the curse of preventing rare problems that we may never really know when we've succeeded. (How could anyone prove conclusively that the kid in Hazleton would have perpetrated a massacre?)

But surely parents can agree that, in the case of school shootings, we'd rather err on the side of too many false positives. The cost of missing those warning signals is simply too high.

"When I think back to the Sandy Hook school tragedy, I know that there was a sequence of events—a chain—that had to link up perfectly for events to unfold as they did," said Hockley in a TEDx talk. Her friend David Wheeler, whose son Ben was killed in the massacre, likened that chain to a set of dominoes, each one of which had to be toppled for disaster to happen.

"When we look at it, we don't see the dominoes, we see the spaces in between," said Hockley in the talk, "when someone could have done something or said something to stop the next domino from falling over."

Hockley, too, lost a child at Sandy Hook. After she learned about the shooting, she hurried to the firehouse near the school, where people were congregating. She remembers the sense of relief that flooded her when she found her eldest son, Jake, there, "the feeling of his arms around my neck—and my reluctance when I had to pull away in order to continue searching for my youngest, my six-year-old, Dylan."

A few hours later, the police delivered the news: Dylan had been murdered in his classroom. Shot multiple times. He was found in the arms of his special education assistant, who died while trying to protect him. He was in first grade.

Hockley wants desperately to stop this moment from happening to another parent. To interrupt another school's chain of dominoes by rushing into the space between them.

CHAPTER 9

How Will You Know You're Succeeding?

A question that bedevils many upstream interventions is: What counts as success? With downstream work, success can be wonderfully tangible, and that's partly because it involves restoration. Downstream efforts restore the previous state. *My ankle hurts—can you make it stop? My laptop broke— can you fix it? My marriage is struggling—can you help us get back to the way we were?* In these situations, there's not much conceptual handwringing about what constitutes success. If your laptop starts working again, that's victory.

But with upstream efforts, success is not always self-evident. Often, we can't apprehend success directly, and we are forced to rely on approximations—quicker, simpler measures that we hope will correlate with long-term success. But because there is a separation between (a) the way we're measuring success and (b) the actual results we want to see in the world, we run the risk of a "ghost victory": a superficial success that cloaks failure.

In this chapter, we'll scrutinize three kinds of ghost victories. To foreshadow the three varieties, let's imagine a long-struggling baseball team that is determined to remake itself as a winner. Because that journey may take years, the manager decides to emphasize power hitting—especially more home runs—as a more proximate measure of success. In the first kind of ghost victory, your measures show that you're succeeding, but you've mistakenly attributed that success to your own work. (*The team applauds itself for hitting more home runs—but it turns out every team in the league hit more, too, because pitching talent declined.*) The second is that you've succeeded on your short-term measures, but they didn't align with your long-term mission. (*The team doubled its home runs but barely won any more games.*) And the third is that your short-term measures *became* the mission in a way that really undermined the work. (*The pressure to hit home runs led several players to start taking steroids, and they got caught.*)

That first type of ghost victory reflects the old expression "A rising tide lifts all boats." If you're in the boat-lifting business, you will be tempted to ignore the tide and proclaim success. That happened in the 1990s as crime fell precipitously across the US. In any particular city, the police chief looked like a miracle worker. A dozen different policing philosophies all looked right because crime was dropping everywhere. "Put it this way: Every police chief in the country who was in office in the '90s has a lucrative consulting company right now," said Jens Ludwig from the University of Chicago Crime Lab (who we met in chapter 7). "And almost no police chief who worked in the late '80s, during the crack cocaine era, has a lucrative consulting company."

This is not to imply, by the way, that the people winning those ghost victories were being deceptive. In their eyes, and in the eyes of the people they were helping, the success was real. In almost every American city, crime really was falling. But their individual stories of causation were likely wrong.

Ghost victories, in all their forms, can fool almost anyone—even (or perhaps especially) the people achieving the "successes." It's only when you examine them very closely that you can spot the cracks—the signs of separation between apparent and real success. For Katie Choe, the chief engineer for the City of Boston's Public Works Department, those first anxiety-making clues came in the form of two maps that she'd commissioned in 2014.

Part of Choe's job was to determine how to spend the city's funds for sidewalk repair, and the first map revealed the current condition of the city's sidewalks. In a herculean feat of cartography, a team had walked all 1,600 miles of sidewalks during a Boston winter, rating the condition of every segment. Thirty percent of the city's sidewalks—labeled in red—were rated in poor condition.

The second city map was a heat map showing where certain 311 calls had originated—specifically, those calls requesting sidewalk repairs. Choe's group had been using the 311 calls to direct the sidewalk-maintenance crews. If a Bostonian called to report a cracked sidewalk, the city would add the complaint to a queue and send construction crews to complete the repairs as resources allowed.

Looking at the maps side by side convinced Choe that something had gone badly wrong. The city's sidewalks were in terrible shape in the lowest-income areas of Boston, but those sidewalks weren't getting fixed, because the 311 calls—which determined how repair dollars were spent—came disproportionately from the rich areas.

In other words, in Boston, the squeaky wheels got the grease—and the squeakiest wheels were rich people.

Choe's team had been unwittingly discriminating against low-income Bostonians. But the inequity had been neatly concealed by the way they'd been measuring themselves. The sidewalks team had evaluated their work in three ways. First, they looked at spending. The city government divided Boston into three zones for ease in administration, and each area was allocated a similar repairs budget for sidewalks, roughly $1.5 million apiece. The second measure was the square footage of sidewalks repaired, which was a measure of the productivity of the repair teams. The third and final measure was the number of 311 cases closed.

Three simple measures. Perfectly reasonable. Together, they reflect the values of equity, productivity, and constituent service. It's easy to see how you could cruise along for years, navigating by these measures and never questioning them. It was only because of the two maps—and the soul-searching it sparked—that Choe realized how distorted the measures were.

For one thing, dividing the city into three parts, and investing in each equally, did not in any way ensure equity, because the money within each area was ultimately spent based on who called 311 to complain. The rich parts of all three areas got served disproportionately. About 45% of the city's repairs were performed on sidewalks rated in *good* condition!

You might ask, well, why didn't the low-income people call? They had equal access to 311. And the simplest answer is that almost everything in their experience had suggested that the city was not interested in investing in them. All you had to do was look around their neighborhoods. Frank Pina, who lived in the low-income Grove Hall area, showed a *Boston Globe* reporter the spider-webbing cracks on the sidewalk in front of his home. The cracks had been there for years. Asked why he didn't call for repairs, he said, "Nothing would get done."

The rich people believed they would get served, so they called, and they were served. The poor people believed they'd be neglected, so they didn't call, and they were neglected. Boston had created two self-fulfilling prophecies.

Compounding the problem was the way jobs were prioritized. Imagine you're part of a construction crew facing more requests for repairs than you could ever complete. And you know you'll be evaluated partly on how many of those requests you complete. Which jobs would you prioritize? The easy ones, of course. The quick fixes. That incentive led to ridiculous outcomes: For instance, 15% of the city's repairs in 2017 were completed on sidewalks in poor condition—*and were still rated in poor condition after the repairs were complete.* (I.e., a crew might have fixed one hole but ignored another one a short distance away.) Kind of like a surgeon who sees a patient with three gunshot wounds, patches one of them, and congratulates herself for speedy service.

To Choe's credit—and she is quick to recognize the mayor and other city leaders for supporting her work—she took decisive action on these issues. Her first question was: What are we trying to accomplish, ultimately, with these repairs? Two goals seemed paramount: walkability and equity. Sidewalks are supposed to allow for easy walking from place to place—repairing a rough patch in a cul-de-sac is far less important than making a similar repair in a high-foot-traffic area. And the places where more walkability was most needed were the places that had been historically neglected.

Before Choe's intervention, somewhere between $3.5 million and $4 million of the city's $4.5 million budget for sidewalk maintenance and small repairs went to serve 311 calls. That number is now about $1 million. The priorities have been flipped: The first people helped are not the ones who ask the loudest but the ones who need it worst. The bulk of the repair budget now goes to strategic, proactive efforts to overhaul damaged sidewalks in the areas where it will make the most difference. "We are serving people who really need it—people who have felt under-invested in and felt like the city may actually have abandoned them at some point," said Choe.

It would be a mistake to assume that this was an easy victory, or that it will be a permanent one. Despite the comparatively low stakes—$4 million to $5 million in a city budget is chicken feed—Choe needed air cover from the mayor. Which tells you something about the political sensitivities involved. And if Boston's squeaky wheels think that it's taking longer for the cracks on their sidewalks to get fixed, they will start calling politicians. What will happen then?

Choe is also struggling with what measures of success should replace those used in the past. The team's aspiration is clear enough: to use sidewalk-repair dollars as leverage to create more practical mobility in the most vulnerable neighborhoods in Boston. But how do you measure that, exactly? Ideally, you'd have tallies of how many people were walking to schools and parks and businesses, before and after the work, and you could celebrate the increases. But how big would those increases have to be to satisfy you? And where would you get those pedestrian counts? Would you try to access surveillance cameras to gather the data, or would privacy issues outweigh your measurement concerns? Would you hire someone to stand at intersections with a counting device, clicking as every human being walks by? (Wacky as it sounds, they're trying that, but it's expensive.)

Part of what made the old metrics in Boston so appealing was how simple they were to access and understand. In his book *Thinking, Fast and Slow*, the psychologist Daniel Kahneman wrote that our brains, when confronted with complexity, will often perform an invisible substitution, trading a hard question for an easy one. "Many years ago I visited the chief investment officer of a large financial firm, who told me that he had just invested some tens of millions of dollars in the stock of Ford Motor Company," wrote Kahneman. "When I asked how he had made that decision, he replied that he had recently attended an automobile show and had been impressed. 'Boy do they know how to make a car!' was his explanation. . . . The question that the executive faced (Should I invest in Ford stock?) was difficult, but the answer to an easier and related question (Do I like Ford cars?) came readily to mind and determined his choice. This is the essence of intuitive heuristics: When faced with a difficult question, we often answer an easier one instead, usually without noticing the substitution."

In Boston, the easy questions to answer were: How much are we spending per area? Are we addressing citizen complaints? And how many square feet of sidewalk are we repairing? Those weren't the right questions, but they were the easy ones.

This substitution—of easy questions for hard ones—is something that happens with both downstream and upstream efforts. But what's distinctive about upstream efforts is their longer timelines, and those timelines force a second kind of substitution. One tech company was considering how to measure its email marketing campaigns, as reported in a research paper by the economists Susan Athey and Michael Luca. Originally, the firm had been measuring the sales generated by its promotional emails, but that was a noisy measure, since it might take weeks before customers placed an order. And it was complicated to link the purchase back to the original email that the customer had received. So the company switched to a new measurement: "open rates," or the percentage of people who opened the company's emails. The open rate could be observed quickly—numbers tallied within hours—and it was useful, in the sense that you could quickly measure the effects of simple tweaks to the email message. Very soon, the open rates increased, thanks to the marketers' creative tweaks.

But within months, the company knew it had a problem: The sales generated per email had declined precipitously. Why? Athey and Luca explained that "the successful emails (using the opening rate metric) had catchy subject lines and somewhat misleading promises." (I.e., just think of every email ever sent by a politician: *Want to have a beer, DAN?*) The short-term measure the leaders chose did not align with their true mission, which was to boost sales.

Choosing the wrong short-term measures can doom upstream work. The truth is, though, that short-term measures are indispensable. They are critical navigational aids. In the Chicago Public Schools example, for instance, the district's leaders ultimately cared about reducing the dropout rate. That was the mission. But they couldn't afford to wait four years to see whether their theories were paying off. They needed more proximate metrics that could guide their work and allow them a chance to adapt. Freshman On-Track (FOT) was the first, but even that was too long-term. (You can't afford to wait until the end of freshman year to see whether students are off track, because if they are, the damage has already been done.) So the school leaders started watching attendance and grades—measures you could examine and influence on a weekly basis. The theory of change was: If we can boost attendance and grades, we can improve a student's On-Track standing, and that will boost her chances of graduating. The short-term measures were well-chosen: The plan worked brilliantly, as we saw.

Getting short-term measures right is frustratingly complex. And it's critical. In fact, the only thing worse than contending with short-term measures is not having them at all.

~~~~~~~~

We've seen two kinds of ghost victories so far—one is caused by an effort that's buoyed by a macro trend, like the local police chief heroes in the '90s who were primarily surfing a nationwide reduction in crime. The second kind of ghost victory happens when measures are misaligned with the mission. That's what Katie Choe realized about Boston's sidewalk repairs: The city had chosen the wrong short-term measures.

There is also a third kind of ghost victory that's essentially a special case of the second. It occurs when measures *become* the mission. This is the most destructive form of ghost victory, because it's possible to ace your measures while undermining your mission.

I've "won" this kind of ghost victory. When I was a boy, my father offered to pay me $1 for every book of the Bible I read. With 66 books in the Bible, I stood to gain a windfall of $66, which could immediately be reinvested into Atari 2600 cartridges. My father intended for me to start with Genesis and read from beginning to end. Instead, I started with Second John, Third John, and Philemon—the three shortest books in the Bible. I can remember the look of disappointment and disbelief on his face as I tried to claim my first $3 installment.

I'd aced the measures and made a mockery of the mission.

In England in the early 2000s, the Department of Health had grown concerned about long wait times in hospital emergency rooms, according to a paper by Gwyn Bevan and Christopher Hood. So the department instituted a new policy that penalized hospitals with wait times longer than four hours. As a result of the policy, wait times began to shrink. An investigation revealed, however, that some of the success was illusory. In some hospitals, patients had been left in ambulances parked outside the hospital—up until the point when the staffers believed they could be seen within the prescribed four-hour window. Then they wheeled the patients inside.

We've all heard stories like this before. People "gaming" measures is a familiar phenomenon. But *gaming* is actually a revealing word, because often these stories are told with an air of playfulness. (I told my own story about books of the Bible that way, mostly to disguise my own embarrassment.) But for many upstream interventions, gaming is not a *little* problem—just a quirky, mischievous aspect of human behavior—it's a destructive force that can and will doom your mission, if you allow it. We need to escalate the rhetoric: People aren't "gaming metrics," they're defiling the mission.

Consider the spectacular drop in crime in New York City. Murders peaked at 2,262 in 1990, and they have fallen in almost every year since, down to 295 in 2018, an 87% drop. Major crimes as a whole declined by more than 80%. Many observers trace the long-term decline to changes made in 1994, when new leadership in the New York City Police Department (NYPD) established a new system called CompStat. (Even as we discuss the CompStat strategy, don't forget the "rising tides" point—crime was falling in other cities that were using very different approaches.)

To simplify somewhat, CompStat had three key components. First, the police began to track crimes obsessively, gathering data and using maps to pinpoint the locations where crime was happening. Second, police chiefs were asked to allocate their resources based on the patterns in the data; in other words, if there was a rash of robberies in a certain neighborhood, they should shift officers there. Third, leaders at the precinct level were held accountable for reducing crime in their areas. It's that last point that created some ter-rible unintended consequences. Recall Joe McCannon's point from chapter 5 about using data for "inspection": When peo-ple's well-being depends on hitting certain numbers, they get very interested in tilting the odds in their favor.

In 2018, *Reply All*, a podcast from Gimlet Media, reported a two-episode series on CompStat and its legacy. It's a stun-ning piece of work—essential listening for anyone who is grappling with the tensions between measures and mission. The podcast host, PJ Vogt, explained how the local chiefs reacted to CompStat's new focus on accountability:

> "If your crime numbers are going in the wrong direction, you are going to be in trouble. But some of these chiefs started to figure out, wait a minute, the person who's in charge of actually keeping track of the crime in my neigh-borhood is me. And so if they couldn't make crime go down, they just would stop reporting crime.
>
> "And they found all these different ways to do it. You could refuse to take crime reports from victims, you could write down different things than what had actually hap-pened. You could literally just throw paperwork away. And so [the chief] would survive that CompStat meet-ing, he'd get his promotion, and then when the next guy showed up, the number that he had to beat was the num-ber that a cheater had set. And so he had to cheat a little bit more. . . .
>
> "The chiefs felt like they were keeping the crime rate down for the commissioner. The commissioner felt like he was keeping the crime rate down for the mayor. And the mayor, the mayor had to keep the crime rate down because otherwise real estate prices would crash, tourists

would go away. It was like the crime rate itself became the boss."

The tendency to lessen the severity of crimes in order to dodge criticism became known as "downgrading." *Reply All* included a chilling example of downgrading. Here's the conversation between the host (PJ) and Ritchie Baez, a 14-year veteran of the NYPD (and a caution to readers: there's a description of rape in the passage ahead):

PJ: Ritchie and his partner had been told to just stand on this one street corner all night. It's this intersection in a commercial part of town, so it's all these retail stores. But it's midnight, so all the stores are closed. It's the kind of assignment where most nights you just stand there and nothing happens until the sun comes up. But that night, this guy runs up to them and says, "Hey, something really bad is going on. You gotta help."

RITCHIE: He says, "Listen, I see a guy dragging a lady into a vacant lot. I think he's gonna rape her." So we got in the car. We drive. And I hear a lady screaming, "Help, help, help." So I see him on top of her. He's punching her, and he's raping her. So I flash my light. I tell him, "Stop." He stopped. And I tell them, both of them, "Come towards me." They both starts walking. So she has a black eye. Both have their pants down.

PJ: The victim starts to tell Ritchie what happened. And he says thinking back now, the thing that still stands out to him is just how precise she was in the way she described it.

RITCHIE: She says, "He raped me. I know I'm a prostitute, but no money was exchanged. He assaulted me, and he inserted his penis inside my vagina without my consent, while he was assaulting me." So she basically broke down the definition of rape. Textbook.

PJ: So Ritchie calls the crime in over the radio, and his boss shows up at the scene.

RITCHIE: And basically, he tried questioning her. The way he was questioning her—they—they question the victim several times and try to see if you change your story slightly.

PJ: Ritchie knew exactly what his boss was up to. His boss did not want to enter this victim's crime into Comp-Stat. And so what he was doing was he was questioning her over and over and over again, trying to find some hole in her story that would give him an excuse to treat the crime as something less than rape. He was trying to downgrade her crime.

PJ: What's the kind of change that would allow a downgrade?

RITCHIE: Well, they was trying to make it as a theft of service.

PJ: Theft of service?

RITCHIE: Yeah.

Think about this: An NYPD official is held accountable for rape statistics. There are two ways to make those numbers look better. The first way is to *actually prevent rape*—to project the police's presence into dangerous areas and thereby deter the violent acts. (That's what would have happened if Ritchie and his partner had arrived at the scene just a few minutes earlier.) The second way to reduce the rape count is to *reclassify actual rapes* as lesser crimes—in this case, Ritchie's boss tries to reframe the incident with the prostitute as a "theft of service." The first way constitutes a victory; the second way is an abomination. But, tragically, both would look the same in the data.

Here's what makes this whole subject even trickier: Crime really did go down—way down—in New York City. But that success became a kind of trap. As it became harder and harder to sustain the real decline in crime, it became more and more tempting to fiddle with the numbers instead.

We cannot be naïve about this phenomenon of gaming. When people are rewarded for achieving a certain number, or punished for missing it, they will cheat. They will skew. They will skim. They will downgrade. In the mindless pursuit of "hitting the numbers," people will do anything that's legal without the slightest remorse—even if it grossly violates the spirit of the mission—and they will find ways to look more favorably upon what's illegal.

All of us won't stoop to this behavior all the time. But most of us will some of the time.

Imagine a high school principal who's getting leaned on, hard, to move the dropout rate. What's the *right way* to reduce the dropout rate? Keep kids engaged, monitor their performance carefully, and support them relentlessly. But that's hard, and this principal is lazy. So how else could the principal make the dropout rate budge? He could telegraph to his teachers that Fs are banned from their gradebooks. Never mind what students learn—if they make even a trivial effort to be present, then they should pass, and they should advance, and they should graduate. That's a ghost victory. More cleverly, the principal could play the downgrading game. Any time a student dropped out, he could consider her situation with the counselor, squint really hard, and come to the determination that she had "TRANSFERRED" (to another school) not "DROPPED OUT." Dropping out counts against you; transferring doesn't. And who's gonna find out?

Who's to say that the student didn't intend, in her heart of hearts, to enroll in a different school in the next semester?

Could the entire success story at Chicago Public Schools be a ghost victory, because of factors like these? The answer is no. But we only know that because CPS had the courage to expose itself to scrutiny. Researchers at the University of Chicago Consortium on School Research, led by Elaine Allensworth, scoured the district's data and found that there was, in fact, reason to believe that gaming had happened—that some dropouts had been falsely relabeled transfers. But the researchers also found that the incidence of gaming was insubstantial relative to the size of the gains in graduation.

The researchers also addressed the first type of ghost victory—those caused by surfing a macro trend. Graduation rates *are* rising nationally—a rising tide is lifting all boats—but the researchers found that CPS's efforts had "outpaced the increases in most other districts."

To address the other risk—that students were graduating just because they got passing grades despite poor performance—the researchers looked at several other indicators. Attendance had improved significantly, suggesting that something real and behavioral had changed. The number of students taking AP (advanced placement) courses and the number scoring well had both increased. But most convincing was the students' performance on the ACT college admissions test, which the state required all students to take. "If schools were simply passing students through to graduation, we would expect the tested achievement levels of students would decline," the researchers wrote. But that didn't happen. ACT scores improved by almost 2 points from 2003 to 2014, where a nearly 2-point gain reflects "the equivalent of almost two years of learning."

CPS's success is no ghost victory. Their measures matched

the mission. And the way the district's leaders accomplished that is instructive. They used what Andy Grove, the former CEO of Intel, called "paired measures." Grove pointed out that if you use a quantity-based measure, quality will often suffer. So if you pay your janitorial crew by the number of square feet cleaned, and you assess your data entry team based on documents processed, you've given them an incentive to clean poorly and ignore errors, respectively. Grove made sure to balance quantity measures with quality measures. The quality of cleaning had to be spot-checked by a manager; the number of data-entry errors had to be assessed and logged. Note that the researchers who assessed CPS used this pairing: They balanced a quantity metric (number of students graduating) with quality ones (ACT scores, AP class enrollments). In New York City in 2017, NYPD finally added some complementary measures to CompStat: questions for local citizens that measure how safe they feel and how much they trust the police.

Any upstream effort that makes use of short-term measures—which, presumably, is most of them—should devote time to "pre-gaming," meaning the careful consideration of how the measures might be misused. Anticipating these abuses before the fact can be productive and even fun, in sharp contrast to reacting to them after the fact. Here are four questions to include in your pre-gaming:

1. The "rising tides" test: Imagine that we succeed on our short-term measures. What else might explain that success, other than our own efforts, and are we tracking those factors?
2. The misalignment test: Imagine that we'll eventually learn that our short-term measures do not reliably predict success on our ultimate mission. What

would allow us to sniff out that misalignment as early as possible, and what alternate short-term measures might provide potential replacements?

3. The lazy bureaucrat test: If someone wanted to succeed on these measures with the least effort possible, what would they do?

4. The defiling-the-mission test: Imagine that years from now, we have succeeded brilliantly according to our short-term measures, yet we have actually undermined our long-term mission. What happened?

There's a fifth question, too, that should be asked, and it's so complicated that we'll spend the next full chapter exploring it:

5. The unintended consequences test: What if we succeed at our mission—not just the short-term measures but the mission itself—yet cause negative unintended consequences that outweigh the value of our work? What should we be paying attention to that's offstage from our work?

As we know, good intentions are not enough to ensure that upstream work succeeds. When we try to prevent future problems, there's always a risk that we'll fail. But beyond that, there's a risk that our efforts to do good might actually cause harm instead. Ahead: the struggle to anticipate the ripple effects of our work.

CHAPTER 10

How Will You Avoid Doing Harm?

Macquarie Island lies about halfway between Australia and the northeast coast of Antarctica. As one of the few islands in the region where animals can breed, it serves as a precious rest and breeding stop for migratory birds. It is also a protected wilderness, uninhabited by humans, other than visiting rangers and researchers. Because of these factors—its remoteness, its unique habitat, and its lack of human beings—the island is home to many rare species, especially seabirds, such as the blue petrel, which lopes across the water to gain speed before it takes off. (The bird is supposedly named for Saint Peter, in honor of the apostle's trusting walk across the water to Jesus.) Huge populations of penguins and seals occupy the island.

Macquarie Island, in short, is a conservationist's paradise. Or it would have been, if it hadn't been ruined in the 19th and 20th centuries by hunters and traders, who sailed to the island repeatedly to capture penguins and seals for their natural oil, which could be used as fuel. Even as the sailors decimated the island's native species, they brought alien species with them: Rabbits served as food, and mice and rats were accidental stowaways. They brought cats to kill the rodents—

and also to provide some company (since clubbing seals all day can be lonely work). These new species had no natural predators on the island, so they treated the island's native flora and fauna as an endless all-you-can-eat buffet.

By the 1960s, conservationists were ready to take aim at the rabbits, whose nonstop grazing and tunneling had caused severe erosion and disrupted the mating habits of seabirds, who like to burrow to breed. Some experiments had been run in the 1960s to see if various poisons would control the rabbits. One virus was thought promising, but it failed to spread, so the conservationists concluded that they needed a vector for the virus. In 1968, they started capturing thousands of fleas from Tasmania, transporting them to Macquarie Island, and releasing them in the rabbit burrows. As the rabbits came in and out of the burrows, the fleas would hop on board.

After about 10 years of this flea-seeding, all the island's rabbits were lousy with them, and in 1978, the deadly myxoma virus was introduced. How do you introduce a virus, you ask? You walk around at night with flashlights and low-powered air rifles, shooting a bunch of rabbits in the bum with cotton-wool pellets soaked with the virus. The fleas took it from there, spreading the virus from rabbit to rabbit. By 1988, over 100,000 rabbits had died, reducing the total population to under 20,000.

Meanwhile, the cats were running out of rabbits to eat. They began to dine on the rare seabirds. So conservationists targeted the cats: Park rangers started shooting them, and by 2000, all cats had been eradicated from the island. Then the rabbit population began to rebound, partly because they had developed resistance to the virus, and partly because they weren't being eaten by cats, which had been shot. Also, the lab that made the rabbit-killing virus stopped making it.

The conservationists decided: We've got to scale this thing

up. They launched a plan to kill all the island's rabbits, mice, and rats. They started by dropping poison bait out of planes, but about 1,000 native birds were killed along with the pests. The conservationists recalibrated. A more ambitious multi-pronged plan was hatched involving: killing the animals with poison bait, shooting them, hunting them with dogs, and unleashing a particularly successful virus called Rabbit Hemorrhagic Disease Virus, which was delivered via laced carrots.

This onslaught worked. By 2014, the last rabbit, mouse, and rat had been eliminated—and of course the cats were long gone. The native species began to rebound. The effort was hailed as a success, nearly 50 years after it had begun. However, the island is now being plagued by invasive weeds. Turns out that the weeds were being held at bay by the nibbling force of thousands of rabbits. Now conservationists are making plans to study and combat the weeds. The war continues.

Of all the stories I researched in writing this book, this is the one that perplexed me the most. I've spent hours trying to make sense of it. Is this the story of an epic fiasco? Or of a stunning conservation victory? Is it a parable about the consequences of "playing God," or is it an inspirational tale about persisting and adapting in the face of failure? Is it a cartoon of downstream activity—constantly reacting to new problems as they emerge—or is it a classic long-term upstream intervention to prevent the extinction of native species?

I couldn't even navigate my way through the morality of it: Is it okay to slaughter an island's worth of animals? Should mankind really be in the business of selecting which species survive and which die? (If you leaned indignantly toward no, are you prepared to doom to extinction a beautiful species of petrel for the sake of preserving thousands of rats that, let's remember, are only on the island in the first place because of some blubber-greedy sailors? [And if you sympathize with the petrel over the rats, then maybe we should question whether our moral judgments might be shaded by a species' cuteness? Imagine if the sailors had brought not rabbits and rats but Labradoodles. One fears the petrels would be in big trouble.*])

Systems are complicated. When you kill the rabbits, the cats start feasting on the seabirds. When you kill the cats, the rabbits start overpopulating. When you kill both, the invasive weeds run rampant. Upstream interventions tinker with complex systems, and as such, we should expect reactions and consequences beyond the immediate scope of our work. In "shaping the water," we will create ripple effects. Always. How can we ensure that, in our quest to make the world better, we don't unwittingly do harm?

"As you think about a system, spend part of your time from a vantage point that lets you see the whole system, not just the problem that may have drawn you to focus on the system to begin with," wrote Donella Meadows in an essay. Meadows was a biophysicist and systems thinker whose work I'll draw on several times in this chapter. She continued, "And realize that, especially in the short term, changes for the good of the whole may sometimes seem to be counter to the interests of a part of the system."

---

* At one point, desperate for insight, I sent a pleading email to Peter Singer, one of the world's leading moral philosophers and the author of the book *Animal Liberation*. What did he make of the Macquarie Island intervention? He replied, "I'm not willing to say that we should let species go extinct rather than kill introduced animals, but if there is extreme suffering (e.g., the deaths of millions of rabbits in Australia because of the introduced virus myxomatosis) then I am doubtful that we ought to do that." He added that "we should develop non-lethal methods of population control, or if that isn't possible, find lethal methods that result in a quick and painless death." I quickly embraced Singer's stance as my own, in hopes of keeping at bay any more cognitive dissonance.

Here's a painful illustration of Meadows's point: In July 2009, a young Google engineer was walking through Central Park when he was struck by a falling oak tree branch, causing brain injuries and paralysis. It seemed like a tragic but fluke injury. Except that, later, the comptroller of New York City, Scott Stringer, started analyzing the claims paid by the city to settle lawsuits, and he discovered an unexpectedly large number of settlements resulting from falling branches. (One was the engineer's lawsuit, which had settled for $11.5 million.) Curious, Stringer investigated further and discovered that the city's pruning budget had been cut in previous years, in an effort to save money. "Whatever money we thought we were saving on the maintenance side, we were paying out on the lawsuit side," said David Saltonstall, the NYC assistant comptroller for policy.

Stringer's office created a program called ClaimStat—its name was inspired by CompStat—that he announced in 2014 would be a "new, data-driven tool that will help to identify costly trouble areas before they become multi-million dollar cases." His team mapped and indexed the roughly 30,000 annual claims made against the city, hunting for patterns. They found, for instance, that the city had paid out $20 million in settlements over a period of years due to injuries to children on playgrounds. ClaimStat revealed that one swing on a Brooklyn playground was responsible for multiple lawsuits—it was hung too low, and five children broke their legs on the swing in 2013. "All someone needed to do was go out and raise the swing six inches, and the big problem would have been eliminated," said Saltonstall. "But nobody thought to do that. . . . When you start to aggregate it, you see what the causes are, and that the fixes are generally not that complicated."

This is what Meadows meant about the interests of the

"part" and the "whole" diverging. You can save money by cutting the pruning budget, and that's good for the parks department. But then you end up paying claims, in amounts far greater than the cuts, to innocent people who got hurt by falling branches. This linkage, though, was invisible to the people involved. It was only when Stringer's team began to compile and study the data that the pattern became apparent.

In planning upstream interventions, we've got to look outside the lines of our own work. Zoom out and pan from side to side. Are we intervening at the right level of the system? And what are the second-order effects of our efforts: If we try to eliminate X (an invasive species or a drug or a process or a product), what will fill the void? If we invest more time and energy in a particular problem, what will receive less focus as a result, and how might that inattention affect the system as a whole?

The Macquarie Island example might have led you to believe that tinkering with ecosystems is too complex to be feasible. But with the right kind of systems thinking, it can work. The international organization Island Conservation, whose mission statement is "to prevent extinctions by removing invasive species from islands," has succeeded many times in ridding islands of rats, cats, goats, and other intruders. As a result, endangered species—often ones that exist nowhere else—have been saved. The organization's tools include sophisticated forms of cost-benefit analysis and conservation models such as a food web, which is essentially an org chart of who eats whom on an island. The food web makes it easier to envision the second-order effects of removing one species from the food chain. "Islands are systems," said Nick Holmes, who was the director of science at Island Conservation for eight years. "If you move things around within the system, there are consequences beyond the direct. . . . If there are goats on an island plus invasive plants, and you remove the goats, will you get an increase in invasive plants?" Holmes said that they use an extensive set of questions about indirect impacts to assess new projects.*

When we fail to anticipate second-order consequences, it's an invitation to disaster, as the "cobra effect" makes clear. The cobra effect occurs when an attempted solution to a problem makes the problem worse. The name derives from an episode during the UK's colonial rule of India, when a British administrator was worried by the prevalence of cobras in Delhi. He thought: *I'll use the power of incentives to solve this problem!* A bounty on cobras was declared: Bring in a dead cobra, get some cash. "And he expected this would solve the problem," said Vikas Mehrotra, a finance professor, on the *Freakonomics* podcast. "But the population in Delhi, at least some of it, responded by farming cobras. And all of the sudden, the administration was getting too many cobra skins. And they decided the scheme wasn't as smart as initially it appeared, and they rescinded the scheme. But by then, the cobra farmers had this little population of cobras to deal with. And what do you do if there's no market? You just release them." The effort to reduce the number of cobras yielded more cobras.

Other examples of the cobra effect are more subtle. Amantha Imber, an organizational psychologist and founder of the Australian innovation firm Inventium, had an unfortunate brush with it. In 2014, her 15-person team was ready to move into a new office space in Melbourne. Imber had spent about $100,000 renovating it, and the results were stunning: a hip open-office plan with two long, custom-made wooden

---

* I should add, to be fair, that Holmes is not skeptical about the Macquarie Island intervention in the way that I am. Don't want it to seem like he's throwing his conservation colleagues under the bus here.

desks, bathed in light from windows stretching up to 12-foot-tall ceilings, with patches of graffiti on the walls. When clients came in, it nailed their conception of what an innovation firm should look like. It was perfect. Except when it came to working.

"I would get to the end of the work day and think to myself, *I haven't really done any work today, I've just spent the day dipping in and out of email, in meetings, being interrupted by coworkers*," said Imber. She started doing her real work at nights or on the weekends.

Imber and her team thought that the open space would encourage face-to-face collaboration, but it backfired. "I'm not going to start face-to-face conversations because everyone else is going to be privy to it," she said. And when people *did* talk, it interrupted every single person in the room, making it impossible to do deep, focused work. Imber started working from cafés in the morning, and she gave her colleagues permission to do the same. As a result, these days there's usually only two or three people in the office at any given time.

A 2018 study by Harvard scholars Ethan Bernstein and Stephen Turban backs up Imber's experience. They studied two Fortune 500 companies who were preparing to transition teams of employees to an open-office floorplan. Before and after the move, many staffers volunteered to wear "sociometric badges," which captured their movements and logged how often they talked and to whom. (Their conversations were not recorded, just the fact they were talking.) The goal was to answer the most basic question about open floorplans: Do they boost face to face (F2F) interactions?

The answer was almost laughably clear: F2F interactions plunged by about 70% in both companies. Meanwhile, email and messaging activity spiked. When people were placed closer together so that they'd talk more, they talked less. The cobra strikes again.

What can be confusing, in situations like these, is that we must untangle contradictory strands of common sense. On one hand, you think: *Of course, moving people closer together will lead them to collaborate more! That's just basic sociology.* On the other hand: *No, look at subways or airplanes—when people are crammed in together, they find ways to retain some privacy through headphones or books or deeply unwelcoming glances.* How can you know in advance which strand of common sense to trust?

We usually won't. As a result, we must experiment. "Remember, always, that everything you know, and everything everyone knows, is only a model," said Donella Meadows, the systems thinker. "Get your model out there where it can be shot at. Invite others to challenge your assumptions and add their own. . . . The thing to do, when you don't know, is not to bluff and not to freeze, but to learn. The way you learn is by experiment—or, as Buckminster Fuller put it, by trial and error, error, error."

Looking back on the open-office miscue, Imber said she wishes she had tried some experiments with her staff in the State Library Victoria in Melbourne. The library has many different kinds of environments, ranging from open, collaborative spaces to more solitary ones. Had the team sampled some of those different areas, observing how they affected the group's productivity and happiness, that experience might have helped them design an office that served them better.

For experimentation to succeed, we need prompt and reliable feedback. Consider navigation as an analogy: To travel somewhere new we need almost constant feedback about our location; we follow the arrow on a compass or the blue dot on Google Maps. Yet that kind of feedback is often missing from upstream interventions. Think of the open-office situation: How would you know whether collaboration was increasing or not? Most employers don't have "sociometric badges" to log conversations. Maybe you'd add a question to the annual employee survey, asking for people's feedback on the transition. But that kind of infrequent, point-in-time feedback isn't enough to navigate. It's like driving a car with no windows and, once every hour or so, getting beamed a photo of the outside environment. You'd never arrive at your destination, and given the risks, you'd be crazy to try.

"The first thing I would say is you just need to be aware that whatever the plan you have is, it's going to be wrong," said Andy Hackbarth, a former RAND Corporation researcher who also helped design measurement systems for Medicare and Medicaid. I had asked him what advice he'd give to people who were designing systems to make the world better. "The only way you're going to know it's wrong is by having these feedback mechanisms and these measurement systems in place."

Hackbarth's point is that we don't succeed by foreseeing the future accurately. We succeed by ensuring that we'll have the feedback we need to navigate. To be clear, there absolutely *are* some consequences we can and should foresee. If we don't anticipate that removing the goats on an island might make the invasive weeds run wild, then that's a clear failure of systems thinking. But we can't foresee everything; we will inevitably be mistaken about some of the consequences of our work. And if we aren't collecting feedback, we won't know how we're wrong and we won't have the ability to change course.

Soon after I talked to Hackbarth, I had another conversation that reinforced his point. I was talking to a physical therapist who works with women who are recovering from mastectomies. The surgeries often cause them muscular pain and movement difficulties. But something she said struck me: "As soon as a woman takes her shirt off for therapy, I can tell which surgeon did the work. Because the scars are so different." One surgical oncologist in particular has a knack for "beautiful" scars, she said, while another consistently leaves unsightly scars.

I felt a bit sad for that less-proficient surgeon (and more sad for his patients). He might well retire never knowing that he could have done more to help women. You could blame the PT for not sharing her observations, but think about it: What would happen if you approached your boss's boss, unsolicited, with a critique of her work? This is a systems problem. There's an open loop in the system: The insight from physical therapists is never getting fed back to the surgeons.

Feedback loops spur improvement. And where those loops are missing, they can be created. Imagine if, in the mastectomy situation, photos of surgical scars were taken automatically at patients' follow-up visits, and those photos were sent back to the surgeons along with a comparison set of their peers' work. (Or even more radically, imagine if the comparison set was shared with patients before their procedures, as an input into their choice of surgeon.*)

Think of all the natural feedback loops involved in, say, selling cars: You've got data on sales and customer satisfaction and quality and market share, and beyond that are exter-

---

*Some nuance here: First, plastic surgeons often *do* show off photos to patients. This physical therapist's experience is with the work of surgical oncologists, who typically handle the mastectomies (removal of the breast) but not the reconstructions. Second, all of the previous chapter's concerns about measurement apply here. Obviously in this situation we're not optimizing for subtle scars. We're optimizing for a woman's healthy recovery from cancer. The hypothesis here is that the right system might allow us to achieve both the health outcomes and the aesthetic ones.

nal assessments to keep you honest, ranging from customer reviews to *Consumer Reports* analyses to J. D. Power studies. Over time, these inputs almost *force* companies to make better cars. It's genuinely difficult to buy a poorly made car these days, especially now that the Pontiac Aztek is gone. But imagine if almost all of these sources of feedback were missing—if you just made cars every day and hoped for the best. That's, in essence, the way our education system works.

Yes, standardized tests scores are a key source of feedback, but *what changes* are made in response to that feedback? If a disproportionate number of eighth graders score poorly on linear equations, for example, do the seventh- and eighth-grade teachers subsequently meet and redesign their approach to the subject for the next semester? (Even if they did, that would still just be 1 point of feedback per year!) Imagine if, instead, teachers had data at their fingertips every day: What if teachers could instantly see which students haven't participated in the last few classes? (And which have hogged too much airtime?) What if they knew, based on the previous night's homework, which concepts the students were struggling with the most? What if they knew, based on school-wide data, which of their colleagues has the best way of teaching a particular lesson? All teachers will have *some* intuition about these things, and some star teachers will engineer their own systems for accomplishing these things, seeking constantly to improve themselves. But improvement shouldn't require heroism! Online marketing messages don't get better because of heroics—they get better because the feedback is so quick and targeted that you almost can't escape improvement.

In short, if we want to make the education system better, we could try to concoct the perfect intervention—the new curriculum, the new model—and hope for the best. Or we could settle for a pretty good solution that's equipped with so many built-in feedback loops that it can't help but get better over time. The second option is the one that systems thinkers would endorse.

How do you build a feedback loop? Let's take a simple example from the business world: the staff meeting. Staff meetings are a great example of a human endeavor—like fistfighting and potty training—that never improve. We get a lot of practice in meetings, but as Michael Jordan said, "You can practice shooting eight hours a day, but if your technique is wrong, then all you become is very good at shooting the wrong way."

One business created a feedback loop for meetings. The owners of Summit CPA Group, a 40-person accounting group founded in Fort Wayne, Indiana, made a decision in 2013 to let everyone work remotely. It was a popular decision, but it had consequences. Because they didn't encounter each other in person anymore, their online meetings became their primary means of contact.

At first, the meetings were problematic in familiar ways. "What happens is you get certain people that will talk forever and dominate the entire conversation," said Jody Grunden, the cofounder of Summit. "You've got certain people that won't say a word, and then you got people in between." Worse, the people who dominated the conversation tended to be the complainers and the critics. The firm actually started losing CPAs because they found the interactions so negative.

So the firm made some changes. They had a facilitator run the meetings, using a new structured agenda that included a segment in which every participant shared something positive from the previous week. It sounds a bit corny, and at first some people tried to pass their turn, but pretty soon it became the norm. The bright-spots focus changed the tone and, better yet, provided a venue for learning: They started sharing advice on everything from handling tough clients to making reports simpler. Beyond the structured agenda, though, they added a feedback loop. At the end of every meeting, every attendee verbally scored the meeting from 1 to 5. Outliers were asked quickly what had made the meeting unusually helpful or unhelpful. When people complained about something—a discussion going on too long, a problem not being resolved—those issues got addressed. As a result, the meetings steadily got better, because now they had a closed loop. The virtual meetings at this accounting firm now consistently score 4.9 out of 5.0. (Whereas Ben Affleck's movie *The Accountant* scored 3.65 out of 5.0 on IMDb. He needed a feedback loop, apparently.)

~~~~~~~

We started with the question: How do we avoid doing harm? We've seen that wise leaders try to anticipate second-order effects beyond their immediate work. (Examples: food webs at Island Conservation and ClaimStat's data patterns in NYC.) We've seen, too, that we can never anticipate everything, so we need to rely on careful experimentation guided by feedback loops.

Based on these ideas, we can formulate some questions to guide a decision about whether or not to stage an upstream intervention. Has an intervention been tried before that's similar to the one we're contemplating (so that we can learn from its results and second-order effects)? Is our intervention "trial-able"—can we experiment in a small way first, so that the negative consequences would be limited if our ideas are wrong? Can we create closed feedback loops so that we can improve quickly? Is it easy to reverse or undo our intervention if it turns out we've unwittingly done harm?

If the answer to any of these questions is no, we should think very carefully before proceeding. To state the obvious, there's a vast difference between an "experiment" where some colleagues try out open-office seating in the Melbourne library and an "experiment" where scientists tinker with a species using gene-editing tools. Please do not mistake this chapter's emphasis on experimentation for the ethos of "move fast and break things."

Upstream work hinges on humility. Because complexity can mount quickly even in simple interventions. Let's take a final example that should be an easy one: trying to cut back on single-use plastic bags. Environmentalists consider these bags a leverage point, because even though they make up only a tiny fraction of the overall waste stream, they do disproportionate harm. They're lightweight and aerodynamic, so they end up blowing into waterways or storm drains. They endanger marine wildlife and befoul beaches. And frankly they're symbolic of an unsustainable mind-set: Factories are manufacturing plastic products—an estimated 100 billion bags are used annually just in the US—that may not degrade for hundreds of years, all for the sake of making it easier for customers to schlep their purchases home, at which point they're immediately considered trash. So this should be a no-brainer: Let's get rid of these bags.

Our starting point for systems thinking demands: What are the likely second-order effects? What will fill the void left by plastic bags, if they're banned? Customers will either: (a) use more paper bags; (b) bring reusable bags; or (c) go without bags.

Here's where we reach our first surprise: While paper bags and reusable bags are far better than plastic ones from the perspective of keeping waterways clean, they are worse in other ways. They require far more energy to produce and ship than do plastic bags, which means they increase carbon emissions. A UK Environment Agency study calculated the "per use" effects of different bags on climate change and concluded that you'd need to use a paper bag 3 times and a cotton reusable bag 131 times to be on par with plastic bags. Not to mention that manufacturing paper and reusable bags causes more air and water pollution than plastic, and they are much harder to recycle. So now we're forced to grapple with part/whole confusion: If protecting waterways and marine life, specifically, is our goal, then a plastic bag ban is a great idea. But if making the whole environment better is the goal, then it's less clear. There are competing effects to consider.

Another twist is that we've got to be very careful how we design the ban. In 2014, Chicago passed a law banning stores from offering thin, single-use plastic bags at checkout. So what did the stores do? They offered *thicker* plastic bags at checkout. The retailers' supposed rationale was that customers could reuse these plastic bags, but of course most didn't. That's the cobra effect again: Trying to rid the environment of plastic led to more plastic.

Experimentation leads to learning, which leads to better experiments. California voters passed a statewide ban in 2016, without the thicker-plastic loophole. One effect of the ban, though, was that sales of small and medium plastic trash bags shot up. (Presumably there were people who reused their grocery store plastic bags as trash bags at home—or for picking up dog poop—so in their absence they had to start buying alternatives.) A study by economist Rebecca Taylor found that 28.5% of the reduction in plastic caused by the ban had been nullified by this shift toward other bags. Still, that's 28.5%, not 100%. The ban had significantly reduced single-use plastics. (And notice that in order to assess this issue at all, someone had to be carefully tracking the sales of substitute products, thus creating a source of feedback.)

Then there were truly unanticipated consequences. Some people attributed a deadly 2017 hepatitis A outbreak in San Diego to the lack of plastic bags. Why? Homeless people had been in the habit of using the bags to dispose of their own waste. When the bags became less plentiful, the other alternatives turned out to be less sanitary.

I wonder if you're feeling now the way I was feeling when I first started trawling through this research: overwhelmed and dispirited, with a spritz of annoyance. What hope do we have of solving the hardest problems facing us when even *plastic bag policies* create a blizzard of complexity?

It was Donella Meadows's quote—about the need "not to bluff and not to freeze but to learn"—that pulled me out of my wallow. Because her point is: It's hard, but we're learning. As a society, we're learning. Think of all the ingredients required even to *analyze* a policy like the plastic bag ban: the computer systems, the data collection, the network infrastructure, not to mention the ecosystem of smart people who know how to structure experiments that can shed light on city- and state-wide policies. This infrastructure of evidence has existed for a mere blip in human history. When it comes to upstream thinking, we're just starting to get in the game.

In 2016, Chicago scrapped the plastic bag ban that had led to the cobra effect. The city council replaced it with a 7-cent tax on all paper and plastic checkout bags that started in early 2017. And you know what? It's working pretty well. A research team led by economist Tatiana Homonoff collected data from several large grocery stores. Before the tax, about 8 out of 10 customers used a paper or plastic bag. After the tax, that dropped to roughly 5 out of 10. What did the other 3 people do? Half the time they brought their own bag and half the time they carried out their purchases without a bag. And for those 5 customers who kept using bags, *ka-ching*, their voluntary tax payments provided the city with extra money to serve citizens.

Chicago's leaders tried an experiment by banning lightweight plastic bags; it failed at first, but they knew why it failed, so they tried a different experiment, which worked better, and hopefully no city on earth has to repeat the dumb version of the ban again. It's slow and tedious and frustrating, but we're collectively getting smarter about systems. Donella Meadows deserves the last word: "Systems can't be controlled, but they can be designed and redesigned. We can't surge forward with certainty into a world of no surprises, but we can expect surprises and learn from them and even profit from them. . . . We can't control systems or figure them out. But we can dance with them!"

CHAPTER 11

Who Will Pay for What Does Not Happen?

In a speech at a health conference in Battle Creek, Michigan, Professor A. Arnold Clark of the state board of health condemned our tendency to shortchange investments in prevention: "But let us see how much we really pay in Michigan for the prevention of disease. How much do you pay in Battle Creek? You have in this city about 45 physicians. I suppose they average an annual income of about $200,000 each. That makes about $9 million which you pay each year to cure you after you get sick.

"Now how much do you pay to prevent your getting sick?" Professor Clark continued. "Probably, not more than $50,000. You have a health officer and you probably pay him about $50,000 a year to stamp out communicable diseases in Battle Creek. Now prevention is better than cure. . . . Some people seem to think that because they always have lived, all money spent to prevent disease and dying, is money wasted. You have heard of the man who dropped his life insurance because he had kept the thing up 20 years, and never derived any benefit from it yet. That seems too often to be the policy of the city, the state, the nation."

Professor Clark delivered this speech in 1890. (I modernized the dollar figures, but otherwise the quote has been left intact.) It's telling that public health experts are still forced to make the same argument today: *Prevention is better than cure.* Actually, it's enraging. Because in the 130 years since Professor Clark made his speech, we have gathered over-whelming evidence of the efficacy of prevention and public health: Just look at our life expectancy.

In 1900, the average life expectancy at birth for Americans was 47.3 years. By 2000, life expectancy had reached 76.8. Clearly a dramatic improvement, but let's be clear about what these numbers mean and don't mean.

"Life expectancy" is an average across a population. In a population of 5, 1 person might live to 75 while the others live to 91, 70, 66, and 82, yielding an average life span of 76.8. The average blurs the variety. (Stick with me here—I know this is obvious so far.)

But sometimes averages don't just blur an underlying reality, they obliterate it. I'm amazed, for instance, by how many perfectly smart people seem to believe that the 47.3-year life expectancy in 1900 is synonymous with "most people lived significantly shorter lives back then." I suppose they picture our ancestors, in their mid-forties, tottering around with canes and false teeth and trying frantically to get their affairs in order. From this perspective, the passage of the Social Security Act in 1935 would have been a cruel joke indeed— *Yes, you can start collecting retirement income at 65—twenty years after you're dead!!* [maniacal laugh]

A representative sample of life spans in that era absolutely did not look like this: 46, 48, 56, 39, and 48, averaging out to 47.4 years. Rather, it looked more like this: 61, 70, 75, 31, and 0. At the turn of the century, in 1900, almost 1 out of every 5 children was dead before reaching their fifth birthday.

The natural life span of human beings today is not that different than it was a hundred years ago. What's different is that we're saving a lot of people—especially babies and children—from dying too early. On this point, you may have noticed that Clark, in his rant above, emphasized "communicable diseases." That's because in his era, about a third of all deaths were due to infectious diseases such as pneumonia, influenza, tuberculosis, and diphtheria. These diseases were disproportionate killers of children. Today, the number of people dying of those infectious diseases has decreased from about 33% in 1900 to less than 3% in 2010.

What's responsible for that decline? Upstream efforts. Better hygiene, cleaner water, pasteurization, and improved living conditions, as well as the advent of sewage systems and the introduction of antibiotics and vaccines. Yet even in the face of this massive success—and by "massive success," I mean *imagine that every fifth child in your family tree would have died were it not for this work*—public health must still plead for resources.

"We under-invest in the services and policies that would keep people healthier so that they would not develop those illnesses or have the injuries or suffer from premature deaths that we know could be avoided," said John Auerbach, the president of the public health policy group Trust for America's Health. "It's tragic." The group pegged the total national spending on public health specifically at $88.9 billion, just 2.5% of total health care spending in the United States in 2017.

Public health efforts suffer from what is effectively a punishment for success. "In public health, if you do your job, they cut your budget, because no one is getting sick," said Julie Pavlin, a physician with experience running global health programs and combating infectious diseases for the

191

Army. And her comment gets to the heart of the matter: The fee-for-service model in health care favors reaction over prevention.

"We'll pay $40,000 a year for the price of insulin, but we won't pay $1,000 to prevent someone from ever getting diabetes," said Patrick Conway, a former deputy administrator at CMS (the Centers for Medicare & Medicaid Services). "We should pay for value. Imagine if a car that took more hours to build was more expensive. That would make no sense. Cars would not become better and cheaper if you paid for them that way."

At one point, I came across a commentary that highlighted American consumers' world-leading access to MRI scans. We get them quicker and more often, apparently, than anyone else in the world. (*USA! USA!*) To take pride in that is a bit like bragging that Americans lead the world in receiving airport security pat-downs. I mean, if there's something to find, it's true that we'd like to find it quickly, but surely, we'd rather be the nation whose people need the least checking-over. (And as the Gil Welch turtles/rabbits logic implies, we might discover things that don't need discovering.) What the MRI statistic illustrates is a simpler idea about our fee-for-service system: When you get paid for something, you do more of it. (No doubt we also "lead the world" in dental X-rays. And just imagine if TSA agents were paid by the grope.)

So, in short, reactive efforts succeed when problems happen and they're fixed. Preventive efforts succeed when nothing happens. Who will pay for what does *not* happen?

That's not an unanswerable question. There *are* people who will pay for what does not happen. (Including you! Presumably all those oil changes are preventing *something*.) But creating payment models to fund upstream efforts can be almost unbelievably complicated, for reasons we will explore in this chapter.

First, though, we should remind ourselves how easy it *should* be to pay for upstream efforts. Take the case of Poppy + Rose, a comfort food restaurant in downtown Los Angeles. Diana Yin, the co-owner, monitored customer reviews carefully, and she noticed a customer had complained online about receiving cold waffles for brunch. She did some detective work and discovered that the restaurant's one waffle maker could not keep up with demand at brunch. So cooks had started making waffles before the rush hit to build up a stash in reserve. A clever workaround—but it led to cold waffles. Nobody likes a cold waffle. So Yin sprung for a second waffle maker.

This is the dream scenario from the perspective of paying for prevention. It's so simple: The person who paid, Diana Yin, is the one who will reap the rewards. Think of it in terms of "pockets": The money was spent from one pocket, and it will be returned to that same pocket. And Yin will probably recoup her investment quickly. This same one-pocket logic would apply, of course, to an investment you made in yourself: a certification or a graduate degree. You might spend thousands of dollars today in the hopes of earning many more thousands in the future.

Our story gets more complicated quickly, though. Having one pocket does not guarantee that wise upstream investments will be made. Here's an example: For decades, caregivers in nursing homes have suffered lower-back injuries from lifting and transferring patients. This is awful for the caregivers, of course, and also costly for their employers, who must contend with lost workdays and workers' compensation claims for the injuries.

Entrepreneurs created mechanical patient-lifting equipment to solve exactly this problem. For the nursing home leader, though, it was not an obvious investment to make. The machines were very expensive, and they required a whole new set of procedures—staffers had to relearn how to transfer patients using the machinery—and they were slower than the old-fashioned, lower-back-fueled technique. So why embrace the nuisance and cost? It's easier to stay in the tunnel and accept that, every now and then, someone's going to get hurt.

Then, in the late 1990s, an evaluation found that if caregivers used specific, research-tested techniques for transferring patients—including the use of that equipment—then nursing homes could cut lost workdays and workers' compensation claims by two-thirds. As a result, the investment in the equipment could be repaid in less than three years. These findings were publicized within the long-term care industry, and nursing homes increasingly adopted the new procedures, leading to a 35% reduction in lower-back injuries between 2003 and 2009, according to a CDC report.

So here's our first wrinkle: The nursing homes had the luxury of a single pocket, but the choice of whether to buy the patient-moving machines was murkier than with the waffle maker example. It was hard to assess the investment from within a single nursing home. A broader perspective, with evidence drawn from across the nursing home industry, was required: *Hey, this equipment is well worth the money.* Even in a simple case like this one, then—where a good payoff awaited an investment—the inertia pushed against prevention.

Now let's swing to the opposite end of the spectrum: the maddening complexity of creating funding models for social services. The Nurse-Family Partnership (NFP) offers a representative case. The program was founded in the 1970s by David Olds, a recent college graduate who had grown disillusioned with the inner-city day care center where he worked. Many of the preschool kids he worked with were suffering because of their parents' bad decisions. One child had developed few language skills, speaking mostly with grunts. When Olds interviewed the child's grandmother, she told him that her daughter (the child's mother) was an addict who had used drugs throughout her pregnancy. Another boy always seemed restless at nap time. Olds later learned that he was beaten by his mother every time he peed in his sleep.

Olds realized that he could have helped these kids much more if he could have intervened earlier in their lives. He could have best served them, he believed, by helping their mothers. The kind of abuse he was witnessing was motivated more by ignorance than by cruelty. These mothers, simply put, didn't have the knowledge or skills they needed to be effective mothers. They didn't have support systems or role models, and they didn't know what to do with the frustration and anger that comes with raising kids.

The program he created, NFP, matches registered nurses with low-income, first-time pregnant women. The same nurse visits the young woman in her home regularly during her pregnancy and throughout the first two years of the child's life. The nurse acts as a mentor, helping the mother deal with the tensions of parenting: what to do when children cry, what to do when they don't sleep, how to get children on a schedule. And the nurse explains the basics: how to breast-feed, swaddle a baby, transition babies to whole foods, brush a child's teeth, and so on. Beyond the parenting instruction, a crucial part of the work is simply to be a caring human being who's there to support the mother. To show her how to take care of herself so that she can care for her child. To help her navigate the complexities of working while raising a child. To listen when the pressures of life seem overwhelming.

Three major randomized controlled trials of NFP have been conducted in the United States: in Elmira, New York; Memphis, Tennessee; and Denver, Colorado. The studies have shown that the program consistently improves maternal health, child safety, and well-being. Among the specific impacts were reductions in smoking during pregnancy, preterm births, infant mortality, child abuse and maltreatment, and criminal offenses by the mother, Food Stamp payments, and closely spaced pregnancies (second births within 18 months of the first). That's quite a laundry list of bad things avoided. One study estimated a return of at least $6.50 for every $1 invested in NFP.

Talk about an easy investment decision! Even if it took you 20 years to earn the $6.50 return, that's still the equivalent of about 10% annual interest. So, we'd expect that, given the results, NFP would be available for every low-income, first-time mother in the country who wants it. No, far from it. Why?

In our simple waffle-iron case, the person who made the investment received the benefits. One pocket. But in this case, notice how splintered the rewards are. The primary beneficiaries, of course, are the child and the mother, in that order. But they can't pay. Who else benefits? All the other institutions who would have had to pay for bad outcomes, if it weren't for NFP. Let's take three examples:

1. Reducing preterm births saves money for Medicaid, which would have paid for the more intensive care needed for those babies;
2. Reducing criminal offenses saves money for the criminal justice system (less burden on the police, courts, and jails) and of course also benefits the general public;

3. Reducing SNAP (Supplemental Nutrition Assistance Program; previously Food Stamps) payments saves money for the federal agriculture department, which administers it.

There are plenty more beneficiaries beyond those three, including ripple effects on health, education, income, and more. Everyone wins!

Let's say a local health system could be persuaded to fund NFP. It's an expensive program, costing roughly $10,000 per woman served. Unfortunately, the health system would receive only a small benefit from the investment, since the primary value goes to all the other parties described above. That's an example of what's called the "wrong pocket problem": a situation where the entity that bears the cost of the intervention does not receive the primary benefit. One pocket pays, but the returns are scattered across many pockets.

Ideally, you'd fix that by passing the hat around to all the relevant parties who'd benefit—taking up a collection to fund NFP. But here are the objections you'll encounter: *There's no precedent for that. There's no line item in my budget for "chipping in for a program that may pay me back eventually."* And, *Let's say you're wrong and we don't save money downstream—does that mean you'll refund my money?* Concerns like these explain why programs like NFP, which could create enormous social benefit, simply can't get funded at the level they deserve.

But there are experiments underway to fix the wrong pocket problem. A group in South Carolina designed a "pay for success" model that could fund a wide expansion of NFP's work. Here's how they set it up: In 2016, NFP received a $30 million infusion of cash to expand its work in the state, and the results of its efforts will be assessed over six years via a randomized control trial. If the work is successful, according to several measures agreed upon in advance, then the state government would be positioned to fund the work permanently. The magic of the arrangement is that the state government doesn't take a big financial risk upfront, because the trial stage was mostly funded from outside. So if NFP proves a valuable investment, South Carolina will reap the rewards; if it doesn't, the state isn't out much.

Conceptually, this arrangement is not difficult to understand, but the intricacies of the deal were exhausting. "We spent three years trying to figure out how to make the rules allow us to do something that everybody in the room understood on day one was the most obvious thing in the world," said Christian Soura, then head of South Carolina's Department of Health and Human Services (DHHS). To get a feel for the difficulty, just look at the list of players involved: The NFP team in South Carolina. The DHHS. The Abdul Latif Jameel Poverty Action Lab. The Harvard Kennedy School of Government Performance Lab. The consulting firm Social Finance. The Duke Endowment. BlueCross BlueShield of South Carolina Foundation. (And honestly, many more—just accept this list as a sampler.)

Soura said the negotiations involved answering "How do we figure out how to get all these different governmental funding streams to let us pay for a thing that all of us know we need more of? And that winds up being this Kafkaesque nightmare of navigating these different federal and state funding restrictions on all these different sources of funding."

The deal has great promise. The initial investment will allow NFP to offer services to an additional 3,200 mothers, supporting them from their pregnancies through the first two years of their children's lives. Those children will be raised in happier, healthier homes as a result of NFP's support. The payoff for those mothers and children should be profound.

Perhaps more important, over the long term, is that the deal could break the wrong-pocket curse. If NFP delivers on expectations, then the state and federal government would want to fund the work on an ongoing basis, since the payoff on the investment would be clear. And since there are 49 other states with high-risk populations of mothers who need help, too, the possibilities for expansion are almost limitless. In that context, three years of laborious haggling over the core contract doesn't look like a poor investment.

We can pay to fix problems once they happen, or we can pay in advance to prevent them. What we need are more business and social entrepreneurs who can figure out how to flip payment models to support the preventive approach. Here's a trivial example of how that can work: A few years ago, my wife and I flipped to "upstream" pest control. We'd had a problem with spiders, so we called an exterminator. When he visited, he offered us a subscription service. The idea was that they'd visit on a regular basis—not requiring an appointment, just spraying outside our home periodically—using the best strategies they'd learned to keep bugs at bay. At first, we were skeptical—"Are we getting ripped off here?"—but ultimately what won us over was the beautiful vision of removing bugs from our life concerns. So we did it, and we removed one small source of drama from our lives. No longer are we cycling from Infestation to Rescue to Inaction (and repeat). Now it's just a quiet and mostly invisible routine: maintain, maintain, maintain.

And it occurred to me, in a similar vein, how many of the world's household repairs are caused by a failure of upstream maintenance. The air-conditioning system breaks prematurely because the air filters weren't changed regularly.

The hot-water heater stops working because it was never flushed.* Toilet problems, gutter problems, roof problems: Aren't many of these faults preventable? Some of us treat our homes like cars that have never had an oil change.

If someone would "own" this work for you—assuming responsibility for the integrity of your major household appliances and systems—would you pay them a regular, monthly fee? Like, forever? It's a concept that at least one major business is exploring. "The home service industry really hasn't changed in the modern era," said Brandon Ridenour, the CEO of ANGI Homeservices, which includes both the websites HomeAdvisor and Angie's List. "It's almost identical to the way it worked 50 years ago. An individual need pops up unexpectedly—it comes up out of the blue and people are left to deal with it reactively. 'I need a plumber, an electrician, a handyman.' That starts the process where they use the phone book or ask friends and then use services like ours."

But Ridenour wondered whether people might be ready for a subscription model, where service is delivered regularly and preventively, without waiting for the moment of crisis. "The extraordinarily wealthy have estate managers," said Ridenour. "They contract for these services and the services are delivered throughout the year." Beyoncé does not call the plumber, in other words. Ridenour believed that a lot of the work that estate managers do could be automated—using data sets to predict when maintenance should happen, and using HomeAdvisor's massive database of contractors to

---

* Here is an actual thing that happened with one of my relatives. Their dryer stopped working, and they sought advice from family members. A round of troubleshooting ensued but was fruitless. Then one final question was asked: "You've cleaned the lint filter, right?" [Silence.] *What's the lint filter?*

match people to the job. "Could we democratize estate management for the masses?" he asked.

Paying for upstream efforts ultimately boils down to three questions: Where are there costly problems? Who is in the best position to prevent those problems? And, how do you create incentives for them to do so? Ridenour's argument seems reasonable: HomeAdvisor (or someone like it), not the homeowner, is in the best position to handle maintenance. Some homeowners are handy and some aren't, but no individual homeowner can leverage the intelligence from *thousands of homes* about which specific types of preventive maintenance to employ. There is untapped value in the system: If major appliances could be prevented from failing too early, the resulting value could be divvied up between homeowners as savings and HomeAdvisor as profits.

Let's apply these three questions to health care. Where is there a costly problem? One example is that Medicare spends a fortune paying for hospital visits that could have been prevented (for instance, if a patient's diabetes had been kept under control). Who is in the best position to prevent those problems? It's not hospitals—they don't have a relationship with the patient before the emergency. Nor is it the patient, really, since a patient isn't a health care expert. (Just as a homeowner isn't a home maintenance expert.) The people best positioned to prevent those problems are primary care doctors. So how do you create incentives for them to do so? Meet the Accountable Care Organization (ACO), one of the models introduced in the 2010 Affordable Care Act.

Here's a highly simplified description of one type of ACO (and trust me when I say there is an endless wormhole of complexity that lies beyond): A bunch of primary care doctors can join together to form an ACO, and Medicare says to the ACO: For the population of patients you serve, we know roughly how many hospital visits to expect this year, and how much those visits will cost us. So if you can reduce those visits by managing your patients' health better, then we'll share the savings with you.

"Before ACOs, doctors didn't get paid a dime for keeping patients out of the hospital," said Farzad Mostashari, the cofounder of Aledade, a company that helps doctors form ACOs. "In this model, it makes sense for the doctors to spend more time sitting with the patient and their family, rather than worrying about how they can see more patients per hour."

I talked with Jonathan Lilly, a primary care doctor in West Virginia, and he said that the ACO model had transformed his practice. He sees fewer patients in a day—maybe 20, rather than 25 or 30—and spends more time with each. He and his partners have become less reactive and more proactive: They're monitoring their patients' blood sugar levels and blood pressure and weight, making sure those diagnostics are trending in the right direction. They've also become more accessible: If you want to keep patients from taking their problems to a hospital, you've got to be available to them. So they now offer evening and weekend hours, as well as a "fast track" visit in which a patient can show up any day, even without an appointment, and get a guaranteed visit.

"I'd never practiced this way," said Lilly. "I've always wanted to be a family doctor, and always wanted to be the gatekeeper, and do it the right way. And this has allowed me to do it." It's working for Lilly and his partners. Their patients are healthier and happier with their care, and they're going to the hospital less. As a result, Medicare saved money, and they shared the savings with the ACO, which meant Lilly got paid more.

There are other positive innovations in paying for upstream health. There's an increasing amount of interest in "capitation," a payment model used by health systems such as Kaiser Permanente, which has over 12 million members. Kaiser Permanente (KP) is unusual in that it's both an insurer and a provider. If you're a member, you pay your monthly premium (or your employer does) to KP, and when you get sick, you go to a KP doctor. This structure allows KP to avoid one of the long-standing tensions in the health care industry: Providers (like your doctors) want to bill insurers for as much as they can, while insurers want to pay for as little as possible, so there's a constant tug-of-war over which procedures will be covered and how they'll be reimbursed.

KP providers get paid a flat fee, per person served, to take care of all that person's needs (on a risk-adjusted basis, so they'd get more to take care of an elderly person than a 25-year-old). That's capitation. KP doctors don't have an incentive to order an unnecessary MRI scan, because they don't get paid any more for doing it. Now, why doesn't capitation lead to *cheating* people of services? After all, the fewer services provided, the greater the profit to the provider. The corrective is that—as with Andy Grove's "paired metrics"— they are also held accountable to quality-of-health metrics and patient-satisfaction metrics. So if they allow their patients' health to deteriorate, or if those patients report being unhappy with the care they receive, the providers will make less money.

Capitation models open the door to upstream interventions, because they make it easier to justify spending money on prevention. At Geisinger Health System, based in Pennsylvania—another integrated system like Kaiser—diabetic patients are invited to use a "Food Farmacy": basically a grocery store full of healthy food where they can shop and take home bags of food for free. Why would Geisinger give away free food? Because, to a diabetic patient, food is medicine. And for Geisinger, it's worth paying for healthy food when it saves the patient from downstream complications that might be far more costly.

Our health system is inching toward a model with better incentives. The success of these efforts provides us a chance to reflect on the lessons of this section of the book. To prevent problems, upstream leaders must unite the right people (caregivers, insurers, patients). They must hunt for leverage points and push for systems change (unnecessary hospitalizations, ACOs). They must try to spot problems early (by, say, monitoring blood sugar levels). They must agonize about how to measure success—avoiding both ghost victories and unintended consequences. And finally they must think about the funding stream: how to find someone who'll pay for prevention.

It's quite a gauntlet of challenges to endure. It's slow and painful. And it's worth it. Because the scale is so great: 1% of the gargantuan $3.5 trillion health care industry is $35 billion—about the same as Nike's 2018 global revenue. Tiny shifts in large systems can have powerful effects. So, together, by wading our way upstream, we can approach a world where the preservation of health is as valuable as the treatment of disease.

SECTION 3

FAR UPSTREAM

~~~~~~~~~

12. THE CHICKEN LITTLE PROBLEM:
DISTANT AND IMPROBABLE THREATS

CHAPTER 12

The Chicken Little Problem:
Distant and Improbable Threats

An ominous video, originally released in 1999 as a VHS tape, features an all-black-clad Leonard Nimoy (of Spock fame) speaking portentously about the future:

> "There is an ancient myth of what may have been the most highly advanced civilization ever to dwell on the planet Earth. . . . But the legend also ends suddenly, with the revelation that this entire ancient civilization vanished. That their great island sank into the sea because their technological innovations were too far ahead of their human judgments, human foresight, and simple human frailties. This legendary civilization was, of course, Atlantis.
>
> "Yet the problem for us, in the year 1999, is that . . . we are now facing very real global issues related to power supply, satellite communications, water, health care, transportation, distribution of food, and other items vital to everyday human survival. These global issues are the direct result of an equally real human oversight many people now refer to as the Y2K or Year 2000 problem, which derives from the fact that billions of lines of computer code and embedded microchips that now run the

very technologies we all depend upon may fail in the briefest moment between December 31, 1999, and January 1, 2000.

"So we recall the fate of Atlantis. The primary question for our civilization as we approach the year 2000 is this: Have we allowed our own highly advanced technological innovations to far outpace our human abilities to control those innovations, and most importantly, to foresee their ultimate consequences?"

As it turns out—spoiler coming—the Y2K bug did not end civilization on January 1, 2000. What did happen, though? Was civilization saved, or did it never need saving at all?

In this chapter, we'll veer away from the kinds of problems we've spent most of our time studying—primarily recurring ones such as the dropout rate, homelessness, disease, and more. These problems aren't mysterious: We can observe them directly, and we can measure their incidence. But now we'll examine upstream efforts to address problems that are unpreventable (like hurricanes) or uncommon (like an IT network being hacked) or downright far-fetched (humanity being extinguished by new technologies).

Y2K was a one-off problem—a new kind of computer bug that humanity had never faced before and wouldn't face again. John Koskinen was the man tasked with preventing the worst from happening. Koskinen had worked in the private sector turning around failed companies and, from 1994 to 1997, had been a senior leader at the Office of Management and Budget. Twenty-two months before the new millennium, in February 1998, Koskinen had accepted President Bill Clinton's invitation to be the nation's Y2K czar.

The Y2K czar role was a classic no-win job, as Koskinen knew. "If everything went smoothly, people would say: 'What was that all about? What a waste of time and money.' On the other hand, if everything were to go poorly, if the power went out, the stoplights didn't work, the phones were dead, the financial systems quit functioning and the communications systems went dark, everyone would want to know: 'What was the name of that guy who was in charge of preventing this?' "

With less than two years to go, and a small staff, Koskinen knew that he had no hope of fixing the government's systems directly. All he could do was convene the right people, get them talking, and encourage them to share information. Early in his tenure, he organized 25 working groups, each reflecting a different sector of the economy: power companies, telecommunications, state and local governments, health care, and more. Each working group was led by a federal agency—the Department of Transportation, for instance, worked with airlines, railroads, truckers, and shipping companies.

A colleague had objected to this approach: *Our job is to fix the Y2K bug in the federal government—not the entire American economy.* Koskinen's reply was "But you know if the federal systems all work and, come January first, the electrical grid fails, the first question everybody's going to ask is: 'What did you do to keep that from happening?' And the answer can't be, 'It wasn't my job.' "

The working groups had an inauspicious start. Many of the companies' lawyers were concerned that, if their firms collaborated closely, they could be at risk of antitrust or liability suits. Koskinen's team actually had to rush a law through Congress to address these concerns. Eventually, though, the groups began working effectively, sharing information freely.* Meanwhile, Koskinen had begun to appreciate that

---

* Upstream game plan: First, soothe lawyers' concerns about potential lawsuits. Second, save civilization.

he was actually addressing not just a technical problem but a psychological one. Public panic was as much of a threat as the technical bugs.

Consider that, according to Koskinen, at any given time about 2% of ATM machines aren't working. They're broken or out of money. But on January 1, 2000, a nonfunctioning ATM might be interpreted as a Y2K problem, fueling fear. One of everyone's biggest concerns was the possibility of a bank run. If customers worried about not being able to get money, or if they worried about banks failing, they might start pulling out money in the weeks before the millennium. And if other customers saw that, they might worry, in turn: *Those people are probably being paranoid, but I don't want them taking all the money before I can get some, so I better make some withdrawals myself.*

Given the fractional banking system in the US, in which a bank might only keep a small percentage of its assets available in cash, it wouldn't take many paranoia-fueled withdrawals to exhaust a local bank's supply. Just imagine the panic that would ensue when rumors start swirling that *the bank is out of money.* In this way, irrational fears of a bank failure could produce an actual bank failure. How seriously did the government take these fears? The Federal Reserve ordered $50 billion in new currency printed and added into circulation nationwide. That's about $500 for every household in the United States.

In the months leading up to the new millennium, Koskinen grew increasingly certain that the Y2K bug would not cause major disruptions. His public communications and interviews were calm and confident. Still, on December 31, 1999, he was not anxiety-free. He worried about the situation globally—every country with IT systems was theoretically at risk from the Y2K bug, and the United States had become the de facto leader of the work internationally. Would there be a foreign country that had neglected Y2K work and saw a critical system collapse? That visible failure—made hysterical by the media—could be enough to spark panic-driven problems in the United States.

As the first day of the new millennium began, the first reports were from New Zealand. One US journalist had flown there to report live on the air about whether his ATM card worked. It did. (Must have been a long flight back.) Koskinen's team breathed a sigh of relief.

Koskinen held press conferences every four hours, and it was an uneventful day. Mostly. The Japanese experienced glitches in monitoring the safety of their nuclear plants. Later, the Defense Department lost touch for several hours with some intelligence satellites. The other issues were more minor: delayed paychecks, stalled payments, repeated charges on credit cards, and so on.

This example, from the final report of the Y2K team a few months later, captures well the day's lack of drama: "Low-level Windshear Alert Systems (LLWAS) failed at New York, Tampa, Denver, Atlanta, Orlando, Chicago O'Hare, and St. Louis airports during the date rollover. The systems displayed an error message. Air transportation system specialists at each site were forced to reboot LLWAS computers to clear the error." (Later, the screenplay about this incident, *Forced to Reboot*, was sold for zero dollars.)

The new millennium arrived. Civilization endured. People returned sheepishly to cities from their rental cabins in the woods.

As Koskinen had predicted, his team's work went uncelebrated. "It was probably no later than forty-eight hours later that people were saying, 'Well, that went pretty smoothly. Must not have been a problem,'" he said.

But might it be possible those skeptics were right—that the Y2K bug was never really much of a threat at all? Some observers, such as the Canadian computer-systems analyst David Robert Loblaw, had been saying that all along: "Planes will not fall out of the sky, elevators will not drop, governments will not collapse. The Year 2000 is going to arrive with a yawn."

When his prediction was proven right, Loblaw took his victory lap. On January 6, 2000, he wrote a piece for the *Globe and Mail* headlined "You Got Conned and I Told You So." "In fact, few systems actually depend on the calendar year, including some of those that were the source of so much hysteria, such as hydro and air-traffic control," he wrote.

Many of the IT leaders who handled the Y2K preparation still get incensed when they hear it called a hoax. "The reason nothing happened is that a huge amount of work was done because people had made a huge amount of fuss," said Martyn Thomas, who worked on Y2K-related issues from within the UK as a consultant and an international partner at (what was then) Deloitte & Touche. He considers the Y2K bug a near-miss—a catastrophe narrowly avoided thanks to a successful global mobilization of talent and energy.

Who's right? It's hard to know, though my own impression is that it was more of a near-miss than a hoax. This uncertainty is a frustrating aspect of upstream work, especially in situations where you're addressing a novel problem. In situations with recurring problems, there's less ambiguity. If there were 500 high school dropouts for 5 years in a row, and then you started a new program, and this year there were only 400 dropouts, then you can have some confidence that your work made an impact. But with Y2K, there's just one data point: January 1, 2000. And, fortunately, by virtue of fortune or preparation or both, it turned out to be no big deal.

~~~~~~~~

Y2K was a situation where we prepared for disaster, and when disaster didn't come, we questioned whether the preparations had been necessary. Think of the opposite scenario: You prepare for a disaster—and it's incredibly destructive anyway. Do you conclude afterward that you blew the preparations, or do you decide that things could have been even worse if you hadn't tried?

A real-world version of that scenario began in early 2004, when two disaster experts met in Washington, DC, for a discussion: Madhu Beriwal, the founder and CEO of Innovative Emergency Management (IEM), a private contractor that helps governments prepare for and respond to disasters, and Eric Tolbert, the director in charge of emergency response for the Federal Emergency Management Agency (FEMA).

Beriwal asked Tolbert, *Out of all the disasters you're considering, which one keeps you up at night?* Tolbert replied: *A catastrophic hurricane striking New Orleans.*

It was the geography of New Orleans that spooked experts. The city rests below sea level and is situated between levees that keep at bay the waters of the Mississippi River and Lake Pontchartrain. Picture the city as at the bottom of a bowl. If the levees were breached, water would rush into the city and stay there.

In the years after 9/11, FEMA's primary focus had been on acts of terrorism, but Tolbert had been lobbying for money to develop plans for natural disasters. When a few million dollars was approved for that purpose in 2004, Beriwal's company, IEM, got a contract for $800,000. The assignment: Create hurricane response plans for New Orleans and the surrounding region.

IEM created a planning exercise at breakneck speed, taking 53 days to complete a process that would ordinarily take much longer. Hurricane season was looming. For a week in July 2004 in Baton Rouge, IEM convened approximately 300 critical players, including representatives from FEMA, over 20 Louisiana state agencies, 13 parishes, the National Weather Service, over 15 federal agencies, volunteer groups, and state agencies from Mississippi and Alabama. (*Surround the problem.*) They were brought together to face Hurricane Pam, a simulation dreamed up by the IEM team.

"Born in the Atlantic Ocean, [Hurricane Pam] hits Puerto Rico and Hispaniola and Cuba, and it grows bigger as it moves through the warm waters of the Gulf of Mexico," wrote Christopher Cooper and Robert Block of the Hurricane Pam simulation in *Disaster: Hurricane Katrina and the Failure of Homeland Security*, an indispensable account of how Katrina was handled. They continue:

> Though there is plenty of time to flee, many residents along the Gulf Coast stay put. And just as predicted, this storm makes a straight track for the tiny camp town of Grand Isle, Louisiana, obliterates it, and moves north toward New Orleans. The hurricane moves upriver for nearly sixty miles, leaving catastrophe in its wake. It passes right over New Orleans, and as it does, the storm tilts nearby Lake Pontchartrain like a teacup and dumps it into the city. A quick rush of brackish water drenches New Orleans and leaves it sitting in as much as twenty feet of

water. And then the hurricane is gone, and everything lies in ruins.

During the simulation in Baton Rouge, the participants formulated their responses in real time, breaking into subgroups according to their specialties: search and rescue, water drainage, temporary housing, triage centers, and more.

One of Hurricane Pam's key organizers, Colonel Michael L. Brown,* had decreed that, in making their plans, there would be "no fairy dust," as Cooper and Block wrote:

> If a job called for 300 boats, participants would have to find those boats and not just wish them to exist. If planners needed fifteen semitrucks to haul generators to New Orleans, they had to identify where they would get them, or at least make a realistic guess at the source. "They were supposed to plan with the resources that were available or that could presumably be brought in," said Beriwal. "They were not supposed to be thinking that magically 1,000 helicopters would show up and do this."

After an intense and dramatic week of grappling with Hurricane Pam, the group had cobbled together a set of emergency-response plans: some richly detailed, some barely fleshed out. It was a start.

Thirteen months after the Hurricane Pam simulation, in late August 2005, Hurricane Katrina hit New Orleans. In her Senate testimony roughly five months after Katrina,

---

* This is not the Mike Brown of "Brownie, you're doing a heckuva job" fame. Different Mike Brown. This Mike Brown's wife is named Pam, and the simulation was named after her.

Beriwal showed a chart comparing the simulation to the reality:

"HURRICANE PAM" DATA	ACTUAL RESULTS FROM HURRICANE KATRINA
20 inches of rain	18 inches of rain
City of New Orleans under 10 to 20 feet of water	Up to 20 feet of flooding in some areas of New Orleans
Overtopping of levees	Levees breached
Over 55,000 in public shelters prior to landfall	Approximately 60,000 people in public shelters prior to landfall
Over 1.1 million Louisiana residents displaced	1 million Gulf Coast residents displaced for the long-term; majority are Louisiana residents
786,359 people in Louisiana lose electricity at initial impact	881,400 people in Louisiana reported to be without electricity the day after impact

The similarities are uncanny. So the obvious question: What in the world happened? How could you gather together exactly the right people, for the sake of rehearsing exactly the right scenario, and then, when the real thing happens a year later, the response is a failure?

"Failure" is understating it—the Katrina response was a national disgrace. Here's an account by journalist Scott Gold of the scene at the Superdome, the stadium used as a shelter:

A 2-year-old girl slept in a pool of urine. Crack vials littered a restroom. Blood stained the walls next to vending machines smashed by teenagers. The Louisiana Superdome, once a mighty testament to architecture and inge-

216

nuity, became the biggest storm shelter in New Orleans the day before Katrina's arrival Monday. About 16,000 people eventually settled in. By Wednesday, it had degenerated into horror. . . . "We pee on the floor. We are like animals," said Taffany Smith, 25, as she cradled her 3-week-old son, Terry. In her right hand she carried a half-full bottle of formula provided by rescuers. Baby supplies are running low; one mother said she was given two diapers and told to scrape them off when they got dirty and use them again.

Here is where I am going to test your patience by asking you to consider how two dissonant ideas might both be true: First, that the disaster response for the people stranded in New Orleans was unspeakably bad, and second, that many thousands of lives were saved because of the planning that was sparked by Hurricane Pam. In short: Hurricane Katrina's effects were terrible, and they could have been much worse.

Because there were two final rows in the chart that Beriwal showed the Senate—two rows that show the biggest points of difference between Hurricane Pam and Hurricane Katrina:

"HURRICANE PAM" DATA	ACTUAL RESULTS FROM HURRICANE KATRINA
Over 60,000 deaths	1,100 deaths reported to date in Louisiana; over 3,000 still missing
36% evacuated prior to landfall	80% to 90% evacuated prior to landfall

In 2019, Beriwal said of Hurricane Pam, "We predicted the consequences almost to the scientific bull's-eye. One thing we got completely wrong was the number of deaths. Our projection was that somewhere over 60,000 people will die. And horrible as it is, the number of deaths was 1,700. So the difference between the two is contraflow." *

"Contraflow" is an emergency procedure in public transportation in which all the lanes of a highway are temporarily switched to flow in the same direction. This sounds logical in theory: All traffic should flow out of a disaster area, after all. But imagine the complexity of reversing the direction of an interstate highway! Every entrance ramp headed the wrong way has to be blocked and monitored; the public has to be informed what's happening; emergency crews have to be on hand to respond quickly to stranded vehicles so that they don't create logjams. And what happens when the contraflow interstate hits the state border and must transition back to a regular-flow interstate? These issues may sound like logistical minutiae, but keep in mind: Beriwal is arguing that contraflow is the main reason that 1,700 people died in Katrina, not 60,000. The details were vital.

New Orleans had experimented with contraflow the prior year during Hurricane Ivan, a less powerful hurricane that hit the Gulf less than two months after the Hurricane Pam simulation. The process had been a fiasco. The highways clogged quickly, leaving some drivers stranded on elevated roadways for up to 12 hours. And then Ivan veered east, missing New Orleans. If it hadn't, thousands of drivers—facing an interstate that had turned into a giant parking lot—might have had to leave their cars behind and seek shelter.

---

* She's citing 1,700 deaths, rather than the 1,100 deaths in her Senate testimony, because the toll grew as some of the people who'd been missing were confirmed dead.

In response to the Hurricane Pam simulation—and the real-world failure with Ivan—the state had overhauled its contraflow plans. Some of the key lessons included tighter collaboration with officials from neighboring states and better communication with the public. For Katrina, the American Red Cross printed up 1.5 million maps to distribute to explain the contraflow process. Other improvements were more subtle: During Ivan, drivers were stopping frequently to ask cops questions, and the cops thought that they were helping by giving good answers. But those conversations were actually creating bottlenecks and contributing significantly to the traffic jam. For Katrina, the lesson was clear: no talking, wave 'em forward.

On Saturday, August 27, 2005, with Hurricane Katrina in the Gulf threatening New Orleans, Louisiana governor Kathleen Blanco ordered contraflow to begin at 4:00 p.m., and it continued nonstop for 25 hours before it was suspended. The traffic flows were far better than with Hurricane Ivan—the trip to Baton Rouge, usually a 1-hour drive, didn't take longer than 3 hours throughout the contraflow period. The flow rate of cars—the number of vehicles per hour—was almost 70% higher than in rush-hour traffic, yet the cars moved steadily. In total, more than 1.2 million people were evacuated, with no significant delays.

The Hurricane Pam simulation is a model example of upstream effort: convening the right people to discuss the right issue in advance of a problem. "The good thing is we know we made a difference," said Ivor van Heerden, the former deputy director of Louisiana State University's Hurricane Center and a participant in the Hurricane Pam simulation. "We know that we saved thousands of lives."

It was the right idea, but unfortunately it was the only time all the major players came together. No single training, no matter how ingenious, is sufficient to prepare for a catastrophe. IEM, the contractor that invented Hurricane Pam, had planned multiple additional exercises in 2005 to push the work forward. "But in a breathtaking display of penny-wise planning," the authors of *Disaster* wrote, "FEMA canceled most of the follow-up sessions scheduled for the first half of 2005, claiming it was unable to come up with money for the modest travel expenses its own employees would incur to attend. FEMA officials have since said that the shortfall amounted to less than $15,000."

FEMA said no to $15,000. Congress ultimately approved more than $62 billion in supplemental spending for rebuilding the Gulf Coast areas demolished by Katrina. It's the perfect illustration of our collective bias for downstream action. To be fair, no amount of preparation was going to stop the Gulf Coast from being damaged by a Category 5 hurricane. But the proportions are so out of whack: We micromanage thousands or millions in funds in situations where billions are at stake. Preparing for a major problem requires practice. In theory, that's not complicated. What makes it complicated in reality is that this kind of practice runs contrary to the tunneling instinct discussed earlier in the book. Organizations are constantly dealing with urgent short-term problems. Planning for speculative future ones is, by definition, not urgent. As a result, it's hard to convene people. It's hard to get funds authorized. It's hard to convince people to collaborate when hardship hasn't forced them to.

Building a habit is one way to counteract this downstream bias. IT leaders, for instance, have learned that, when it comes to network security, the weakest links are often their colleagues. Phishing schemes—in which people are sent fraudulent emails that trick them into supplying personal information such as credit card numbers or passwords—have become common, involved with 32% of the security breaches examined by the 2019 *Verizon Data Breach Investigations Report*. A cottage industry has sprung up to send fake phishing emails to employees in hopes of training them not to fall for the real attacks. (Sign of the times: There's an industry for fraudulent fraudulence.)

Don Ringelestein, director of technology of West Aurora School District No. 129, in Illinois, was concerned about phishing attacks, so he accepted a free trial from a vendor called KnowBe4. In January 2017, he sent his first phishing test to the district's staffers from a weird email address they'd never seen before. The email announced that a suspected security breach had happened earlier in the week and encouraged them to click a link to change their passwords. Ringelestein had frequently warned his staff about such schemes and figured most people would see through the scam. No: 29% of his colleagues clicked it.

"Surprised is one word. Panic was another," he said of his reaction. Phishing is a particular concern in school districts because—beyond the value of the district's financial data—the students' personal data can be "pure" for identity theft purposes. A thief might use a student's information for years to open up accounts before the student ever realizes there's a problem, according to the FBI and others.

"There's no way we can block all this email with hardware—there's no hardware that will do it," said Ringelestein. "So really the best way for us to close that last door—that last opportunity for phishing schemes to work—is to train our people."

He began crafting emails that tempted his colleagues to click. A free Amazon Prime subscription, just for you—click here! A free drink from Starbucks—download this coupon!

You're way overdue on your E-ZPass toll charges—click to pay now! The click rate on that latter one was 27%, which was particularly discouraging, since Illinois doesn't have E-ZPass. It's I-Pass. (Had Ringelestein offered "free interns to grade student papers," the click rate might have cleared 90%. . . .)

When someone clicks on one of these links, the system diverts the person to a screen where he or she is schooled about internet safety practices. Meanwhile, Ringelestein could monitor which staffers were clicking, and it soon became clear that there were some people on staff who were almost infinitely gullible. Even his least-creative efforts were sufficient to draw their clicks. Ringelestein would drop by their schools to discreetly offer a tutorial.

For more than two years, Ringelestein has been testing and educating his colleagues, and they have slowly raised their guard. The disastrous 29% click rate on the first email has declined to averages of more like 5% in recent attempts.

It's progress. And it's intended to be *generalized* progress—the goal, in other words, is not to arm employees only against fake Starbucks promotions, but to boost their defenses against scams of many colors. If a West Aurora teacher got a suspicious *phone call* asking for sensitive information, they'd be on guard, Ringelestein hopes, even though the medium was different.

That's the vision, too, for disaster preparedness. Emergency simulations aren't supposed to be perfect predictions, just credible ones, and ideally, the parties involved get multiple opportunities to practice. Because they're building knowledge and skills that the parties involved will need in *any* emergency. When disaster strikes, they will already know the players involved. They'll understand the linkages in the system. They'll know where to go for resources. One person

I interviewed, who'd been part of a community-wide preparedness event, said it well: "You don't want to be exchanging business cards in the middle of an emergency."

In these efforts to prepare for uncertain or unpredictable problems—like Y2K or hurricanes—we're seeing familiar themes. An authority convenes the right players and aligns their focus. They escape their tunnels and surround the problem. And they try to make tweaks to the system—like improvements to contraflow—that will boost their readiness for the next disaster.

But now a much more difficult question: What if, for certain kinds of problems, being "prepared" isn't good enough? What if avoiding a problem requires *perfection*?

Think again about Ringelestein's colleagues, who started with a fool-me rate of 29% and improved through education to 5%. That's a big change by behavioral standards. But is it enough? "Education doesn't work when security depends on your weakest link," said Bruce Schneier, a computer security expert, commenting generally on defense against hacking. In other words, if a hacker was dead set on breaking into West Aurora School District No. 129—or any other specific institution, for that matter—then the difference between 29% and 5% is immaterial. For many hacking purposes, you just need one open door. Just that one gullible person who will click on *anything*.

Nick Bostrom, a Swedish philosopher at the University of Oxford, contemplates whether technological innovation has left modern society on the verge of a similar kind of vulnerability—a situation in which the fate of everyone could hinge on a single bad break or bad actor. The context of his comments is mankind's tendency to keep pushing for new innovations almost without regard for the consequences. Scientists and technologists rarely cross a formal threshold where they ask themselves, *Should* this thing be invented? If it *can* be invented, it will be. Curiosity and ambition and competitiveness push them forward, forward, forward. When it comes to innovation, there's an accelerator but no brake.

Sometimes their discoveries are of immense value: antibiotics, say, or the smallpox vaccine. Other times, the inventions are a mixed bag: guns, the automobile, air conditioning, Twitter. We never really know in advance what these technologies will yield, whether they will be mostly good or mostly bad. We just fumble our way forward and deal with the consequences.

Bostrom conjured a metaphor for this fumbling-forward habit: Imagine that humanity is pulling balls out of a giant urn, where the balls represent inventions or technologies. The urn contains some white balls, which represent beneficial technologies like antibiotics, and some gray balls, which represent the mixed-blessing types. The point is: When we reach into the urn, we don't know which color we're going to draw. We just keep reaching in; it's our compulsion. But what if one of those balls turns out to be catastrophic? In his paper "The Vulnerable World Hypothesis," Bostrom considers whether there might be a black ball in the urn, representing a technology that will destroy the civilization that invents it.

Bostrom notes that we haven't drawn a black ball so far, but "The reason is not that we have been particularly careful or wise in our technology policy. We have just been lucky. . . . Our civilization has a considerable ability to pick up balls, but no ability to put them back into the urn. We can invent but we cannot un-invent. Our strategy is to hope that there is no black ball."

This black ball idea may sound absurdly sci-fi: a technology that can destroy civilization. But it's hardly far-fetched: Bostrom contends that our civilization could be put at risk if we ever draw a ball from the urn that puts mass destruction in the hands of small groups. This is, in essence, the "ISIS with a nuclear weapon" scenario. It requires only two conditions: first, a set of actors who would welcome mass destruction, and second, a technology that makes mass destruction available to the masses. Does anyone doubt that the first condition holds? The presence of countless terrorist groups and school shooters and mass murderers provides convincing proof.

As for the second condition—mass destruction being available to the masses—Bostrom asks us to consider an alternate history in which nuclear weapons had not required the sophistication and resources of nation-states to develop. What if, instead, there had been "some really easy way to unleash the energy of the atom—say, by sending an electric current through a metal object placed between two sheets of glass." If people could assemble a nuclear bomb with materials acquired from Home Depot, who doubts the disastrous consequences? Could it be one of our species' luckiest breaks that nuclear weapons turned out to require a lot of money/expertise/resources to harness?

Bostrom's point is that there's no guarantee that we will continue to get lucky in the same way. Already, at this moment, there are DNA "printers" that allow companies to produce stretches of DNA quickly and cheaply for research purposes. Imagine if, someday, those DNA printers could be brought into the home—perhaps in the spirit of offering genetically tailored medicine—and someone could home-cook a copy of the 1918 Spanish flu. One human being could trigger the end for all of us.

We began the chapter with this quote from Leonard Nimoy: "So we recall the fate of Atlantis. The primary question for our civilization as we approach the year 2000 is this: Have we allowed our own highly advanced technological

225

innovations to far outpace our human abilities to control those innovations, and most importantly, to foresee their ultimate consequences?" I'll admit, when I first saw this video, in all of its cheesy synthesized glory, there was nothing but mockery in my heart. Now, though, the smirk is gone. Spock might be right.

There's a concept called "the prophet's dilemma": a prediction that prevents what it predicts from happening. A self-defeating prediction. What if Chicken Little's warnings actually *stopped* the sky from falling? The Y2K bug was an example of the prophet's dilemma. The warnings that the sky would fall triggered the very actions that kept the sky from falling. Maybe what society needs is a new generation of enlightened Chicken Littles. Not the conspiracy theorists who use hate to sell gold and vitamins. Not the fear-entrepreneurs using hysteria to hock consulting services. But people like Bostrom, who founded the Future of Humanity Institute to attract interest in research about existential risks and humanity's long-range future. Or writers like the computer security guru Bruce Schneier—quoted earlier about the "weakest link" problem in network security—whose book *Click Here to Kill Everybody* is essential reading for anyone involved in setting the policy or norms for networked technology.

And maybe we need to start building a system that can act on the warnings of these enlightened Chicken Littles. Does every inhabitant of Earth need access to a DNA printer? And should it be the companies that produce DNA printers that get to make that choice—and if not, whose should it be?

Believe it or not, we have a historical model that can provide some inspiration: an effort in which parties around the globe came together in the 1950s and 1960s to address an ambiguous scientific threat. The threat? The possibility of bringing back destructive alien life from a mission to the

Moon. "Thousands of concerned citizens wrote NASA letters, worried that they were at risk from Moon germs," wrote Michael Meltzer in his fascinating book *When Biospheres Collide*.

It might be tempting to mock these fears now, with the infallibility of hindsight, but this concern was no joke. We simply did not know what was on the Moon. And existential risk was in the air. It was the era of the Cold War, nuclear fallout shelters, biological warfare agents, the Cuban missile crisis, "duck and cover" exercises in schools. (Feeding the fears was a 1969 bestseller by Michael Crichton, *The Andromeda Strain*—released about two months before the Moon landing—which concerned a deadly alien organism brought back to earth by a fallen satellite.)

In the 1950s, just before the launch of the USSR's Sputnik program, a group of scientists began to warn of the dangers of contamination from space exploration. The scientists, including the biologist J. B. S. Haldane and the Nobel laureates Melvin Calvin and Joshua Lederberg, warned of two types of contamination: backward and forward. "Backward contamination" is the contamination of Earth by a returning spaceship—aka the Andromeda scenario—and "forward contamination" is the contamination of another planet with organisms from Earth. (We are in far upstream territory here.)

The interest in these issues sparked a new scientific field that Lederberg labeled "exobiology." (It's now called astrobiology.) "Exobiology profoundly influenced the way space exploration was conducted," wrote the astronomer Caleb Scharf in *Nautilus*. "Strict protocols were developed for the sterilization of spacecraft, and for quarantines to restrict what they might bring back. NASA built clean rooms, and technicians swabbed and baked equipment before sealing it up for launch. Scientists got to work and hurriedly computed the acceptable risks for biological contamination of other worlds."

When the Apollo astronauts came back from the Moon, they were immediately put into quarantine. To be clear, most scientists did not think the Moon was capable of supporting life. They weren't unduly worried that the astronauts would bring back deadly Moon bugs. But, to their credit, they worried about what they didn't know. Why take life-and-death chances in a domain (space travel) we barely understand? They put in place a number of obsessive protocols to try to protect against an improbable risk. Humanity wasn't forced to do this; we did it voluntarily. Perhaps these were our first baby steps upstream to work collectively on the civilization-threatening problems we may face in the years ahead.

The person in charge of these efforts was a NASA employee called the Planetary Protection Officer (originally the Planetary Quarantine Officer). The office still exists; the Planetary Protection Officer in 2019 was Lisa Pratt. One of her predecessors, Catharine Conley, said something striking about the office's history: "So far as I can tell, planetary protection is the first time in human history that humans as a global species decided to prevent damage before we were capable of doing something."

May there be a second time.

CHAPTER 13

You, Upstream

In 2005, Tricia Dyal's husband, Justin, a Marine in a special operations role, was deployed to Iraq. They had two girls, three-year-old Elena Grace and eight-month-old Elissa Faith. Before he left, Justin told her, "You know, I'm not afraid of going over there. I don't fear for my life. I fear that my children won't know who I am when I come back."

A few weeks later, both girls contracted a rotavirus and had to be hospitalized. Elena Grace was a mess—physically exhausted from the virus and terribly sad about her dad being gone. Tricia had given her a photo of Justin, but Elena Grace had handled it so much that it was falling apart.

Desperate to give her daughter some comfort, Tricia called her great-aunt Mary, a gifted crafter, and asked if she could rig up a doll with Justin's picture on it. Mary used a photo of Justin in his uniform. She found a way to imprint his photo on some fabric, and she sewed it up into the form of a doll. When Tricia shared the daddy doll with Elena Grace, she lit up. The doll never left her bedside.

When they returned home from the hospital, the daddy doll became part of everyday life. Elena Grace carted him around with her everywhere: He sat next to her in the shopping cart at Target. He played with her at the park. He joined countless tea parties. And at night before bedtime, he prayed with her.

Elissa Faith also had a daddy doll. He slept next to her in the crib every night. After the nine-month tour, when Justin returned, he was worried how Elissa Faith would react to him. She'd been a baby when he left, and he didn't know if she would remember him. Other Marines had shared stories about coming home to find that their kids were scared of them for a few weeks after they returned.

He arrived home at night, when the girls were asleep, and went directly into Elissa Faith's room, eager simply to set eyes on her. She woke up and stared. He was still wearing his uniform. Then she looked at her doll. "She threw her Daddy doll down and she put her hands up to him and said, 'Daddy!' " said Tricia. "It was the first time I'd ever seen my husband cry."

Whenever other people saw the daddy doll, they'd say what a good idea it was. During the girls' hospital stay, the nurses had asked whether it would be possible to provide dolls for a few other children in the ward. Tricia and Nikki Darnell, a fellow Marine spouse and neighbor, worked together to create more.

It gradually dawned on Tricia that the dolls shouldn't be just for her daughters, or for friends of friends. The dolls were for every family that suffered from the absence of a loved one. "Even if you've never experienced a deployment, you can relate to a child missing someone so much—and that parent not having a choice in having to be away from their kids," she said. "It's heart-wrenching and it doesn't get easier."

She and Darnell started a business, Daddy Dolls. Within a year, they had distributed more than 1,000 Daddy Dolls to military kids. They later expanded the concept beyond military fathers to include military mothers, departed loved ones, and more. They're now called Hug-a-Hero Dolls. Their dolls are on some deployment checklists—the list of things soldiers need to address before they depart, ranging from setting up a Skype account to writing a will.

Liz Byrne, the wife of an Air Force lieutenant colonel, bought Hug-a-Hero Dolls for her daughters. "As adults, we handle things a little bit better," she said. "You go through the stages: The first couple days he's gone, you're just crying, you don't want to do anything. And then it gets easier, and you just kind of fall into your routine. But for the girls, I think having [the dolls] definitely helped. . . . I feel like, when they had their daddy doll and hugged it . . . there was a connection there. Somehow, it makes a difference for them."

The pain of deployments wasn't a problem created by Tricia Dyal. But it was one that she could help fix.

That's the spirit of upstream thinking: With some forethought, we can prevent problems before they happen, and even when we can't stop them entirely, we can often blunt their impact. A group of Icelandic parents and politicians and researchers asked: How can we create a society where teenagers don't abuse alcohol? A team of executives at Expedia asked: How can we keep customers from needing to call us for help? Administrators and teachers across Chicago Public Schools asked: How can we prevent students from dropping out?

So many of the stories in this book have involved the work of groups, small and large: businesses and school districts and cities. But it's also worth asking a simpler question: What can one person do? Tricia Dyal acted as an individual—a mother who wanted to ease her own daughters' pain. The founding father of astrobiology, Joshua Lederberg, raised such a stink about backward and forward contamination that he willed an entire scientific discipline into existence. And you'll recall that I once ingeniously bought a second power cord for my laptop, thereby extinguishing a substantial burden of cord-shuffling. Heroes, all of us.

How can you, personally, move upstream? Consider your own problem blindness. Which problems have you come to accept as inevitable that are, in fact, nothing of the kind? Maybe it's something small: say, the irritation of finding a place to park in a crowded parking lot. I met a woman who told me about an epiphany: "I literally have a step-counter on my wrist and yet I was driving myself crazy trying to find a close space. It was madness. So now I always park in the most remote spot in the lot. I think of it as a 'VIP spot,' away from the other cars. I get some extra steps and don't stress about finding a spot. It's such a wonderful sense of relief, like I've purged that concern forever from my life."

For Jake Stap, a tennis coach, it was the nuisance of picking up tennis balls at the summer camps he ran in Wisconsin. Once you've bent over a few hundred times to retrieve balls, and suffered from the ensuing back pain, you're ready for a better solution. So he put a tennis ball on the passenger seat of his car—to serve as a reminder of the problem—and as he drove around, he brainstormed solutions. What if I had an arm extender, he wondered, that would allow me to grab balls without bending over? No, that wasn't quite right—it would still be laborious, handling one ball at a time. "Finally, during one of his meditations," wrote Pagan Kennedy in *Inventology*, "Stap reached over and pinched the tennis ball on the seat next to him. When the rubber yielded under his fingertips, he had a new idea: the ball could squeeze through metal bars, taking a one-way trip into a wire bin."

And that's how the familiar tennis ball hopper was dreamed into the world, born of back pain and irritation. Stap solved his own problem—and that of every other tennis player since.

Have you come to accept problems in your relationships that might be avoidable? Sometimes a bit of upstream thinking can open up new possibilities. "After twenty-five years of marriage, my wife and I thought we had very little in common and rarely had meaningful conversation," said Steve Sosland of Fredericksburg, Texas. "When we did talk, it often sent me into fight-or-flight (typically flight) mode. My wife just wanted to talk things through. We had no ground rules for working through the issue."

Several couples close to them had divorced, and it spooked both of them. "Over coffee one morning on our back porch, we discussed our friends' divorces. One of us asked the other, 'Are we headed in that direction?' The answer seemed obvious. We decided to sit together and discuss what we could do to prevent it. We really didn't have an answer, so we agreed to return the next morning to discuss it again, and the next, and the next."

What they both wanted was a way to have safe discussions—to talk through any issue, no matter how hard, without remorse or regret or hard feelings. It made sense to them to have a physical place where these conversations would happen. So they bought a hot tub, and that's where they had complicated conversations. It just seemed to work.

"After several years, we built the home we always wanted and of course we put a Jacuzzi on the back deck for our 'hot tub' conversations," he said.

Daddy Dolls. VIP parking places. Tennis ball hoppers. Hot tub conversations. Upstream thinking is not just for organizations, it's for individuals. Where there's a recurring problem in your life, go upstream. And don't let the problem's longevity deter you from acting. As an old proverb goes, "The best time to plant a tree is 20 years ago. The second-best time is now."

Maybe you're also motivated to help solve a bigger problem in society. There are countless places you could invest your time or money: How do you choose? Let me offer three suggestions based on what I've learned about upstream efforts:

1. *"Be impatient for action but patient for outcomes."* That's a quote from Maureen Bisognano, the president emerita of the Institute for Healthcare Improvement, and it struck me as the perfect motto for upstream efforts. The world is full of groups who engage in lofty discussions—and feel virtuous doing so—but never create meaningful change. Change won't come without action.

   At the same time, it can take a while for action to bear fruit. Downstream work is narrow and fast. Upstream is broad and slow(er). You can bring a homeless person a meal today, and you'll feel good immediately. But to figure out how to reduce evictions, in order to prevent people from becoming homeless—that might take years. What kind of work do you care so much about that you could stick with it for 5 years? Or 10 years?

   When I think of the conviction—and stubbornness—it takes to sustain upstream efforts, I think of advocates like Sally Herndon, who worked for years in North Carolina for an anti-smoking initiative called Project ASSIST. She joined the organization in 1990, her team spent two years preparing plans, and just as they began to roll out their campaign, they suffered a terrible defeat. In 1993, the tobacco industry persuaded the state legislature to pass a law mandating that 20% of the space in government buildings be reserved for smoking. Even more devilishly, the law forbade local governments from passing stricter regulations. Herndon called it the "Dirty Air Law."

Her mandate, and that of her allies, was to improve the public's health by reducing smoking. That's classic upstream work. But how could they prevail against one of the world's most powerful lobbies—on its home soil in North Carolina? It was clear they weren't going to deliver a knockout blow. Herndon knew that their only hope was to chip away at the problem.

And they did. They started by picking a fight they thought they could win: making schools smoke-free. "Even tobacco farmers didn't want their kids to smoke," said Herndon. For years, they won tough victories at the local level—persuading school boards, one at a time, to banish smoking. By 2000, they'd convinced 10% of the state's school districts to go tobacco-free.

Think of it: It took her team a full decade to succeed in *one-tenth* of the state's districts. And this was supposed to be the *easy* fight. That's stamina.

But then there was a radical acceleration. During the second decade of her team's work, from 2000 to 2010, the dynamics swung in their favor. A state-wide smoke-free ban in schools was passed. Then a ban in hospitals, then in prisons, then in the state's General Assembly, and, finally, in 2009, restaurants and bars. Chip, chip, chip. And that's how upstream victories are won. An inch at a time, and then a yard, and then a mile, and eventually you find yourself at the finish line: systems change. *Be impatient for action and patient for outcomes.*

2. *Macro starts with micro.* When we think about big
problems, we're forced to grapple with big numbers.
What would it take to solve problems for 1,000 people? Your first instinct might be to say: *We'll have to
think about the big picture, because we can't very
well intervene individually with 1,000 people.* But
that notion, as it turns out, is exactly wrong. Notice
how often the heroes in this book actually organized
their work on a name-by-name basis. The teachers
in Chicago assisted ninth graders using a by-name
list. The team in Rockford housed homeless people
using a by-name list. The domestic violence high-
risk team protected women using a by-name list. All
of these efforts were also aided by systems change,
to be clear, but those changes were often sparked
by a familiarity with individual cases. (The domestic violence team discovered that abusers needed to
have their GPS bracelets added before they were
released from jail—not two days later.) The lesson is
clear: You can't help a thousand people, or a million,
until you understand how to help one.

That's because you don't understand a problem
until you've seen it up close. Until you've "gotten
proximate" to the problem, as we explored in the
chapter on leverage points. The leaders of the University of Chicago Crime Lab read the medical examiner's reports on 200 homicide victims. How many
people develop strong opinions about crime without
bothering to train their intuition in that way? How
many people develop strong opinions about homelessness without knowing any homeless people?

It's true that it's harder to imagine this "by-
name" methodology working with millions of peo-

ple rather than hundreds or thousands. To affect millions requires systems change. But even systems change usually starts up close: Someone understands a problem so well that they formulate and lobby for a new policy at the city or state level, and it works, and later other state leaders see that the policy works and they embrace it, too. Remember the efforts of Dr. Bob Sanders in Tennessee, who lobbied for mandatory car seats? *Macro starts with micro.*

If you want to help solve big problems in the world, seek out groups who have ambitious goals coupled with close-up experience.

3. *Favor scoreboards over pills.* I believe the social sector has been misled by a bad mental model: that running social interventions is a bit like distributing pills. First, you formulate a great "drug": Maybe it's a mentoring program or a behavioral therapy or a job-training model. Then you conduct a randomized control trial (RCT) of the "drug," and if it proves effective, you attempt to spread it far and wide.

It's not that this kind of testing is a bad idea. It's a great idea. It's how we learn which interventions work and which don't. But the problem comes when the obsession with testing becomes a hindrance to scale and learning. Take the South Carolina Nurse-Family Partnership experiment as an example. It's a perfect example of the Pill Model: a six-year RCT to assess the program. I argued that it was a noble experiment (and two chapters later, I still stand by that!). But the formality of the experiment also has real costs. For six years, the people doing the most important job—the nurses who support the mothers—won't have access to the data. Only at the end will they receive the results. Imagine being kept in the dark for six long years and then, at the end, attending a sort of surprise party where some academics inform you whether you succeeded or failed. That's hard to bear, particularly in the latter case.

Worse, the cardinal rule of the Pill Model is: Don't change the pill in the middle of a test. Even if you've had an epiphany—*Aha! A different formulation of this pill would be much better!*—you can't replace people's supply with the new-and-improved version, because then you've confounded the whole experiment. So, in South Carolina, nurses are essentially forbidden from learning/improving/innovating during the six-year span of the trial.

Contrast the Pill Model with a mind-set focused on continuous improvement—what I'll call the Scoreboard Model. In the Scoreboard Model, you get a group of people together who've agreed to take ownership of a problem, and you arm them with data to assess their progress. We've encountered this idea before in chapter 5. This is what Joe McCannon meant by "data for learning" rather than "data for inspection": The people in the field who are doing the hard work should receive timely, useful data that allows them to learn and adapt. I'm using a scoreboard as a metaphor for this continuous flow of data, which provides a way to judge in real time whether you're succeeding or failing.

To be clear, it's possible to have the best of both worlds. You can use the Pill Model to establish that an intervention works but, when it comes time to scale it, people should be *encouraged to tweak it* (not discouraged from changing the formulation). The Domestic Violence High Risk Team is a great example of this: They started with an evidence-based tool (the Danger Assessment) and then surrounded it with a team of people who used it to watch over specific women, in ever-changing ways, on an ongoing basis. The movement in Iceland, too, incorporated both: using evidence-based "pills" for reducing substance abuse (for instance, by encouraging formal sports participation) but ultimately relying on their own scoreboard—the annual survey data—to guide and calibrate their work.

In the Scoreboard Model, the question is: How can we make progress this week? The Scoreboard Model was used by Expedia to reduce the number of calls to its customer service center; by Rockford to eliminate its homelessness problem; by Chicago Public Schools to increase the graduation rate by 25 percentage points.

So if you're looking for a place to contribute your talents, *favor Scoreboards over Pills*. Don't obsess about formulating the perfect solution before you begin your work; instead, take ownership of the underlying problem and start slogging forward.

~~~~~~~

A final way you can apply upstream thinking, as an individual, is to change the organization you work for. Could you be the person who improves a system from within?

In 2015, Darshak Sanghavi was working in the federal government as the director of Preventive and Population Health at the Center for Medicare and Medicaid Innovation (CMMI). CMMI is part of CMS (the Centers for Medicare & Medicaid Services)—and hang in there, it gets more interesting—which is the federal agency that runs Medicare and Medicaid. Translation: Sanghavi's job was to consider how to use Medicare and Medicaid money to fund upstream health efforts.

The federal government had a rule that a particular health care innovation could be expanded nationally—and funded through CMS—if it delivered quality care *and* saved money (or if it improved one of those factors while keeping the other neutral). This is a high bar. When Sanghavi joined CMS in 2014, not a single prevention program had met that threshold for expansion.

But Sanghavi and his colleagues were tracking the Diabetes Prevention Program (DPP) in hopes that it could clear the bar. The DPP had been designed to help "prediabetic" people—those who are at high risk of developing diabetes but don't currently have it. People could enroll in the program at a local YMCA or other community organization, and they were challenged to do two things: lose at least 5% of their body weight and engage in physical activity (the equivalent of brisk walking) for at least 2.5 hours per week. In pursuit of those goals, they attended a series of classes on healthy habits taught by a lifestyle coach, who also consulted with them one-on-one. A major study of DPP found that a decade after participants had completed the program, they were still one-third less likely to develop type 2 diabetes than a control group, and even those who did advance to diabetes had the onset delayed for an average of four years. A pretty stunning success, especially given the terrible track record of most diet- and exercise-focused programs.

Bureaucracy being bureaucracy, CMMI decided to *retest* DPP using its own methodology, and by late 2015, the results were finally in. Just as they expected, the program had stopped or delayed patients from advancing to diabetes. The results suggested that DPP might clear the daunting double hurdle of improving quality while saving money. So Sanghavi and his colleagues roped in CMS's actuaries, the people entrusted to certify a program as cost-saving. With their blessing, the program could be expanded nationally. Sanghavi was elated: Finally, a major prevention success story!

Then came a fateful meeting at which the actuaries revealed that they couldn't, in fact, certify DPP as a cost-saving program. The reason? It helped people live longer. And when people live longer, their health care costs more.

That's not a sick joke. That was the official logic of the federal government, which is the largest payer for health care in the United States. (Under this logic, the best-scoring interventions would have been programs teaching people to chain-smoke cigarettes, unplug traffic signals, and skydive "organically.")

"I was sitting there in disbelief," said Sanghavi. "Seriously? This is what's gonna take it down?" Patrick Conway, then the deputy administrator of CMS and Sanghavi's boss at CMMI, remembers thinking, *This is crazy. We can't not invest in a program because it saves people's lives!*

So Sanghavi and Conway appealed to the chief actuary, hoping to overturn this method of computing savings. And then something happened that should give hope to anyone who has ever felt like an insignificant cog in a giant wheel.

Before Christmas in 2015, a letter was delivered to

CMS's chief actuary on CMS letterhead. It had been written by one of the chief's own employees, an actuary who was on the cusp of retirement. The end of the letter's first paragraph foreshadowed what was ahead: "Because this is a cry of the heart, the language may be more passionate than usual."

In the letter, the actuary argued that the way CMS was computing cost savings was perverse. He said it's as if the actuaries were "explicitly calling attention to the increased life expectancy declaring it is a bad thing with the most powerful weapon in our arsenal: our numbers."

He speculated about how the public would react if they knew about the policy. He imagined the media headlines:

→ A "Do Not Resuscitate" Order Has Now Been Stamped on the Head of Every Older American
→ Actuaries: More Important to Save the Trust Fund Than to Save Lives
→ Medicare Lives, Seniors Die

But ultimately, in the letter, he made a moral case for change, not one based on public relations. He closed the memo with a paragraph so perfect that you can almost hear the soaring orchestral music playing in the background:

The first rule of medicine "*Primum non nocere*," "First do no harm," binds not just doctors but all who serve in the health field, including actuaries. Perhaps especially actuaries since a bad doctor can only harm a few people but a bad actuary can harm millions. Therefore, the office should adopt a firm rule of never calculating in an estimate the resulting added cost resulting from saving a person's life. Calculators are appropriate for determining how much doctors and hospitals should be paid, calculators are not appropriate for determining how long people should be allowed to live.

Justice prevailed. Some combination of this actuary's letter and the appeal by Sanghavi and Conway led to the following legal language being added to government regulations: "The Centers for Medicare & Medicaid Services has made a determination that costs associated with expected improvements in longevity are not appropriate for consideration in the evaluation of net program spending."

As the climax of a story, that's awfully flat. There's no gunfight or airlift or resuscitation or redemption. It's just a sentence, and a boring one at that. A bit of legalistic prose that got added to a federal rulebook.

Yet it captures so well what an upstream success looks like. Quiet but powerful, with effects that ripple across time. A modest sentence that will extend and save lives.

"Try and leave this world a little better than you found it," goes a famous quote, but until I researched it, I never realized that the source was Robert Baden-Powell, founder of the movement that gave us the Boy Scouts, Girl Guides, and Girl Scouts, and someone who taught multiple generations of kids to "Be Prepared." That is to say: Anticipate the future and be ready to shape it.

We are drawn to the glory of the rescue and the response. But our heroes shouldn't only be the people who restore things to normal, extinguishing fires and capturing felons and fishing drowning kids out of rivers. Our heroes should also include a teacher who skips lunch to help a freshman with math, in hopes that she'll get back on track to graduate. And a cop who makes himself a conspicuous presence around an abused woman's home, ensuring her ex-husband will think twice before coming around. And an activist who rallies an underserved community to fight for the parks and investments they've always been denied.

These should be our heroes, too: The people who are unsatisfied with normal. People who clamor for *better*.

Next Steps

If you've finished *Upstream* and are interested in learning more, visit the website:

http://www.upstreambook.com/

Check out the "Resources" section. When you sign up for the Heath Brothers newsletter, you'll get access to *free* materials like these:

- **Upstream Summary.** You can download a bigger, prettier, color version of the 1-page summary of this book. (The smaller, monochrome version is on page 247, if you want to glance at it.) Perfect for tacking up next to your desk.

- **Book Club Guide.** If you're reading *Upstream* as part of a book club, this Guide offers suggested questions and topics to guide your discussion.

- **Next-Steps Reading List.** All my sources are available to you in the endnotes, of course. But in this list I share my favorite books, articles, and videos, categorized by chapter. So if you want more depth on any of the topics in the book—problem blindness, early detection, systems thinking, and so on—check out this document. All the resources are clickable for quick access.

- **The *So You Want to Go Upstream* . . . podcast.** If you're feeling inspired to prevent a problem in your work, but aren't quite sure where to start, listen to this podcast. I offer some simple tips on how to take those first few steps upstream.

"So often we find ourselves reacting to problems, putting out fires, dealing with emergencies. We should shift our attention to preventing them."

Summary of
UPSTREAM
by **DAN HEATH**

7 QUESTIONS TO ASK YOURSELF

Where to find a point of leverage? Get closer to the problem.
⚠ Notion that prevention must save money

How to get early warning of the problem? Deploy sensors. Look for predictors.
⚠ False positives

How to know you're succeeding? Pre-game your measures. Use paired measures.
⚠ Ghost victories

How to change the system? Fight for systems change. Shape the water.
⚠ Enabling a flawed system

How to avoid doing harm? Look beyond the immediate. Close feedback loops.
⚠ Failing to test and overconfidence

How to unite the right people? Surround the problem. Use data for learning.
⚠ Data for inspection

Who will pay for what doesn't happen? Align incentives. Stitch together pockets of value.
⚠ The wrong pocket problem

3 BARRIERS TO OVERCOME

Problem blindness I don't see the problem; or, it seems inevitable

Lack of ownership That's not my problem to solve

Tunneling I can't deal with that right now

Appendix 1

Scaling Programs in the Social Sector

As mentioned in chapter 7, the Becoming a Man (BAM) program delivered very positive results in the first 2 RCTs and much weaker results in a third study, one which involved a much larger student population. The data on BAM suggests that the more teenagers who participate in BAM, the lower the average impact and the greater the variability in their experience.

Simply put—and this is true across the social sector—we don't know very much about how to scale up successful programs. Imagine a world with only one McDonald's outlet. A world where Starbucks stayed in Seattle and never grew. That's essentially the norm in social science. You would be hard-pressed to find a specific social program that has been "franchised" as successfully as KFC. (Kindergarten is one possible example.)

There's good reason for that difficulty, of course. There are probably six billion people who could be properly trained to fry up a batch of fries. How many people could aspire to do what Tony D does? Six million—1 in 1,000—if we're lucky? When it comes to the messiness and complexity of human lives, it's very hard to deliver solutions as reliably as businesses deliver products.

"More and more people are starting to wrestle with this question of scale, but it's still very, very early days," said the Crime Lab's Jens Ludwig. "We're very far from knowing: Here's the recipe for getting this social program that works really well for one thousand kids to work really well for five thousand kids."

My own take is that this is largely an unsolvable problem—that there are few programs for improving the lives of human beings that are as easy to reproduce on a large scale as fried chicken or lattes. (Here I'm thinking of programs in the sense of BAM—those that rely on people providing services to other people. Certainly there are more systemic approaches, from Social Security to stoplights, that scale very well indeed.) And because of that, in the social sector, we've eventually got to shift from a mind-set of "scaling a specific program by reproducing it faithfully" to "owning a problem and adapting a program as needed to achieve results." For more on that idea, see my "Pill vs. Scoreboard" rant toward the end of chapter 13.

Acknowledgments

First and foremost, thanks to the readers who provided feedback on an early draft of the book in the summer of 2019. You were incredibly generous with your time and your insights. The book got a lot better thanks to your suggestions and criticisms—I am grateful.

There were many people whose wisdom and guidance I drew on repeatedly during this project, chief among them my brother and collaborator, Chip Heath, who contributed countless ideas to the book. Also on that list of advisors were Joe McCannon, Rosanne Haggerty, Nick Carnes, Maureen Bisognano, Becky and Christine Margiotta, Jeff Edmondson, Jens Ludwig, Farzad Mostashari, Justin Osofsky, and my colleagues at Duke's CASE, Erin Worsham and Cathy Clark.

Several thank-yous for specific expertise: Roosa Tikkanen of the Commonwealth Fund coached me through international patterns of health care spending; Byron Penstock helped me calculate Interface's returns; Lyle Ungar tutored me on the components of life expectancy; Bridget Jancarz and Jennifer Blatz of StriveTogether turned me on to the CPS story; and Melissa Wiggins helped me collect reader feedback.

Thanks to the social sector leaders who flew to Durham to join me for a day of upstream brainstorming: Beth Sandor,

ACKNOWLEDGMENTS

Jennifer Blatz, Kate Hurley, Michelle Pledger, Anne Eidelman, Susan Rivers, Katie Hong, Talma Shultz, Alison Marczuk, Brigid Ahern, and Karthik Krishnan.

I am so thankful to Peter Griffin and Janet Byrne for their editing prowess. Any sloppy passages in the book are likely the result of me ignoring their advice.

I am forever grateful to my core team of researchers, whose fingerprints are all over this book: Evan Nesterak, Sarah Ovaska-Few, and Rachel Cohn. Week in, week out, you helped me push *Upstream* downstream. Thank you so much. And a sincere thanks as well to the other researchers who made major contributions: Emily Calkins, Stephanie Tam, Marian Bihrle Johnson, Julianna Garbo, and J. J. McCorvey.

For about 15 years, I've been lucky to work with the peerless Christy Fletcher, who has a knack for giving the right feedback at the right time. Thanks to Christy and her team for their ongoing support. And it's an honor to count *Upstream* among the first generation of books to be published by Avid Reader Press, co-helmed by my brilliant editor, Ben Loehnen. I am so appreciative, too, of the Avid team members who helped launch the book: Meredith Vilarello, Alex Primiani, Jordan Rodman, and Jofie Ferrari-Adler.

A heartfelt thank you to the Heath clan and the Albertson clan for your constant love and support. And I would be nowhere without my wonder of a wife, Amanda, and our daughters, Josephine and Julia.

Notes

Chapter 1: Moving Upstream

1 **A public health parable:** John B. McKinlay, "A Case for Refocusing Upstream: The Political Economy of Illness," in Peter Conrad, Valerie Leiter, eds., *The Sociology of Health & Illness: Critical Perspectives*, 10th ed. (New York: Sage, 2018), 578.

1 **For every 100 customers:** The Expedia story is drawn from multiple interviews: Ryan O'Neill, June 2018, July 2018, and August 2019; Tucker Moodey, June 2018 and August 2019; and Mark Okerstrom, August 2018.

3 **top priority:** Written communication with Khosrowshahi, September 2019.

3 **58% to roughly 15%:** Note that, per O'Neill, the specific percentage varies depending on the type of reservation—vacation packages, for instance, spawn many more calls than hotel reservations. O'Neill, interview, August 8, 2019.

6 **two police officers:** Deputy chief, interview, November 2009.

8 **certain kinds of behavioral therapy:** Council of Economic Advisers, *Returns on Investments in Recidivism-Reducing Programs* report, Executive Office of the White House: 2018, 11–12, https://www .whitehouse.gov/wp-content/uploads/2018/05/Returns-on-Invest ments-in-Recidivism-Reducing-Programs.pdf.

8 **criminal is still in his mother's tummy:** Richard Tremblay, "Developmental Origins of Chronic Physical Aggression: From Social Learning to Epigenetics," Talk at Picower New Insight Symposium, Massachusetts Institute of Technology, November 29, 2014, https:// www.youtube.com/watch?v=Br3OeGwGxuY, audio location: 00:17:20.

8 **Tremblay points to a cluster of risk factors:** Ibid., audio location: 00:17:20–17:44. This research was brand-new to me. Here's a bit

more detail if you're curious. In another paper, Tremblay et al. write: "The child inherits a mix of their parent's genes, and their mother's smoking, stress, poverty, and depression during pregnancy impact the fetus' brain development through epigenetic mechanisms. From the postnatal period onwards, the physical and social environments created by a poor, young, depressed woman with low education, behavior problems, and coercive parenting in a dysfunctional family clearly fail to provide the care and education needed by the brain of a young child to learn to control their emotions and behavior." And "Parents who have had behavior problems carry with them pervasive high-risk environmental conditions (e.g., low education, low income, poor neighborhoods, and risky lifestyle choices such as use of tobacco, alcohol, and drugs, and unhealthy nutrition), which impact childhood and adulthood psychopathology through many interrelated channels, including impacts on the children's DNA methylation." Richard E. Tremblay, Frank Vitaro, and Sylvana M. Côté, "Developmental Origins of Chronic Physical Aggression: A Bio-Psycho-Social Model for the Next Generation of Preventive Interventions," *Annual Review of Psychology* 69 (April 2018): 383–407, https://doi.org/10.1146 /annurev-psych-010416-044030.

8   **they can be *changed*:** Ibid., 17:40.

8   **"we need to focus on females":** Stephen S. Hall, "Behaviour and Biology: The Accidental Epigeneticist," *Nature* 505, no. 7481 (December 30, 2013), 14–17, https://www.nature.com/news/behaviour-and-bi ology-the-accidental-epigeneticist-1.14441.

10   **$3.5 trillion health care industry which constitutes almost a fifth of the American economy:** Centers for Medicare & Medicaid Services, National Health Expenditure Accounts, 2017 data, https://www.cms .gov/research-statistics-data-and-systems/statistics-trends-and-re ports/nationalhealthexpenddata/nationalhealthaccountshistorical .html.

11   **convened two focus groups in Charlotte:** Focus group results from data summary provided by The Health Initiative. "The Health Initiative (THI)—Public Opinion Research Key Insights to Date," December 2018.

11   **"spending patterns were stunning":** Rocco Perla, interview, February 11, 2019.

11   **for every $1 we spend on downstream health care:** Elizabeth Bradley, Heather Sipsma, and Lauren A. Taylor, "American Health Care Paradox—High Spending on Health Care and Poor Health," *QJM: An International Journal of Medicine* 110, no. 2 (2017): 61–65; 62, fig. 2; 63. Jennifer Rubin et al., *Are Better Health Outcomes*

Related to Social Expenditure?: A Cross-national Empirical Analysis of Social Expenditure and Population Health Measures, RAND, 2016, 11, fig. 1.

12 **we spend roughly $1 upstream:** Bradley, Sipsma, and Taylor, "American Health Care Paradox," 61–65, 63, fig. 2.

12 **9th out of 34 countries:** Ibid.

12 **RAND research report,** figure 6 (descriptions) and figure 7 (percentages of spending).

12 **Meanwhile, we spend about 30% more:** Jennifer Rubin et al., *Are Better Health Outcomes Related to Social Expenditure?*, 15, table 6; 16, table 7.

13 **The US is a world leader in knee replacements:** Elizabeth Bradley and Lauren Taylor, *The American Health Care Paradox: Why Spending More Is Getting Us Less* (New York: Public Affairs, 2013), 5.

13 **Let's consider some evidence from Norway:** Bradley et al., "American Health Care Paradox—High Spending on Health Care and Poor Health," *QJM: An International Journal of Medicine* 110, no. 2 (2017): 63, fig. 1.

13 **Norway's spending priorities are radically different:** Ibid.

13 **Norwegian woman will pay nothing:** "Pregnancy and Maternity Care in Norway," Norway Health Agency, https://helsenorge.no/other-languages/english/pregnancy-and-maternity-care. https://www.irishtimes.com/news/health/norway-shows-the-way-in-child care-1.467444.

13 **entitled to a whole slew of leave:** "Norway's 'Daddy Quota' Means 90% of Fathers Take Parental Leave," September 17, 2018, Apolitical, https://apolitical.co/solution_article/norways-daddy-quota -means-90-of-fathers-take-parental-leave/.

13 **full-time, high-quality day care:** "Age 1, Kindergartens and Schools," New in Norway: Practical Information from Public Agencies, http://www.nyinorge.no/en/Familiegjenforening/New-in-Norway/Fam ilies-and-children-in-Norway-/Kindergarden-and-schools/. Cost, "Prices and Payment, Kindergarten," Oslo commune website, https://www.oslo.kommune.no/english/kindergarten/prices-and-pay ment/#gref.

13 **a little over $100 per month:** "Child Benefit," Norwegian Labor and Welfare Administration, https://www.nav.no/en/Home/Bene fits+and+services/Relatert+informasjon/child-benefit#chapter-1. See "Rates" for monthly amount.

14 **college tuition is free in Norway:** Rick Noack, "7 Countries Where Americans Can Study at Universities, in English, for Free (or Almost Free)," *Washington Post*, October 29, 2014, https://www .washingtonpost.com/news/worldviews/wp/2014/10/29/7-coun

tries-where-americans-can-study-at-universities-in-english-for-free
-or-almost-free/.

14 **infant mortality:** OECD data, infant mortality rates, https://data
.oecd.org/healthstat/infant-mortality-rates.htm, accessed on October 3, 2019.

14 **Life expectancy:** OECD data, life expectancy at birth, https://data
.oecd.org/healthstat/life-expectancy-at-birth.htm#indicator-chart,
accessed on October 3, 2019.

14 **Least stressed:** Bloomberg analysis in "Most Stressed-Out: Countries," Best (and Worst), 2013, https://www.bloomberg.com/graphics
/best-and-worst/#most-stressed-out-countries.

14 **Happiness:** John F. Helliwell, Richard Layard, and Jeffrey D. Sachs,
World Happiness Report 2019, 24–25, fig. 2.7.

15 **City officials in 1989 banned . . . driving:** Lucas W. Davis, "The
Effect of Driving Restrictions on Air Quality in Mexico City," *Journal of Political Economy* 116, no. 1 (2008): 38–81.

15 **smallpox . . . killed an estimated 300 million:** Colette Flight, "Smallpox: Eradicating the Scourge," BBC, February 17, 2011, https://
www.bbc.co.uk/history/british/empire_seapower/smallpox_01
.shtml.

15 **vaccination of 54,777 people:** Ibid. Also David Brown, "The Last
Case of Smallpox," *Washington Post*, January 26, 1993, https://www
.washingtonpost.com/archive/lifestyle/wellness/1993/01/26/the-last
-case-of-smallpox/46e21c4c-e814-4e2c-99b5-2a84d53eefc1/.

Chapter 2: Problem Blindness

21 **Marcus Elliott:** All quotes from interviews with Marcus Elliott,
August and September 2019. Details also come from those interviews unless otherwise noted below.

21 **fatalistic mind-set about injuries:** Ian McMahan, "Why Hamstring Injuries Are So Common in NFL Players, During Presea-
son Play," *Sports Illustrated*, August 18, 2016, https://www.si.com
/edge/2016/08/18/hamstring-injuries-nfl-training-camps-new-en
gland-patriots.

22 **22 hamstring injuries:** Ibid.

23 **graduation rate . . . was 52.4%:** Elaine Allensworth, Kaleen Healey,
Julia Gwynne, and René Crispin, *High School Graduation Rates
Through Two Decades of Change: Research Summary* (Chicago: Uni-
versity of Chicago Consortium on School Research, June 2016), 13.

23 **"Every system is perfectly designed":** Paul Batalden, senior fellow at

Institute of Healthcare Improvement, http://www.ihi.org/communi
ties/blogs/origin-of-every-system-is-perfectly-designed-quote.

23 **sprawling mass of CPS:** CPS statistics from https://cps.edu/About
_CPS/At-a-glance/Pages/Stats_and_facts.aspx; Green Bay School
enrollment: https://www.gbaps.org/our_district; City of Seattle budget portal, https://openbudget.seattle.gov.

23 **"high school, you're gonna make it or break it":** Interview with Elizabeth Kirby, August 2018.

24 **you could predict, with 80% accuracy:** Elaine Allensworth, "The
Use of Ninth-Grade Early Warning Indicators to Improve Chicago
Schools," *Journal of Education for Students Placed at Risk (JESPAR)*
18:1 (2013): 68–83, doi: 10.1080/10824669.2013.745181, 69.

24 **two surprisingly simple factors:** Ibid. Also author communication
with Paige Ponder, September 2019.

24 **were 3.5 times more likely to graduate:** Elaine Allensworth and John
Easton, "The On-Track Indicator as a Predictor of High School
Graduation" (Chicago: University of Chicago Consortium on Chi-
cago School Research, June 2005), 18.

25 **"Freshman On-Track matters more":** Interview with Paige Ponder,
March 2019.

25 **68% chance of graduating:** Allensworth and Easton, "The On-Track
Indicator," 7.

25 **in Chicago, there's no junior high:** Chicago Public Schools, "Elementary
and High School Guide," https://cps.edu/SiteCollectionDocuments
/gocps/GoCPS-ES-and-HS-Guide-2019-20-English.pdf.

25 **"People are vulnerable during transitions":** Interview with Sarah
Duncan, March 2018.

26 **"kids got suspended":** Ibid.

27 **"changes relationships between teachers and students":** Interview
with Elaine Allensworth, March 2018.

27 **Freshman Success Teams:** Interview with Paige Ponder, March 2019.

27 **"you care about Michael":** Ibid.

28 **Managing attendance is one of the most important:** Ibid.

28 **graduation rate had vaulted to 78%:** "Mayor Emmanuel and CPS
Announce Record High Graduation Rate of 78.2 Percent," Chicago
Public Schools, news release, September 3, 2018, https://cps.edu
/News/Press_releases/Pages/PR1_9_3_2018.aspx.

28 **an additional 30,000 students:** Communication with Elaine
Allensworth, June 2019. I had prodded Allensworth for a ballpark
figure; this is an informed estimate only.

28 **lifetime wages increase . . . $300,000 to $400,000:** "Education and
Lifetime Earnings," Social Security Administration, https://www.ssa

.gov/policy/docs/research-summaries/education-earnings.html, fig. 1, using gross numbers (without controls).

29 **Yes, that's a tiny gorilla:** The study: Trafton Drew, Melissa L.-H. Vo, and Jeremy M. Wolfe, "The Invisible Gorilla Strikes Again: Sustained Inattentional Blindness in Expert Observers," *Psychological Science* 24, no. 9 (2013): 1848–53. I am grateful to Drew for allowing me to reproduce the gorilla image here.

31 **"A married man usually likes attractive":** Helen Gurley Brown, *Sex and the Office* (1964), Kindle version, location 1426. Quote found in an article by Tamar Lewin, "Sexual Harassment in the Workplace: A Grueling Struggle for Equality," *New York Times*, November 9, 1986.

31 **30% of 2,000 companies surveyed:** Lewin, "Sexual Harassment in the Workplace."

31 **The term *sexual harassment*:** Lin Farley, "I Coined the Term 'Sexual Harassment.' Corporations Stole It," *New York Times*, October 17, 2018.

31 **"consciousness raising" session . . . Brooke Gladstone:** Brooke Gladstone, "Sexual Harassment, Revisited," *On the Media*, WNYC radio, October 27, 2017, https://www.wnyc.org/story/sexual-harassment-revisited/?tab=transcript.

32 **"Working women immediately took up the phrase":** Farley, "I Coined the Term 'Sexual Harassment.'"

33 **"buried under nine feet of manure":** Stephen Davies, "The Great Horse-Manure Crisis of 1894," Fee, September 1, 2004, https://fee.org/articles/the-great-horse-manure-crisis-of-1894/.

33 **horse manure crisis was the talk of the conference:** Elizabeth Kolbert, "Hosed: Is There a Quick Fix for the Climate?," *The New Yorker*, November 8, 2009.

33 **a Brazilian activist named Deborah Delage:** Quotes and details from interview in January 2019 and written communication in May 2019.

34 **C-section rates vary quite a bit around the world:** Cesarean section rates in OECD countries, in 2016 (per 1,000 live births), https://www.statista.com/statistics/283123/cesarean-sections-in-oecd-countries/.

34 **In Brazil . . . 84% of children:** Agência Nacional de Saúde Suplementar (Brasil), *Cartilha nova organização do cuidado ao parto e nascimento para melhores resultados de saúde: Projeto Parto Adequado—fase 1*, Agência Nacional de Saúde Suplementar, Sociedade Beneficente Israelita Brasileira Hospital Albert Einstein, Institute for Healthcare Improvement. Rio de Janeiro: ANS, 2016, 11.

34 **manicures and massages to go with the C-sections:** Olga Khazan,

"Why Most Brazilian Women Get C-Sections," *The Atlantic*, April 14, 2014, https://www.theatlantic.com/health/archive/2014/04/why -most-brazilian-women-get-c-sections/360589/. Also: https://www .thestar.com/news/world/2015/10/07/luxury-birthing-spawns-cae sarean-section-epidemic-in-brazil.html.

34 **Obstetricians could make much more money:** Interview with Paulo Borem, July 2015. Also Marina Lopes, "Brazilian Women Are Push- ing Back Against Rampant C-sections," Vice, December 7, 2016, https://www.vice.com/en_us/article/9a38g8/brazil-c-sections-natural -births.

35 **"Childbirth is . . . primitive":** Khazan, "Why Most Brazilian Women Get C-Sections."

35 **In a survey of 1,626 women:** C. C. Palma and T. M. S. Donelli, "Violência Obstétrica em Mulheres Brasileiras," *Psico* 48, no. 3 (2017): 216–30, table 3.

35 **Parto do Princípio submitted a 35-page document:** *Denúncia da Parto do Princípio motiva Ação do Ministério Público Federal*, Parto de Princípio website, https://www.partodoprincipio.com.br /den-ncia—altas-taxas-de-ces-reas.

36 **Jacqueline Torres, an obstetric nurse:** "Reducing Health Inequities in Brazil," Institute for Healthcare Improvement, http://www.ihi.org /communities/blogs/reducing-health-inequities-in-brazil-institution al-racism-and-the-effects-on-maternal-outcomes.

36 **Borem was working . . . in Jaboticabal:** Interview with Paulo Borem, July 2015. Also: interview with Joelle Baehrend, December 3, 2015. "Changing Culture, Changing Care: Reducing Elective C-Section Rates in Brazil," http://www.ihi.org/communities/blogs/_layouts/15 /ihi/community/blog/itemview.aspx?List=7d1126ec-8f63-4a3b -9926-c44ea3036813&ID=179.

36 **more frequently sent to the neonatal intensive care unit (NICU):** From email exchange with Paul Borem, September 2019. "NICUs After Elective C-section," Clinical Perinatology 35, no. 2 (June 2008): 373–vii, doi: 10.1016/j.clp.2008.03.006.

36 **rate of natural childbirth . . . 3%:** Joelle Baehrend, "Changing Cul- ture, Changing Care: Reducing Elective C-Section Rates in Brazil," IHI blog, December 3, 2015.

36 **"system was designed to produce C-sections":** Interview with Paulo Borem, November 20, 2018.

37 **natural childbirth . . . 40%:** Pedro Delgado, Paulo Borem, and Rita Sanchez, "The Birth of the Parto Adequado Collective in Brazil," Presentation for Institute for Healthcare Improvement National Forum 2015, Orlando, Florida, http://app.ihi.org/FacultyDocu

ments/Events/Event-2613/Presentation-12655/Document-10253 /Presentation_C11_Collaborative_to_Reduce_CSection_Rates_in _Brazil.pdf.

37 **18-month phase . . . 20% to 37.5%:** Agência Nacional de Saúde Suplementar (Brasil), *Cartilha nova organização do cuidado ao parto e nascimento para melhores resultados de saúde: Projeto Parto Adequado—fase 1,* 33; 35 hospitals: "Parto Adequado" project website, Agencia Nacional de Saúde Suplementar, accessed September 7, 2019: http://www.ans.gov.br/gestao-em-saude/parto -adequado.

37 **decrease in NICU admissions:** Agência Nacional de Saúde Suplementar (Brasil), *Cartilha nova organização do cuidado ao parto e nascimento para melhores resultados de saúde: Projeto Parto Adequado—fase 1,* 34.

37 **10,000 C-sections were avoided:** Projeto Parto Adequado project website, Agencia Nacional de Saúde Suplementar, http://www.ans .gov.br/gestao-em-saude/parto-adequado, accessed September 7, 2019.

37 **over three times as many hospitals:** Ibid.

37 **"The results of phase 1 offer hope":** Communication with Pedro Delgado, September 2019.

37 **Brazil's 6,000+ hospitals:** 6,400 hospitals, "Brazil-Healthcare," International Trade Administration, US Department of Commerce, https://www.export.gov/article?id=Brazil-Healthcare, accessed September 19, 2019. This source says 6,300: https://thebrazilbusiness .com/article/healthcare-industry-in-brazil.

37 **waiting list of hospitals:** Interview with Jacqueline Torres, December 2018.

37 **the campaign struck a chord with her:** Interview with Rita Sanchez, November 2018.

38 **The seed of improvement is dissatisfaction:** I'm grateful to Steve Spear, a senior lecturer at MIT who helps organizations build cultures of learning and improvement, for this insight. He said something that stuck with me: Improvement efforts must start with an "insufferable frustration."

Chapter 3: A Lack of Ownership

39 **Until 1994, Ray Anderson:** Richard Todd, "The Sustainable Industrialist: Ray Anderson of Interface," *Inc.*, November 6, 2016, https:// www.inc.com/magazine/20061101/green50_industrialist.html.

39 **$800 million:** Ibid.

39 **He'd taken it public:** https://www.interface.com/US/en-US/about /mission/The-Interface-Story-en_US.

39 **Raised in a small town in Georgia:** Anderson was born in West Point, Georgia. From Ray Anderson, *Mid-course Correction. Toward a Sustainable Enterprise: The Interface Model* (White River Junction, VT: Chelsea Green, 1998), 23. Attended Georgia Tech on football scholarship: Ibid., 24. Early career in the carpet industry: Spent roughly 14 years working in the carpet industry at Deering-Milliken and Callaway Mills before starting Interface: https://www.raycander sonfoundation.org/biography.

39 **In 1969, on a trip to Kidderminster:** Anderson, *Mid-course Correction*, 29.

39 **modular carpet tiles made changes easy:** David Grayson, Chris Coulter, and Mark Lee, *All In: The Future of Business Leadership* (New York: Routledge, 2018), 138.

39 **didn't even require glue:** Anderson, *Mid-course Correction*, 36.

39 **founded Interface in 1973:** https://www.interface.com/US/en-US /about/mission/The-Interface-Story-en_US. Age 38, bring carpet tiles to the US: Anderson, *Mid-course Correction*, 28, 34. Technically, at first incorporation, Interface was two different entities with names that have since been abandoned. We'll call it Interface for simplicity.

39 **one of the largest carpet companies in the world:** Grayson, Coulter, and Lee, *All In,* 132.

39 **company's stance on "environmental sustainability":** Interview with Connie Hensler, November 2018, call notes.

40 **received a copy of Paul Hawken's book:** Grayson, Coulter, and Lee, *All In,* 133–34.

40 **man-made environmental collapse:** Paul Hawken, *The Ecology of Commerce: A Declaration of Sustainability* (New York: Harper-Collins, 1993).

40 **Anderson wept:** Paul Vitello, "Ray Anderson, Businessman Turned Environmentalist, Dies at 77," *New York Times*, August 10, 2011.

40 **"a spear in my chest":** Anderson, *Mid-course Correction*, 40.

40 **nylon is a plastic:** Charles Fishman, "Sustainable Growth—Interface, Inc.," *Fast Company*, March 31, 1998, http://www.fastcompany .com/33906/sustainable-growth-interface-inc. Also: interview with Connie Hensler, November 2018, call notes. Nylons are plastics: https://www.explainthatstuff.com/nylon.html.

41 **Her memory of the chair-moving moment:** Jeannie Forrest, written communication, December 2018.

42 **Tobacco companies are in the best position:** World Health Organization, "Fact Sheet: Tobacco," https://www.who.int/news-room/fact-sheets/detail/tobacco.

43 **"psychological standing":** D. T. Miller, D. A. Effron, and S. V. Zak, "From Moral Outrage to Social Protest: The Role of Psychological Standing," in D. Ramona Bobocel, Aaron C. Kay, Mark P. Zanna, and James M. Olson, eds., *The Psychology of Justice and Legitimacy* (New York: Psychology Press, 2010), 117–38.

44 **auto safety advocate Annemarie Shelness and the pediatrician Seymour Charles:** A. Shelness and S. Charles, "Children as Passengers in Automobiles: The Neglected Minority on the Nation's Highways," *Pediatrics* 56, no. 2 (1975): 271–84.

44 **The number one killer of kids:** A. Shelness and S. Charles, "Children as Passengers," 271.

44 **More . . . killed and injured *inside*:** Ibid.

44 **all new cars were required to have seat belts:** J. Hedlund, S. H. Gilbert, K. A. Ledingham, and D. F. Preusser, *How States Achieve High Seat Belt Use Rates*. US Department of Transportation, National Transportation Safety Administration, August 2008, publication no. HS–810 962, https://crashstats.nhtsa.dot.gov/Api/Public/View Publication/810962. Most didn't use seat belts: A. Shelness and S. Charles, "Children as Passengers," 271.

44 **car seats . . . not widely adopted:** https://crashstats.nhtsa.dot.gov /Api/Public/ViewPublication/810962; A. Shelness and S. Charles, "Children as Passengers," 272.

44 **early seats had been designed not to boost safety:** A. Shelness and S. Charles, "Children as Passengers," 272.

45 **"No one is in a better position":** A. Shelness and S. Charles, "Children as Passengers," 282.

45 **call to take ownership . . . was well received:** Harvard public health professor David Hemenway wrote in *While We Were Sleeping: Success Stories in Injury and Violence Prevention* (Berkeley and Los Angeles, CA: University of California Press, 2009) that the *Pediatrics* article "served as a wake-up call for pediatricians and advocates nationwide."

45 **"That article was a stunner":** Robert Grayson, "Robert S. Sanders, MD: Interviewed by Robert Grayson, MD," Oral History Project, Pediatric History Center, American Academy of Pediatrics, April 20, 2004, 33. Thanks to Larry Cohen for suggesting I investigate this story.

45 **pediatrician and county health director:** Ibid.

45 **"The whole idea of prevention and care":** Interview with Pat Sanders, September 2018.

45 **legislation to require . . . car seats in Tennessee:** Interview with Pat Sanders, September 2018; Robert Sanders Jr., *Dr. Seat Belt: The Life of Robert S. Sanders, MD, Pioneer in Child Passenger Safety* (Armstrong Valley: 2008).

46 **legislation . . . for those under four:** Robert Grayson, "Robert S. Sanders," 31, 32.

46 **On the weekends, Bob Sanders would call them:** Interview with Pat Sanders, September 2018.

46 **"in a rocket to the Moon":** Ibid.

46 **Child Passenger Protection Act . . . two-thirds support:** House and Senate journals of the State of Tennessee's General Assembly (1977).

46 **Tennessee became the first state:** Bill Mitchell, "Is Your Child Riding in a Safe Seat?" *Tennessean*, July 16, 1978.

46 **a "Babes-in-Arms" amendment:** Robert Grayson, "Robert S. Sanders."

47 **"Now why go and strap it into a seat belt?":** Mitchell, "Is Your Child Riding in a Safe Seat?"

47 **referring to the . . . amendment as the "Child Crusher" amendment:** Robert Grayson, "Robert S. Sanders."

47 **in 1981, two parents testified:** Larry Daughtrey, "Child Death Told at Auto Hearing," *Tennessean*, February 18, 1981.

47 **11 children under the age of 3 died:** Associated Press, "Youngsters Fight Car Safety Seats: Troopers," *Tennessean*, October 29, 1980.

47 **in 1981, it was repealed:** Larry Daughtrey, "House Passes Bill Closing Loophole in Child Seat Law," *Tennessean*, March 5, 1981.

47 **West Virginia became the third state:** J. Y. Bae, E. Anderson, D. Silver, and J. Macinko, "Child Passenger Safety Laws in the United States, 1978–2010: Policy Diffusion in the Absence of Strong Federal Intervention," *Social Science & Medicine* 100 (2014): 30–37, table 2.

47 **By 1985, all 50 states:** S. P. Teret, A. S. Jones, A. F. Williams, and J. K. Wells, "Child Restraint Laws: An Analysis of Gaps in Coverage," *American Journal of Public Health* 76, no. 1 (1986): 31–34, 31.

47 **1975 to 2016, 11,274 children under the age of four had their lives saved:** National Center for Statistics and Analysis, Occupant protection in passenger vehicles. *Traffic Safety Facts 2016*, Report No. DOT HS 812 494 (Washington, DC: National Highway Traffic Safety Administration, 2018), 7, table 6.

48 **"It hit me right between the eyes":** Anderson's epiphany and the story of the kick-off speech from Anderson, *Mid-course Correction*, 39–40.

48 **"When he first came up with this idea":** Vitello, "Ray Anderson, Businessman Turned Environmentalist, Dies at 77."

48 **still recovering from a recession:** David Grayson, Chris Coulter, and

Mark Lee, *All In: The Future of Business Leadership* (New York: Routledge, 2018), 132.

49   **reduce, reuse, reclaim:** Anderson, *Mid-course Correction*, 43.

49   **"first $200 million":** Boilers/emissions detail, revenue increase, and "first $200 million" quote from Charles Fishman, "Sustainable Growth—Interface, Inc.," *Fast Company*, March 31, 1998, http://www.fastcompany.com/33906/sustainable-growth-interface-inc.

49   **In 1997, at a company meeting:** Interview with David Gerson, November 2018, 00:14:20; interview with Connie Hensler, November 2018, call notes. Ray Anderson, speech, 1997, https://youtu.be/Uos8SQi9Vqc?t=1277. Mission Zero: https://www.interface.com/EU/en-GB/about/index/Mission-Zero-en_GB#.

49   **seven-part plan for achieving Mission Zero:** https://www.interface.com/EU/en-GB/about/index/Mission-Zero-en_GB#; Gray, Coulter, and Lee, *All In*, xvi.

50   **technology that could recycle carpets:** Interview with Eric Nelson, January 2019.

50   **"a culture of dreamers and doers":** Gray, Coulter, and Lee, *All In*, xvii.

51   **"If you'd told me then":** Interview with David Gerson, October 2015.

51   **Anderson scored Interface as having traveled about halfway:** Stats on fossil fuel use and water usage, as well as Anderson's assessment of Interface's progress, from Cornelia Dean, "Executive on a Mission: Saving the Planet," *New York Times*, May 22, 2007, http://www.nytimes.com/2007/05/22/science/earth/22ander.html.

51   **Anderson passed away at the age of 77:** Vitello, "Ray Anderson, Businessman Turned Environmentalist, Dies at 77."

51   **"extraordinarily credible":** Grist staff, "Paul Hawken Pays Tribute to Green-Biz Visionary Ray Anderson," Grist, August 13, 2011, https://grist.org/sustainable-business/2011-08-12-paul-hawken-pays-tribute-to-green-biz-visionary-ray-anderson/.

51   **fishermen were paid to retrieve abandoned fishing nets:** Interview with Miriam Turner, December 2015. Also: http://net-works.com/about-net-works/locations/philippines/; https://www.econyl.com/blog/architecture-design/net-works-fishing-nets-arrived-in-aj dovscina-for-regeneration/; https://www.youtube.com/watch?time_continue=10&v=1HCfLMVgub8.

52   **return would have been 3.6%:** Via calculations on Bloomberg, TILE versus SPX Index, December 31, 1993, to December 31, 2018.

53   **untangle a dispute between staff members:** Interview with Jeannie Forrest, February 2019, and follow-up via email March 2019. The

quotes from "Dawn" and "Ellen" reflect Forrest's recollection of the conversation.

Chapter 4: Tunneling

57 **John Thompson . . . had been forgetting:** John Thompson, November 21, 2018, response to survey from author.

57 **Rich Marisa had a similar upstream epiphany:** Rich Marisa, November 20, 2018, response to survey from author; interview with Marisa, January 2019.

59 **Eldar Shafir and Sendhil Mullainathan . . . call this "tunneling":** Sendhil Mullainathan and Eldar Shafir, *Scarcity: Why Having Too Little Means So Much* (New York: Henry Holt, 2013), 28.

60 **"poverty reduces anyone's bandwidth":** Ibid., 13.

60 **"Scarcity . . . put off important but not urgent things":** Ibid., 117.

60 **shadowing 22 nurses in 8 hospitals:** Interview with Anita Tucker, January 2019. Original research in Anita L. Tucker, Amy C. Edmondson, and Steven Spear, "When Problem Solving Prevents Organizational Learning," *Journal of Organizational Change Management* 15, no. 2, (2002): 122–37.

63 **a morning "safety huddle":** Risha Sikka, Kate Kovich, and Lee Sacks, "How Every Hospital Should Start the Day," *Harvard Business Review*, December 5, 2014, https://hbr.org/2014/12/how-every -hospital-should-start-the-day.

64 **Daniel Gilbert argues that a focus on the immediate:** Dan Gilbert, "If Only Gay Sex Caused Global Warming," *Los Angeles Times*, July 2, 2005, http://articles.latimes.com/2006/jul/02/opinion/op-gilbert2.

65 **Let's go back to 1974:** Mario J. Molina and F. S. Rowland, "Stratospheric Sink for Chlorofluoromethanes: Chlorine Atom-Catalysed Destruction of Ozone," *Nature* 249 (1974), 810–12, https://www .nature.com/articles/249810a0.

66 **The scientists had discovered something:** Wendy Becktold, "'Ozone Hole' Shows That We Avoided Planetary Disaster Before," Sierra Club, April 10, 2019, https://www.sierraclub.org/sierra /ozone-hole-shows-we-avoided-planetary-disaster-before-pbs-docu mentary.

66 **nonflammable and nontoxic:** This comes from the PBS film *Ozone Hole: How We Saved the Planet*, 2019, https://www.pbs.org/show /ozone-hole-how-we-saved-planet/.

66 **would eat up the world's ozone layer:** Ibid. Also Justin Gillis, "The Montreal Protocol, a Little Treaty That Could," *New York Times*,

December 9, 2013, https://www.nytimes.com/2013/12/10/science /the-montreal-protocol-a-little-treaty-that-could.html.

66 **disruption of the world's food supply and skin cancer:** Ibid.

66 **"It didn't make any noise":** PBS, *Ozone Hole: How We Saved the Planet*, https://www.pbs.org/show/ozone-hole-how-we-saved -planet/ at 00:11:50.

66 **"a tap on the brakes":** Sean Davis, "Lessons from the World Avoided," TEDxTalk, October 11, 2017, https://www.youtube.com /watch?v=sTCnJa_P8xY at 00:08:17.

66 **ozone layer is not "fixed":** Brad Plumer, "The Ozone Layer Is On Pace for a Full Recovery by 2050, Scientists Say," Vox, September 10, 2014, https://www.vox.com/2014/9/10/6132991/ozone-lay er-starting-to-recover.

67 **About 21.5 million Americans file their taxes:** Ben Casselman, "Everyone Files Their Taxes at the Last Minute," FiveThirtyEight, April 15, 2016, https://fivethirtyeight.com/features/everyone-files -their-taxes-at-the-last-minute/.

68 **became vocal advocates for action:** Shari Roan, "F. Sherwood Rowland Dies at 84; UC Irvine Professor Won Nobel Prize," *Los Angeles Times*, March 12, 2012, https://www.latimes.com/local/obituaries /la-me-sherwood-rowland-20120312-story.html.

68 *All in the Family*: "Gloria's Shock," *All in the Family*, season 5, episode 7, 1974; Stephen O. Anderson and K. Madhava Sarma, *Protecting the Ozone: The United Nations History* (London: Earthscan, 2012), 375.

68 **The sale of aerosol sprays dropped:** PBS, *Ozone Hole: How We Saved the Planet*, April 10, 2019.

68 **the term** *ozone hole*: Sebastian Grevsmühl, "Revisiting the 'Ozone Hole' Metaphor: From Observational Window to Global Environmental Threat," *Environmental Communication* 12, no. 1 (2018): 71–83.

68 **Some scientists objected to the term:** Kerri Smith, "Past Cast: Discovering the Ozone Layer Hole," *Nature*, May 31, 2019, https:// www.nature.com/articles/d41586-019-01582-z#MO0.

68 **"it certainly made it easier":** Ibid.

69 **DuPont had become a supporter:** PBS, *Ozone Hole: How We Saved the Planet*, April 10, 2019.

69 **"DuPont's support for the protocol":** James Maxwell and Forest Briscoe, "There's Money in the Air: The CFC Ban and DuPont's Regulatory Strategy," *Business Strategy and the Environment* 6, no. 5 (1998): 276–86, 282.

69 **Other opponents included the leaders of developing nations:** Rich-

ard E. Benedick, "Human Population and Environmental Stress in the Twenty-First Century," *Environmental Change & Security Project Report* 6 (2000): 5–18, 13.

69 **Margaret Thatcher . . . led the charge:** PBS, *Ozone Hole: How We Saved the Planet*, April 10, 2019.

69 **Donald Hodel was quoted as speaking critically:** Guy Darst, "Hodel Offends Environmentalists with Lotion-and-Hats Policy," *Associated Press*, May 30, 1987, https://www.apnews.com /006054380f941f9735f0fb0201ef2056.

70 **Hodel backpedaled:** PBS, *Ozone Hole: How We Saved the Planet*, at 00:33:20, April 10, 2019.

70 **"helps us to contemplate the world we've avoided":** Davis, "Lessons from the World Avoided," TEDxTalk, https://www.youtube.com /watch?v=sTCnJa_P8xY, 00:08:39.

Chapter 5: How Will You Unite the Right People?

75 **In 1997, a photograph was taken in downtown Reykjavík:** Inga Dóra Sigfúsdóttir, Planet Youth Workshop presentation, March 2019.

75 **the photo was shot at 3:00 a.m.:** Interview with Inga Dóra Sigfúsdóttir, June 2019.

75 **42% of Icelandic 15- and 16-year-olds reported having been drunk:** I. D. Sigfúsdóttir, A. L. Kristjánsson, T. Thorlindsson, and J. P. Allegrante, "Trends in Prevalence of Substance Use Among Icelandic Adolescents, 1995–2006," *Substance Abuse Treatment, Prevention, and Policy* 3, no. 1 (2008), 12; Inga Dóra Sigfúsdóttir, Planet Youth Workshop presentation, March 2019, graph, p. 35.

75 **quarter smoked cigarettes daily, and 17% had already tried cannabis:** Ibid.

75 **"helped a friend of mine to puke in an alley":** Mayor Dagur Eggertsson, Planet Youth Workshop lecture, March 2019.

76 **second-highest rate of accidents or injuries:** European School Survey Projection Alcohol and Other Drugs (ESPAD), 1995 report, Eggertsson appendix II, 62 (p. 223 of document).

76 **percentage who'd been drunk at the age of 13 or younger:** ESPAD report, 1995, 71.

76 **been drunk 10 or more times during the previous year:** Ibid., 67.

76 **rate of substance abuse crept up:** Sigfúsdóttir, Kristjánsson, Thorlindsson, and Allegrante, "Trends in Prevalence of Substance Use," 21; Inga Dóra Sigfúsdóttir, Planet Youth Workshop presentation, March 2019, graph, p. 11. Concerned leaders: *Drug-free Iceland*

Final Report, May 2003, https://www.landlaeknir.is/servlet/file /store93/item10661/IAE_final2003.pdf.

76 launched an anti-substance-abuse movement called Drug-free Iceland: *Drug-free Iceland Final Report*, 7, https://www.landlaeknir.is /servlet/file/store93/item10661/IAE_final2003.pdf.

77 help from anyone who was willing to assist: Ibid.

77 most Icelanders live in or around the capitol city of Reykjavík: Andie Fontaine, "Population Figures: Reykvikingar Vastly Outnumber Other Icelanders," *Reykjavík Grapevine*, January 29, 2019, https://grape vine.is/news/2019/01/28/population-figures-reykvikingar-vastly -outnumber-other-icelanders/.

77 the key distinguishing features from Kentucky: Comparea, http:// www.comparea.org/ISL+US_KY.

77 "saying no" missed the big picture: Inga Dóra Sigfúsdóttir, Planet Youth Workshop lecture, March 2019; interview with Alfgeir Krist-jansson, January 2019.

77 "We wanted to change communities": Interview with Inga Dóra Sig-fúsdóttir, June 2019.

77 risk factors for teenage substance abuse: Sigfúsdóttir, Kristjánsson, Thorlindsson, and Allegrante, "Trends in Prevalence of Substance Use," 12; friends who drink/smoke: I. D. Sigfúsdóttir, T. Thorlinds-son, Á. L. Kristjánsson, K. M. Roe, and J. P. Allegrante, "Substance Use Prevention for Adolescents: The Icelandic Model," *Health Promotion International* 24, no. 1 (2008): 16–25, 17, 24.

77 having lots of unstructured time: Ibid., 24.

77 *protective* factors that reduce the risk: Sigfúsdóttir, Kristjánsson, Thorlindsson, and Allegrante, "Trends in Prevalence of Substance Use," 12.

78 having better ways for teens to spend their time: Ibid., 12, 8.

78 quantity of time spent matters more than quality: Planet Youth Workshop presentation, March 2019, at 00:16:56–19:16.

78 Change the culture surrounding teenagers: Sigfúsdóttir, Kristjáns-son, Thorlindsson, and Allegrante, "Trends in Prevalence of Sub-stance Use," 12.

78 worked to change the culture around popular festivals: *Drug-free Iceland Final Report*, May 2003, 23–26, https://www.landlaeknir.is /servlet/file/store93/item10661/IAE_final2003.pdf.

78 friendlier version of a curfew: Inga Dóra Sigfúsdóttir, personal com-munication.

78 they were all breaking the rules: Interview with Inga Dóra Sigfúsdót-tir, March 2019.

78 encouraging them to honor the outside hours: *Drug-free Iceland Final Report*, 23.

Notes

78 **letter also included a refrigerator magnet:** Ibid.; interview with Inga Dóra Sigfúsdóttir, March 2019.

79 **made a villain of the lonely parents trying to stick to the policy:** Interview with Inga Dóra Sigfúsdóttir, March 2019.

79 **compliance increased significantly:** Sigfúsdóttir, Thorlindsson, Kristjánsson, Roe, and Allegrante, "Substance Use Prevention for Adolescents," 22; *Drug-free Iceland Final Report*, 23; interview with Inga Dóra Sigfúsdóttir, March 2019.

79 **took organized walks at night:** BBC News, "How Iceland Saved Its Teenagers," December 3, 2017, https://www.youtube.com/watch ?v=cDbD_JSCrNo.

79 **arose from the research of Harvey Milkman:** Biography: Metropolitan State University of Denver, MSU Denver Experts Guide, "Harvey Milkman," https://www.msudenver.edu/experts/allexperts /milkman-harvey.shtml.

79 **"corollary to that was natural highs":** Interview with Harvey Milkman, March 2019.

79 **"sports clubs":** Emma Young, "Iceland Knows How to Stop Teen Substance Abuse, But the Rest of the World Isn't Listening," *Mosaic Science*, January 17, 2017, https://mosaicscience.com/story/iceland -prevent-teen-substance-abuse/; Margret-Lilja-Gudmundsdottir, Planet Youth workshop presentation, March 2019, 16–17.

79 **a paid, experienced veteran:** Margret-Lilja-Gudmundsdottir, Planet Youth Workshop presentation, March 2019.

80 **To support participation:** Young, "Iceland Knows How to Stop Teen Substance Abuse."

80 **An annual survey, "Youth in Iceland":** ICSRA website, Youth in Iceland survey, http://www.rannsoknir.is/en/youth-in-iceland/.

80 **The steering committee alone met 101 times:** *Drug-free Iceland Final Report*, 9.

80 **Participation in formal sports:** Sigfúsdóttir, Thorlindsson, Kristjánsson, Roe, and Allegrante, "Substance Use Prevention for Adolescents," 22.

80 **Time spent with parents:** Ibid., 21; Inga Dóra Sigfúsdóttir, Planet Youth Workshop presentation, March 2019, graph, p. 31.

80 **Compliance with outside hours:** Sigfúsdóttir, Thorlindsson, Kristjánsson, Roe, and Allegrante, "Substance Use Prevention for Adolescents," 22; Inga Dóra Sigfúsdóttir, Planet Youth Workshop presentation, March 2019.

80 **teenage culture had been transformed:** Inga Dóra Sigfúsdóttir, Planet Youth Workshop presentation, March 2019; Sigfúsdóttir, Kristjánsson, Thorlindsson, and Allegrante, "Trends in Prevalence of Substance Use," 12.

81 **Most teenagers today aren't really aware of it:** Interview with Harvey Milkman, March 2019; interview with Inga Dóra Sigfúsdóttir, March 2019.

81 **Iceland's campaign became the envy of the world:** Q&A, Planet Youth website, https://planetyouth.org/the-method/qa/.

81 **"one element ... that is the most important, and it's empowerment":** Interview with Inga Dóra Sigfúsdóttir, March 2019.

82 **In 1997, Kelly Dunne ... had just arrived:** Dunne's entry into domestic violence work: All quotes from interview with Kelly Dunne, October 2018. Some details from Rachel Louise Snyder. Rachel Louise Snyder, "A Raised Hand," *The New Yorker*, July 15, 2013, 35.

83 **the Jeanne Geiger Crisis Center:** The center's original name was the Women's Crisis Center. It was renamed after Jeanne Geiger, a hotelier based in nearby Plum Island, who died in a bizarre fall. After her death, her family donated $1 million to the center to honor her; https://jeannegeigercrisiscenter.org/about-us/who-is-jeanne-geiger/; http://archive.boston.com/news/local/articles/2005/02/27/fatal_fall_stirs_more_questions/.

83 **murdered by her estranged husband:** Description of Dorothy Giunta-Cotter's death in Snyder, "A Raised Hand," 34.

83 **a crisis of faith for Dunne:** Interview with Kelly Dunne, October 2018.

84 **Campbell had had her own awakening:** Jacquelyn Campbell's entry into domestic violence work: Interview with Jacquelyn Campbell, October 2018.

84 **If a woman is murdered:** E. Petrosky, J. M. Blair, C. J. Betz, K. A. Fowler, S. P. Jack, and B. H. Lyons, "Racial and Ethnic Differences in Homicides of Adult Women and the Role of Intimate Partner Violence: United States, 2003–2014," *Morbidity and Mortality Weekly Report* 66, no. 28 (July 21, 2017): 741–46.

84 **contained crime-scene photographs:** Interview with Jacquelyn Campbell, October 2018.

85 **Campbell developed a "Danger Assessment" tool:** J. Campbell, D. Webster, and N. Glass, "The Danger Assessment: Validation of a Lethality Risk Assessment Instrument for Intimate Partner Femicide," *Journal of Interpersonal Violence* 24 (2009): 653–74.

85 **The current version of the tool:** Danger Assessment questionnaire (2018 version), https://www.dangerassessment.org/uploads/DA_2018%20pdf.pdf.

85 **represented an early-warning system:** Interview with Kelly Dunne, October 2018.

85 **she would have scored an 18 out of 20:** Snyder, "A Raised Hand," 37.

86 **she organized the Domestic Violence High Risk Team:** Ibid.

86 **13 to 15 people met once a month:** Interview with Robert (Bobby) Wile, October 2018.

86 **create an emergency plan:** Interview with Kelly Dunne, October 2018.

86 **Police officers would start driving by:** Interview with Robert (Bobby) Wile, October 2018.

87 **"where are they?":** Ibid.

87 **"Twenty years ago, if you told me":** Jeanne Geiger Crisis Center promotional video, *Doug Gaudette: DV Advocacy*, https://vimeo .com/117406066.

87 **172 high-risk cases . . . no subsequent re-assault:** Domestic Violence High Risk Team website, http://dvhrt.org/impact. Numbers for first 12 years (2005–2017).

87 **8 domestic violence–related deaths:** Dave Rogers, "Stats Show Need for Domestic Violence Team," *(Newburyport) Daily News*, November 2, 2013, https://www.newburyportnews.com/news/lo cal_news/stats-show-need-for-domestic-violence-team/article_e86 c086b-6f3b-530a-84a2-0a237bbeb7a8.html; communication with Kelly Dunne, June 13, 2019.

87 **not one woman has been killed:** Interview and communications with Kelly Dunne. From Dunne in a June 2019 email: "Prior to the team, there were 8 DV-related deaths in a ten-year span. All of these deaths occurred in the town of Amesbury, Massachusetts. Amesbury is adjacent to Newburyport and one of the communities that is part of the DVHRT. Since the creation of the team, there have been no DV-related homicides in any of the communities that are members of the DVHRT (including Amesbury). Although we don't consider this a DV-related homicide, in 2014 an officer shot a suspect after he attempted to murder his wife in Salisbury, MA."

89 **"data for the purpose of learning":** Interview with Joe McCannon, March 2019.

89 **McCannon is an expert:** McCannon is the cofounder of the Billions Institute and the former director of Learning and Diffusion at the Center for Medicare & Medicaid Innovation. Previously, he led an amazing campaign—called the 100,000 Lives Campaign—to make health care safer: "Overview of the 100,000 Lives Campaign," https://www.ihi.org/Engage/Initiatives/Completed/5MillionLives Campaign/Documents/Overview%20of%20the%20100K%20 Campaign.pdf.

90 **challenged by a colleague to take the Mayor's Challenge:** US Interagency Council on Homelessness, "Mayor's Challenge to End Veteran Homelessness," https://www.usich.gov/solutions/collaborative -leadership/mayors-challenge/.

90 **working on the issue of homelessness:** Interview with Larry Morrissey, November 2018.

90 **"Rockford is now the nation's underwater capital":** Conor Dougherty, "Crisis Plus Five: Welcome to Rockford, the Underwater Mortgage Capital of America," *Wall Street Journal*, September 7, 2013.

90 **population ... had been shrinking:** US Census Quick Facts, https://www.census.gov/quickfacts/rockfordcityillinois.

90 **"We were addicted to mediocrity":** Interview with Larry Morrissey, October 2018.

91 **"What's gonna change?":** Interview with Larry Morrissey, November 2018.

91 **He reluctantly ... agreed to attend a training session:** Ibid.

91 **"The lightbulb went off":** Interview with Larry Morrissey, October 2018.

91 **ended homelessness among local veterans:** Erica Snow, "A City Solves Veteran Homelessness," *Wall Street Journal*, December 5, 2018.

91 **"'I believe in fairies' moment":** Interview with Jennifer Jaeger, November 2018.

92 **I met with Jaeger in the fall:** Description of Jaegar's office, based on author observations during November 2018 visit.

92 **the team ... made three critical shifts:** Interview with Larry Morrissey, October 2018.

92 **"Housing first" flips that sequence:** Community Solutions, "Housing First: The Cheapest, Most Effective Solution to Homelessness," https://www.community.solutions/sites/default/files/housingfirstfact sheet-zero2016.pdf.

92 **"thinking of them as people without houses":** Interview with Jennifer Jaeger, November 2018.

92 **what's known as "coordinated entry":** Interview with Angie Walker, November 2018.

93 **an annual "point in time" census:** US Department of Housing and Urban Development, "PIT and HIC Guides, Tools and Webinars," https://www.hudexchange.info/programs/hdx/guides/pit-hic/#general -pit-guides-and-tools.

93 **"Nobody ... to actually count unsheltered people":** Interview with Angie Walker, November 2018.

93 **"by-name list" ... meet to discuss homelessness:** Ibid.

94 **the meetings had been "bitch sessions":** Interview with Larry Morrissey, November 2018.

94 **"The data itself feels like ... a living creature":** Interview with Jennifer Jaeger, November 2018.

95 **"You can't solve a dynamic problem with static data":** Interview with Beth Sandor, October 2018.

95 **achieved . . . "functional zero":** Interview with Angie Walker, November 2018. The fact that 156 veterans were housed: interview with Jennifer Jaeger, November 2018.

95 **In 2017, they achieved functional zero:** Interview with Angie Walker, November 2018. Youth homelessness: interview with Jennifer Jaeger, November 2018.

95 **"Every day is hard":** Interview with Angie Walker, November 2018.

95 **the problem of "inflow":** Interview with Jennifer Jaeger and Angie Walker, November 2018.

96 **the eviction rates are as high as 24%:** Ibid. Rockford has one of the highest eviction rates in the state and the country. It's ranked within the top 50 on Eviction Lab's list of large US cities by eviction rate: Eviction Lab, "Eviction Rankings," https://evictionlab.org/rankings/#/evictions?r=United%20States&a=0&d=evictionRate&l=50.

96 **city conducted a pilot program:** Email correspondence with Jennifer Jaeger, May 2019.

96 **In some cases, the city negotiated:** Interview with Angie Walker, November 2018.

96 **decreased the . . . homeless due to eviction by 30%:** Interview with Jennifer Jaeger, June 2019.

Chapter 6: How Will You Change the System?

97 **Anthony Iton moved to Baltimore:** Interview with Anthony Iton, April 2019.

98 **It was all there on the county's death certificates:** Anthony Iton, "Change the Odds for Health," TEDxSanFrancisco, November 4, 2016, https://www.youtube.com/watch?v=0H6yte4RXx0.

98 **"Shortened Lives":** Suzanne Bohan and Sandy Kleffman, "Day I: Three East Bay ZIP Codes, Life-and-Death Disparities," *East Bay Times*, December 2, 2009, https://www.eastbaytimes.com/2009/12/02/day-i-three-east-bay-zip-codes-life-and-death-disparities/. Assisted by Matt Beyers: https://www.eastbaytimes.com/2009/12/03/how-bay-area-news-group-examined-health-inequities-in-the-east-bay/.

98 **The same pattern was unearthed in other cities:** Iton, "Change the Odds for Health."

99 **23 years of life expectancy vanished:** Julie Washington, "Where You Live Determines How Long You Live," *Plain Dealer*, December 19,

2018, https://www.cleveland.com/healthfit/2018/12/where-you-live
-determines-how-long-you-live.html.

99 **"Sweden and Afghanistan in the same city":** Interview with Anthony
Iton, November 2018.

99 **"They're literally under siege":** Michael Krasny, "Tony Iton on How
to Fix California's Health Care Gap," KQED, July 5, 2018, https://
www.kqed.org/forum/2010101866101/tony-iton-on-how-to-fix
-californias-health-care-gap.

99 **"incubators of chronic stress":** Iton, "Change the Odds for Health."

100 **In 1962, the San Francisco Giants:** Noel Hynd, "Giant-Sized Con-
fession: A Groundskeeper's Deeds," *Sports Illustrated*, August 29,
1988, https://www.si.com/vault/1988/08/29/118286/giant-sized-con
fession-a-groundskeepers-deeds.

102 **"I get irritated":** Interview with Anthony Iton, November 2018.

103 **David Foster Wallace once told a story:** "This Is Water," Kenyon College Commencement Address, 2005, https://fs.blog/2012/04/david
-foster-wallace-this-is-water/.

103 **1 of the 10 greatest public health achievements:** Centers for Disease
Control and Prevention (CDC), "Ten Great Public Health Achievements: United States, 1900–1999," *Morbidity and Mortality Weekly
Report* 48, no. 12 (1999): 241; Centers for Disease Control and Prevention (CDC), "Achievements in Public Health, 1900–1999: Fluoridation of Drinking Water to Prevent Dental Caries, *Morbidity and
Mortality Weekly Report* 48 (1999): 933–40. J. O'Connell, J. Rock-
ell, J. Ouellet, S. L. Tomar, and W. Maas, "Costs and Savings Associated with Community Water Fluoridation in the United States,"
Health Affairs 35, no. 12 (2016): 2224–32.

103 **5 people died:** National Highway Traffic Safety Administration,
"Motor Vehicle Traffic Fatalities and Fatality Rates, 1899–2017,"
2019, https://cdan.nhtsa.gov/tsftables/tsfar.htm.

103 **1 death:** Ibid. List of improvements: Susannah Locke, "You're Less
Likely to Die in a Car Crash Nowadays—Here's Why," Vox, April 6,
2014, https://www.vox.com/2014/4/2/5572648/why-are-fewer-peo
ple-dying-in-car-crashes.

104 **more than 37,000 people:** National Highway Traffic Safety Administration, "Motor Vehicle Traffic Fatalities and Fatality Rates, 1899–
2017."

104 **high friction surface treatments (HFSTs):** Federal Highway
Administration, "High Friction Surface Treatments: Frequently
Asked Questions," March 2014, https://www.fhwa.dot.gov/inno
vation/everydaycounts/edc-2/pdfs/fhwa-cai-14-019_faqs_hfst
_mar2014_508.pdf.

104 **crashes have been reduced almost 80%:** Ibid.

104 **VanMoof received complaints:** Story from Bex Rad, "Our Secret's Out," *Medium*, September 6, 2016, https://medium.com/vanmoof /our-secrets-out-f21c1f03fdc8. Also: May Bulman, "What Happened When a Bike Company Started Putting TVs on the Sides of Its Delivery Packages," *Independent*, September 25, 2016, https://www .independent.co.uk/news/world/europe/vanmoof-bikes-flatscreen -tv-huge-reduction-delivery-damages-printing-giant-tv-side-of -box-a7328916.html.

105 **"Any idiots out today, Dad?":** Charlie Shaw, "32 People Share the Funniest Thing They've Heard a Kid Say," *Thought Catalog*, April 15, 2014, https://thoughtcatalog.com/charlie-shaw/2014/04/32-people -share-the-funniest-thing-theyve-heard-a-kid-say/.

107 **DonorsChoose is a website:** DonorsChoose, "Impact," https://www .donorschoose.org/about/impact.html, accessed September 13, 2019.

108 **"go beyond what you'd expect":** Written communication with Charles Best, August 2019.

110 **Building Healthy Communities:** The California Endowment, Building Health Communities, https://www.calendow.org/build ing-healthy-communities/.

110 **their vision was to start with *power*:** Ibid.

110 **"part of something bigger than yourself":** Interview with Anthony Iton, November 2018.

110 **BHC's theory of change:** The California Endowment, Building Health Communities, https://www.calendow.org/building-healthy-commu nities/.

111 **The city manager vetoed the ad:** KFSN ABC 30, "#Parks4All Bus Ad Controversy," 2015, https://www.youtube.com/watch?v=F_4q8yZ RXG4.

111 **Sandra Celedon posed in front:** KFSN ABC 30, "#Parks4All Initiative for More and Better Parks," 2015, https://www.youtube.com /watch?v=asV3d6uYCrI.

111 **"too controversial and too political":** Ezra David Romero, "City of Fresno Rejects Controversial Bus Banner," KVPR, May 27, 2015, https://www.kvpr.org/post/city-fresno-rejects-controversial -bus-banner.

111 **a new Parks Master Plan:** Suzanne Bohan, *Twenty Years of Life: Why the Poor Die Earlier and How to Challenge Inequity* (Washington, DC: Island Press, 2018), Kindle edition, location 1334 of 4552.

111 **a new skateboard park:** George Hostetter, "Skate Park Is First Taste of City's Parks Pivot," *Sun*, April 13, 2016, http://sjvsun.com/news /fresno/skate-park-is-first-taste-of-citys-parks-pivot/.

111 **district agreed to open up 16 school playgrounds:** Tim Sheehan, "Some Fresno Schools Will Double as Parks on Weekends," *Fresno Bee*,

April 29, 2016, https://www.fresnobee.com/news/local/article7477 8512.html.

111 **18-acre . . . soccer park:** Tim Sheehan, "There's a Shortage of Parks in Southeast Fresno: One Group Steps Up with Plans to Help," *Fresno Bee*, February 8, 2018, https://www.fresnobee.com/news/local/article 199207409.html.

112 **a cap-and-trade law:** California Climate Investments, "About California Climate Investments," http://www.caclimateinvestments .ca.gov/about-cci; TCC grants: California Strategic Growth Council, "Transform Fresno: Transformative Climate Communities," and, http://sgc.ca.gov/programs/tcc/docs/20190201-TCC_Awardee _Fresno.pdf.

112 **allocate $70 million to Fresno:** Johnny Magdaleno, "How This Community Fought for $70 Million in Cleanup Funds—and Won," Next City, August 13, 2018, https://nextcity.org/features/view/how -this-community-fought-for-70-million-in-cleanup-funds-and-won.

112 **controversy about how it would be spent:** Interview with Sarah Reyes, January 2019.

112 **Fresno City College . . . MLK Magnet Core Park:** Brianna Calix, "How Much Good Can Be Done in Five Years with $66 Million in Southwest Fresno?" *Fresno Bee*, February 26, 2019, https://www .fresnobee.com/article226807669.html.

113 **I also met Kieshaun White:** Brianna Calix, "Teen's Data Shows Air Quality Is Worse in South Fresno. He's Taking His Work to Schools," *Fresno Bee*, December 17, 2018, https://www.fresnobee.com/news /local/article222580890.html.

113 **asthma, a common health problem:** Central Valley Health Policy Institute, "Community Benefits Needs Assessment in South Fresno," California State University, Fresno, 2017, http://www.fres nostate.edu/chhs/cvhpi/documents/Community%20Benefits%20 Report%20CVHPI%208-3.pdf.

113 **321 policy wins and 451 systems changes:** From document provided by Anthony Iton, September 2019.

113 **"you've got to change the power inputs":** Interview with Anthony Iton, April 2019.

113 **about a fifth of their employees turn over:** Tracy Vanderneck, "Does the Nonprofit Industry Have an Employment Problem?," *NonProfit PRO*, May 18, 2017, https://www.nonprofitpro.com/post/nonprofit -industry-employment-problem/.

113 **"It took 50 years for us to get Medicare":** Interview with Sandra Celedon, April 2019.

Chapter 7: Where Can You Find a Point of Leverage?

116 **in the midst of a crime wave:** Steven Gray, "Chicago Confronts a Crime Wave," *Time*, August 3, 2008, http://content.time.com/time /nation/article/0,8599,1828287,00.html.

116 **build an evidence base that policymakers could rely on:** Background on the founding and early days of the Crime Lab from multiple interviews with Jens Ludwig and Roseanna Ander in 2018 and 2019, and an interview with Harold Pollack in August 2018. Also: see University of Chicago Urban Labs, "Our Approach," https://urbanlabs .uchicago.edu/about.

116 **pored over medical examiner reports:** Ibid. Also: see University of Chicago Crime Lab, "Testimony of Harold Pollack, PhD, March 13, 2013," https://blogs.chicagotribune.com/files/mandatory-minimums -testimony20130313.pdf.

116 **a kid . . . had stolen a bike:** Interview with Roseanna Ander, March 2018.

117 **"My fundamental equation":** Interview with Harold Pollack, August 2018.

117 **better known as Tony D:** Rob Waters, "A Conversation with Tony D: How 'Becoming a Man' Got to the White House," *Forbes*, March 9, 2016, https://www.forbes.com/sites/robwaters/2016/03/09/a -conversation-with-tony-d-how-becoming-a-man-got-to-the-white -house/#5c0f2e81666b.

118 **He started inviting young men:** Interview with Tony D, August 2018.

119 **One was called The Fist:** S. B. Heller, A. K. Shah, J. Guryan, J. Ludwig, S. Mullainathan, and H. A. Pollack, "Thinking, Fast and Slow? Some Field Experiments to Reduce Crime and Dropout in Chicago," *Quarterly Journal of Economics* 132, no. 1 (2017): 1–54, 3.

119 **a tradition called the "check-in":** Interview with Tony D, August 8, 2018, 00:14:30, 00:17:30; J. Lansing and E. Rapoport, *Bolstering Belonging in BAM and Beyond: Youth Guidance's Becoming a Man (BAM) Program Components, Experiential Processes, and Mechanisms*, a Report to Youth Guidance (Chicago: Chapin Hall at the University of Chicago, 2016), 43–44.

119 **"it's calming":** J. Lansing and E. Rapoport, *Bolstering Belonging in BAM and Beyond*, 44.

120 **"instead of freaking out . . . I accepted it":** Ibid., 63.

120 **they saw a connection:** Interview with Jens Ludwig, August 2018.

121 **scale up its work to 18 schools:** S. B. Heller, A. K. Shah et al., "Thinking, Fast and Slow?," 1–54.

122 **convert his home-brewed course notes:** Interview with the Youth Guidance team, August 2018.

122 **27 one-hour, weekly BAM sessions:** S. B. Heller, A. K. Shah, et al., "Thinking, Fast and Slow?," 8.

122 **learn that one of their students had been arrested:** Interview with Harold Pollack, August 8, 2018.

123 **arrests were down 28%:** RCT results from S. B. Heller, A. K. Shah, et al., "Thinking, Fast and Slow?," 20.

123 **"one of the greatest moments of my entire career":** Interview with Harold Pollack, August 2018.

123 **BAM program had been successful:** S. B. Heller, A. K. Shah, et al., "Thinking, Fast and Slow?," 2.

124 **A similar strategy was used by the Permanente Medical Group:** From Chip Heath and Dan Heath, *Decisive: How to Make Better Choices in Life and Work* (New York: Random House, 2013), 70.

124 **reduced mortality for patients with sepsis by 60%:** Kaiser Permanente Institute for Health Policy, "Saving Lives Through Better Sepsis Care," *Kaiser Permanente Policy Story*, 1, no. 4 (2012), https://www.kpihp.org/wp-content/uploads/2019/03/KP-Story-1.4-Sepsis-Care.pdf.

124 **anticipate the problems that elderly people:** Corgan, "About Corgan," https://www.corgan.com/about-corgan/. Anticipate: Robin Young and Jack Mitchell, "40 Years in 5 Minutes: Age Simulation Suit Aims to Increase Empathy in Building Design," WBUR, June 3, 2019, https://www.wbur.org/hereandnow/2019/06/03/age-simulation-suit.

126 **Five thousand people is about 0.2%:** Chicago's population estimate, 2,716,540; City of Chicago, "Facts & Statistics," https://www.chicago.gov/city/en/about/facts.html, accessed October 2019.

126 **17% of them:** Jens Ludwig, "Crime in Chicago: Beyond the Headlines," presentation to the City Club of Chicago, January 29, 2018.

126 **social cost of a single gunshot injury is $1.5 million:** Philip J. Cook and Jens Ludwig, *Gun Violence: The Real Cost* (New York: Oxford University Press, 2000), 112. Note: Book cites $1 million, but that figure is in 1998 dollars, which is the equivalent of about $1.5 million in 2018 dollars.

126 **given a fresh start:** Interview with Roseanna Ander, March 2018. Also: Patrick Smith, "A Program Gives Jobs to Those Most at Risk for Violence: Can Chicago Afford It?," NPR, June 6, 2019, https://www.npr.org/local/309/2019/06/06/730145646/a-program-gives-jobs-to-those-most-at-risk-for-violence-can-chicago-afford-it.

126 **heavy utilizers of emergency medicine:** Diane Hasselman, Center for Health Care Strategies, *Super-Utilizer Summit: Common Themes from Innovative Complex Care Management Programs*, October

2013, https://www.chcs.org/media/FINAL_Super-Utilizer_Report .pdf.

129   **"the tiniest part of the health equation":** Interview with Carmela Rocchetti, August 2019.

129   **ask their patients if they often go hungry:** Mahita Gajanan, "US Doctors Advised to Screen Child Patients for Signs of Hunger," *Guardian*, October 23, 2015, https://www.theguardian.com/us-news/2015 /oct/23/doctors-child-patients-hunger-food-pediatricians. Marissa Cabrera and Maureen Cavanaugh, "Report Explores How Doctors Can Help Patients Fight Food Insecurity," KPBS, November 16, 2016, https://www.kpbs.org/news/2016/nov/16/report-how-doctors -can-help-fight-food-insecurity/.

130   **reinventing the way doctors are trained:** The story of the Hackensack Meridian Health School of Medicine comes from interviews with Carmela Rocchetti, August 2019; Dean Bonnie Stanton, August 2019; and student Aamirah McCutchen, September 2019. Rocchetti shared documents explaining more about the curriculum. A few details from Laurie Pine (May 30, 2018). "Seton Hall University and Hackensack Meridian Health Celebrate Opening of School of Medicine with Ribbon-Cutting Attended by Gov. Murphy and Key Lawmakers," Hackensack Meridian School of Medicine at Seton Hall University, https://www.shu.edu/medicine/news/celebrating-opening -of-school-of-medicine.cfm.

133   **Bryan Stevenson . . . calls this the "power of proximity":** Bryan Stevenson, "The Power of Proximity," Fortune CEO Initiative 2018, https://www.youtube.com/watch?v=1RyAwZIHo4Y.

Chapter 8: How Will You Get Early Warning of the Problem?

135   **the "churn" was high:** Story of LinkedIn and early warning of churn from interviews with Dan Shapero, September 2018; Roli Saxena, September 2019; and Archana Sekhar, September 2019.

137   **Northwell Health . . . EMS (Emergency Medical Services) leaders:** The story of Northwell's EMS and its forward-deployed ambulances comes from interviews with Alan Schwalberg and Jonathan Washko in August 2019 and a subsequent visit to the command center—and an additional interview with Washko—in September 2019. Details from other sources cited separately below.

138   **run by the fire department:** US Department of Transportation, "EMS System Demographics," NHTSA, June 2014, https://www.ems.gov /pdf/National_EMS_Assessment_Demographics_2011.pdf, 5.

139 **Northwell's average response time is about 6.5 minutes:** Written communication with Jonathan Washko, October 2019. The national average from Howard K. Mell et al., "Emergency Medical Services Response Times in Rural, Suburban, and Urban Area," *JAMA Surgery* 152, no. 10 (October 2017): 983–84.

139 **a metric called the ROSC:** "Return of Spontaneous Circulation," *EMT Prep*, 2018, https://emtprep.com/free-training/post/return -of-spontaneous-circulation-rosc.

140 **world's best early-detection systems for earthquakes:** Alex Greer, "Earthquake Preparedness and Response: Comparison of the United States and Japan," *Leadership and Management in Engineering* 12, no. 3 (2012): 111–25.

140 **TV commercial for IBM:** IBM Watson TV commercial, *Watson at Work: Engineering*, 2017, https://www.ispot.tv/ad/wIha/ibm-watson -watson-at-work-engineering, accessed April 30, 2019.

141 **elevator companies today offer "smart" elevators:** Oscar Rousseau, "AI, Sensors, and the Cloud Could Make Your Buildings Lift Safer," *Construction Week Online,* February 18, 2019, https://www.con structionweekonline.com/products-services/169357-ai-sensors-and -the-cloud-could-make-your-buildings-lifts-safer.

142 **"time it takes a door to close":** George Nott, "IoT, Cloud and Machine Learning Giving Elevator Giants a Lift," *Computerworld,* November 26, 2018, https://www.computerworld.com.au/article /649993/iot-cloud-machine-learning-giving-elevator-giants-lift/.

142 **Smart watches that detect atrial fibrillation:** "Heart Rhythm Monitoring with a Smartwatch," *Harvard Heart Letter,* Harvard Health Publishing, April 2019, https://www.health.harvard.edu/heart -health/heart-rhythm-monitoring-with-a-smartwatch.

142 **"smart pigs":** Phil Hopkins, "WTIA/APIA Welded Pipeline Symposium," *Learning from Pipeline Failures* (March 2008), 12.

142 **bus driver is falling asleep:** Alex Dunham, "Dubai Buses Get Safer Thanks to Facial Recognition Technology," *TimeOut Dubai*, October 18, 2016, https://www.timeoutdubai.com/aroundtown/news /74054-dubai-buses-get-safer-thanks-to-facial-recognition-techno logy.

142 **trains 16 million people to perform CPR:** "CPR Statistics," American Heart Association, https://cprblog.heart.org/cpr-statistics/.

142 **"'Loose Lips Sink Ships'":** Manny Fernandez, "A Phrase for Safety After 9/11 Goes Global," *New York Times*, May 10, 2010, https:// www.nytimes.com/2010/05/11/nyregion/11slogan.html?pagewant ed=1&hp.

143 **butterfly-shaped gland:** "Thyroid Cancer," *Mayo Clinic*, https://

www.mayoclinic.org/diseases-conditions/thyroid-cancer/symp
toms-causes/syc-20354161.

143 **rising precipitously:** Hyeong Sik Ahn, Hyun Jung Kim, and
H. Gilbert Welch, "Korea's Thyroid-Cancer 'Epidemic': Screening and Overdiagnosis," *New England Journal of Medicine* 371
(November 6, 2014):1765–67, https://www.ecmstudy.com/up
loads/3/1/8/8/31885023/nejm-koreas_thyroid-cancer_epidemic
-screening_&_overdiagnosis.pdf.

143 *15-fold* **since 1993:** Ibid., 1766.

143 **five-year survival rate:** Gil Welch, "Cancer Screening & Overdiagnosis," 2018, YouTube, https://www.youtube.com/watch?v=lwfZF
skoifw, 00:24:59.

143 **promoted "medical tourism":** Ibid., 00:24:15.

144 **"only a matter of time until it killed":** Gil Welch, *Less Medicine,
More Health*: 7 *Assumptions That Drive US Medical Care* (New
York: Beacon Press, 2015), 57.

144 **the analogy of a barnyard pen of cancers:** Ibid., 57–58.

144 **if they were symptomatic:** Sohee Park, Chang-Mo Oh, Hyunsoon
Cho, Joo Young Lee, et al., "Association Between Screening and the
Thyroid Cancer 'Epidemic' in South Korea: Evidence from a Nationwide Study," *BMJ* 355 (November 30, 2016), https://www.bmj.com
/content/355/bmj.i5745.

145 **South Korea began encouraging more people to get screened:**
Gina Kolata, "Study Points to Overdiagnosis of Thyroid Cancer," *New York Times*, November 5, 2014, https://www.nytimes
.com/2014/11/06/health/study-warns-against-overdiagnosis-of-thy
roid-cancer.html.

145 **surgery to remove the thyroid gland:** Welch, "Cancer Screening &
Overdiagnosis," YouTube, https://www.youtube.com/watch?v=lw
fZFskoifw, 00:22:50.

145 **99.7% of them were still alive!:** Ibid., 00:24:59.

145 **That's alarm fatigue:** B. J. Drew, P. Harris, J. K. Zègre-Hemsey,
T. Mammone, D. Schindler, R. Salas-Boni, et al., "Insights into the
Problem of Alarm Fatigue with Physiologic Monitor Devices: A
Comprehensive Observational Study of Consecutive Intensive Care
Unit Patients," *PLoS ONE* 9, no. 10 (2014): e110274, https://doi
.org/10.1371/journal.pone.0110274.

146 **the aftermath of the massacre at Sandy Hook Elementary School:**
Sandy Hook Advisory Commission, *Final Report of the Sandy Hook
Advisory Commission* (March 6, 2015), http://www.shac.ct.gov
/SHAC_Final_Report_3-6-2015.pdf.

146 **They wanted action:** Unless noted otherwise, the story of Sandy

Hook Promise's work is drawn from multiple interviews with Nicole
Hockley and Paula Fynboh in fall 2018 and 2019, as well as written
communication with Fynboh and other staffers. Two documents,
produced by Sandy Hook Promise for their training, were particularly helpful for this account: "Gun Violence in America Fact-
sheet" and "Know the Signs." Also see Hockley's powerful 2016
speech: "All Gun Violence Is Preventable If You Know the Signs,"
TEDxWakeForestU, https://www.youtube.com/watch?v=2DD4wm
wBUzc.

146 **"We've tried [gun] policy for a few decades":** Lois Beckett, "Sandy
Hook Mom: 'For Christ's Sake, Why Be So Defeatist?,'" *Guardian*, October 4, 2017, https://www.theguardian.com/us-news/2017
/oct/04/sandy-hook-mother-nicole-hockley-gun-control.

147 **"one developed country":** David Frum, "The American Exception,"
The Atlantic, August 4, 2019, https://www.theatlantic.com/ideas
/archive/2019/08/guns-are-american-exception/595450/.

147 **a video in 2016 called *Evan*:** Sandy Hook Promise, *Evan*, 2016,
https://www.youtube.com/watch?v=A8syQeFtBKc.

149 **Say Something Anonymous Reporting System:** "Organizational
Accomplishments," Sandy Hook Promise, https://www.sandyhook
promise.org/impact_historical; "Say Something Anonymous Reporting System," https://www.saysomething.net/.

149 **178,000 students:** "Press Release: Attorney General Shapiro
Announces Strong Start for Safe2Say School Safety Reporting
Program," Office of Attorney General Josh Shapiro, January 23,
2019, https://www.attorneygeneral.gov/taking-action/press-releases
/attorney-general-shapiro-announces-strong-start-for-safe
2say-school-safety-reporting-program/.

149 **615 tips and calls:** Myles Snyder, "New School Safety Hotline Gets
Over 600 Tips in First Week," ABC27, January 23, 2019, https://
www.abc27.com/news/pennsylvania/new-school-safety-hotline
-gets-over-600-tips-in-first-week/.

149 **46 suicide interventions, 3 major drug busts:** Email correspondence
with SHP team, January 2019.

149 **police received a referral:** WLYN News, Facebook post, January 24,
2019, https://www.facebook.com/wylnnews/photos/a.16525993022
5293/2112671945484072/?type=3&theater.

150 **"we don't see the dominoes":** Nicole Hockley, "All Gun Violence
Is Preventable," TEDxWakeForestU, https://www.youtube.com
/watch?v=2DD4wmwBUzc.

Chapter 9: How Will You Know You're Succeeding?

154 **"A rising tide lifts all boats"**: Commonly attributed to John F. Kennedy; from the JFK Library: https://www.jfklibrary.org/learn/about -jfk/life-of-john-f-kennedy/john-f-kennedy-quotations.

154 **as crime fell precipitously across the US**: Matt Ford, "What Caused Crime to Decline in the US?," *The Atlantic*, April 15, 2016, https:// www.theatlantic.com/politics/archive/2016/04/what-caused-the -crime-decline/477408/.

154 **"Every police chief in the country"**: Interview with Jens Ludwig, April 2019.

155 **For Katie Choe, the chief engineer**: Story from interview with Katie Choe, January 2019, and interview with Choe, Ramandeep Josen, and Christopher Coakley in March 2019, subsequent written exchanges, and documents provided by Choe and Coakley. Facts from other sources are noted in the endnotes below.

155 **sidewalks . . . were rated in poor condition**: Meghan E. Irons, "Boston's Rich and Poor Neighborhoods Show Sidewalk Repair Disparity," *Boston Globe*, March 4, 2018.

156 **"Nothing would get done"**: Ibid.

159 **"when faced with a difficult question"**: Daniel Kahneman, *Thinking, Fast and Slow* (New York: Farrar, Straus and Giroux, 2011), 12. Google Books link: https://books.google.com/books?id=TA7Q27RWlj0C&printsec =frontcover&dq=kahneman+fast+and+slow&hl=en&sa=X&ved=2a hUKEwiG1b3bo6vkAhXic98KHeGuCM8Q6AEwAHoECAAQA g#v=onepage&q=kahneman%20fast%20and%20slow&f=false.

159 **measuring the sales generated by its promotional emails**: Susan Athey and Michael Luca, "Economists (and Economics) in Tech Companies," *Journal of Economics* 33, no. 1 (Winter 2019): 209– 30, https://doi.org/10.1257/jep.33.1.209.

161 **long wait times in hospital emergency rooms**: Gywn Bevan and Christopher Hood, "What's Measured Is What Matters: Targets and Gaming in the English Public Health Care System," *Journal of Public Administration* 84, no. 3 (2006): 517–38, http://citeseerx .ist.psu.edu/viewdoc/download?doi=10.1.1.454.2524&rep=rep1 &type=pdf.

162 **spectacular drop in crime in New York City**: Police Department, City of New York, *CompStat Report*, August 25, 2019, https:// www1.nyc.gov/assets/nypd/downloads/pdf/crime_statistics/cs-en -us-city.pdf. Note that the people who died from the attacks on 9/11 are not counted in these figures (even though they were clearly murdered).

162 **established a new system called CompStat**: Chris Smith, "The

Controversial Crime-Fighting Program That Changed Big-City Policing Forever," *New York*, March 2, 2018, http://nymag.com /intelligencer/2018/03/the-crime-fighting-program-that-changed -new-york-forever.html.

162 **allocate their resources based on the patterns:** "NYPD and CompStat," *Big Data in New York City Management*, School of International and Public Affairs Case Consortium at Columbia, Columbia University, http://ccnmtl.columbia.edu/projects/caseconsortium/case studies/127/casestudy/www/layout/case_id_127_id_886.html.

162 **accountable for reducing crime:** New York City Police Department, "6th Precinct," https://www1.nyc.gov/site/nypd/bureaus/patrol/pre cincts/6th-precinct.page.

163 **In 2018, *Reply All*:** PJ Vogt and Alex Goodman, "The Crime Machine: Vols. 1 and 2," *Reply All*, October 12, 2018, https://gimlet media.com/shows/reply-all/76h967/127-the-crime-machine-part-i. A sincere thanks to Gimlet Media for allowing me to share these excerpts.

163 **"he had to cheat a little bit more":** Ibid., vol. 2, https://gimletmedia .com/shows/reply-all/n8hwl7.

164 **Ritchie Baez, a 14-year veteran:** Ibid. Note that Baez was part of a lawsuit in which several black and Latino POC officers sued NYPD, claiming they were unfairly punished because they didn't hit their "quotas" of arrests and summonses. See: Dana Sauchelli, Frank Rosario, and Leonard Greene, "NYPD Targets Minority Officers with Quota Punishments: Suit," *New York Post*, March 2, 2015, https://nypost.com/2015/03/02/nypd-targets-minority-officers -with-quota-punishments-suit/. The suit was later thrown out.

164 **"Hey, something really bad is going on":** Ibid.

167 **success story at Chicago Public Schools:** Elaine Allensworth, Kaleen Healey, Julia Gwynne, and René Crispin, *High School Graduation Rates Through Two Decades of Change: Research Summary* (Chicago: University of Chicago Consortium on School Research, June 2016).

168 **called "paired measures":** Andrew S. Grove, *High Output Management* (New York: Random House, 1978; rev. ed. 2015), 18.

168 **NYPD finally added some complementary measures:** Al Baker, "Updated NYPD: Anti-Crime System to Ask: 'How We Doing?,'" *New York Times*, May 8, 2017, https://www.nytimes .com/2017/05/08/nyregion/nypd-compstat-crime-mapping.html.

Chapter 10: How Will You Avoid Doing Harm?

171 **Macquarie Island lies about halfway:** Macquarie Island station information page, Australian Antarctic Division, Australian Department of the Environment and Energy, http://www.antarctica.gov.au /living-and-working/stations/macquarie-island.

171 **breeding stop for migratory birds:** 3.5 million and 80,000 elephant seals arrive each year. Macquarie Island World Heritage Area information page, Tasmania Parks and Wildlife Service, https://www .parks.tas.gov.au/index.aspx?base=394.

171 **a protected wilderness:** Australian Government Department of the Environment and Energy, "World Heritage Places—Macquarie Island," https://www.environment.gov.au/heritage/places/world /macquarie-island; Macquarie Island is actually a UNESCO World Heritage Centre, "World Heritage List," https://whc.unesco.org/en /list/629/.

171 **home to many rare species:** Australian Government Department of the Environment, "Macquarie Island: From Rabbits and Rodents to Recovery and Renewal," Commonwealth of Australia, 2014, 1; Blue Petrel, Species Profile and Threats Database, Australian Department of the Environment and Energy, http://www.environment.gov.au /cgi-bin/sprat/public/publicspecies.pl?taxon_id=1059.

171 **named for Saint Peter:** Craig Campbell, "'Miraculous' St. Peter Bird Is Able to Walk on Water," *Sunday (Glasgow) Post*, September 16, 2016.

171 **penguins and seals occupy:** Australian Government Department of the Environment, "Macquarie Island: From Rabbits and Rodents," 1.

171 **capture penguins and seals for their natural oil:** Australian Department of the Environment and Energy, Australian Antarctic Division, "Macquarie Island Station: A Brief History," http://www.antarctica .gov.au/about-antarctica/history/stations/macquarie-island.

171 **Rabbits served as food:** "The Pest Problem," Macquarie Island Pest Eradication Project, Tasmania Parks and Wildlife Service.

171 **cats to kill the rodents:** Miss Cellania, "Messing with Mother Nature: The Macquarie Island Ecosystem," Mental Floss, March 27, 2012, http://mentalfloss.com/article/30307/messing-mother-nature -macquarie-island-ecosystem; Nick Holmes, "Unintended Consequences," *The Pulse*, July 27, 2018, podcast, at 36:53.

172 **they needed a vector for the virus:** The Macquarie story is based on interviews in September 2018 with Keith Springer, Dana Bergstrom, Aleks Terauds, Jamie Kirkpatrick, Keith Broome, Sue Robinson, and Nick Holmes. Also these four sources: Dana Bergstrom, Arko Luc-

ier, Katie Kiefer, et al., "Indirect Effects of Invasive Species Removal Devastate World Heritage Island," *Journal of Applied Ecology* 46, no. 1 (2009): 73–81. Tasmania Parks and Wildlife, "Plan for the Eradication of Rabbits and Rodents on Subantarctic Macquarie Island," Biodiversity Conservation Branch, Department of Primary Industries and Water, Tasmania, March 2007. Tasmania Parks and Wildlife Service, *Evaluation Report: Macquarie Island Pest Eradication Project*, "Timeline," August 2014, https://parks.tas.gov.au /Documents/Evaluation_Report_Macquarie_Island_Pest_Eradica tion_Project.pdf. Tasmania Parks and Wildlife Service, "Macquarie Island Pest Eradication Project," August 2014, https://www.parks .tas.gov.au/file.aspx?id=31160.

173 **plagued by invasive weeds:** Funny side note: The park rangers are also helping to keep the weeds at bay by eating them—turns out chickweed is tasty. See Laura Williams and Alex Fergus, "Macquarie Island Weed Hunters," This Week at Macquarie Island, February 17, 2017, http://www.antarctica.gov.au/living-and-working/stations /macquarie-island/this-week-at-macquarie-island/2017/this-week -at-macquarie-island-17-february-2017/macquarie-island -weed-hunter.

174 **"vantage point that lets you see the whole system":** Donella Meadows. "Dancing with Systems," Donella Meadows Archives, Donella Meadows Project, Academy for Systems Change, http://donella meadows.org/archives/dancing-with-systems/.

175 **a young Google engineer:** Benjamin Weiser, "Comptroller Aims to Curb Personal-Injury Claims Against New York City," *New York Times*, July 9, 2014, https://www.nytimes.com/2014/07/09/nyre gion/comptroller-aims-to-curb-personal-injury-claims-against-new -york-city.html.

175 **settlements resulting from falling branches:** Office of the New York City Comptroller Scott M. Stringer, *ClaimStat: Protecting Citizens and Saving Taxpayer Dollars*, July 2014, 2.

175 **settled for $11.5 million:** Benjamin Weiser, "Comptroller Aims to Curb Personal-Injury Claims," *New York Times*, July 9, 2014.

175 **"Whatever money we thought we were saving":** Interview with David Saltonstall, August 2019.

175 **"new, data-driven tool":** Office of the New York City Comptroller Scott M. Stringer, "Comptroller Stringer Releases ClaimStat: New Data-Driven Analysis of Legal Claims to Help Save Taxpayer Dollars and Make the City Safer," press release, July 9, 2014, https:// comptroller.nyc.gov/newsroom/comptroller-stringer-releases-claim stat-new-data-driven-analysis-of-legal-claims-to-help-save-taxpayer -dollars-and-make-the-city-safer/, accessed September 25, 2019.

175 **roughly 30,000 annual claims:** Interview with Saltonstall, August 2019.

175 **injuries to children on playgrounds:** Office of the New York City Comptroller Scott M. Stringer, "ClaimStat Alert: Protecting Kids on NYC Playgrounds," March 2015, https://comptroller.nyc.gov /wp-content/uploads/documents/ClaimStat_Playground_February _2015.pdf.

175 **"All someone needed to do":** Interview with Saltonstall, August 2019.

176 **"to prevent extinctions":** Island Conservation, "Mission and History," https://www.islandconservation.org/mission-and-history/.

176 **models such as a food web:** E. S. Zavaleta, R. J. Hobbs, and H. A. Mooney, "Viewing Invasive Species Removal in a Whole-Ecosystem Context," *Trends in Ecology & Evolution* 16, no. 8 (2001): 454–59.

176 **"Islands are systems":** Interview with Nick Holmes, December 2015.

177 **The cobra effect occurs:** Dale Hartley, "The Cobra Effect: Good Intentions, Perverse Outcomes," *Psychology Today*, October 8, 2015, https://www.psychologytoday.com/us/blog/machiavellians-gull ing-the-rubes/201610/the-cobra-effect-good-intentions-per verse-outcomes.

177 **"And he expected this would solve the problem":** Stephen Dubner and Steven Levitt, "The Cobra Effect," *Freakonomics* podcast, October 11, 2012, episode 96.

177 **examples of the cobra effect are more subtle:** Story from interview with Amantha Imber, November 2018, and subsequent communication, August 2019.

178 **A 2018 study by Harvard scholars:** Interview with Ethan Bernstein, November 2018. Also: Ethan S. Bernstein and Stephen Turban, "The Impact of the 'Open' Workspace on Human Collaboration," *Philosophical Transactions of the Royal Society B: Biological Sciences* 373 (1753), July 2, 2018, https://royalsocietypublishing.org/doi/full /10.1098/rstb.2017.0239.

179 **"Remember, always, that everything you know":** Donella Meadows, "Dancing with Systems," 3.

179 **her staff in the State Library Victoria:** Communication with Imber on August 15, 2019. State Library Victoria website, https://www.slv .vic.gov.au.

180 **"The first thing I would say":** Interview with Andy Hackbarth, March 2019.

183 **"You can practice shooting eight hours a day":** Jim Afremow, *The Champions Comeback: How Great Athletes Recover, Reflect and Re-Ignite* (New York: Rodale, 2016), Google https://books.google

.com/books?id=8iu5CwAAQBAJ&pg=PA76&dq=#v=onep
age&q&f=false, p. 76.

183 **The owners of Summit CPA Group:** The story of the Summit CPA
group and its overhauled meetings comes from interviews with Jody
Grunden and Jamie Nau, August 2019.

184 *The Accountant* **scored 3.65:** "*The Accountant*, 2016," IMDb website, https://www.imdb.com/title/tt2140479/.

185 **100 billion bags are used:** Tatiana Homonoff, Lee-Sien Kao, Doug
Palmer, and Christina Seybolt, *Skipping the Bag: Assessing the
Impact of Chicago's Tax on Disposable Bags*, Chicago Mayor's
Office, September 2018, 3.

186 **they are worse in other ways:** Ibid.

186 **need to use a paper bag 3 times:** Chris Edwards and Jonna Mey-
hoff Fry, *Life Cycle Assessment of Supermarket Carrier Bags: A
Review of the Bags Available in 2006*, UK Environmental Agency,
2011, 8.

186 **They offered** *thicker* **plastic bags:** Alexia Elejalde-Ruiz, "The Result
of Chicago Plastic Bag Bank: Shopping Bags to Be Sturdier," *Chicago Tribune*, June 20, 2015, https://www.chicagotribune.com
/business/ct-plastic-bag-ban-0622-biz-20150622-story.html.

186 **California voters passed a statewide ban:** "State Plastic and Paper Bag
Legislation," National Conference of State Legislatures, August 15,
2019, http://www.ncsl.org/research/environment-and-natural-re
sources/plastic-bag-legislation.aspx.

186 **sales of . . . plastic trash bags shot up:** Greg Rosalsky, "Are Plastic Bags Garbage," *Planet Money* newsletter, April 9, 2019, https://
www.npr.org/sections/money/2019/04/09/711181385/are-plastic
-bag-bans-garbage.

186 **28.5% of the reduction:** Rebecca L. C. Taylor, "Bag Leakage: The
Effect of Disposable Carryout Bag Regulations on Unregulated
Bags," *Journal of Environmental Economics and Management* 93
(2019): 254–71, 17 in downloaded version.

187 **deadly 2017 hepatitis A outbreak:** Paul Sisson, "What Is Causing
an Outbreak That Has Infected 181 People and Killed Four?," *San
Diego Union-Tribune*, June 24, 2017.

187 **"not to bluff and not to freeze":** Donella Meadows, "Dancing with
Systems," 3.

187 **a 7-cent tax:** Tatiana Homonoff et al., *Skipping the Bag*.

188 **"Systems can't be controlled":** Donella Meadows, "Dancing with
Systems," 2.

Chapter 11: Who Will Pay for What Does Not Happen?

189 **In a speech at a health conference:** A. A. Clark, "Restriction and Prevention of the Dangerous Communicable Diseases," *Proceedings of the Sanitary Convention*, Battle Creek, Michigan, June 25 and 26, 1890, 23.

190 **In 1900, the average life expectancy:** These calculations drawn from E. Arias, J. Xu, and K. D. Kochanek, "United States Life Tables, 2016," *National Vital Statistics Report* 68, no. 4 (2019), 48, table 19; 49, table 20.

191 **The natural life span:** Amanda Ruggeri, "Do We Really Live Longer Than Our Ancestors?" BBC, October 3, 2018, http://www.bbc.com /future/story/20181002-how-long-did-ancient-people-live-life-span -versus-longevity.

191 **deaths were due to infectious diseases:** Rebecca Tippett, "Mortality and Causes of Death, 1900 vs. 2010," Carolina Demography, University of North Carolina at Chapel Hill, June 16, 2016, https:// demography.cpc.unc.edu/2014/06/16/mortality-and-cause-of-death -1900-v-2010.

191 **disproportionate killers of children:** Centers for Disease Control and Prevention, "Achievements in Public Health, 1900 to 1999: Control of Infectious Diseases," *Morbidity and Mortality Weekly Review*, July 30, 1999, https://www.cdc.gov/mmwr/preview/mmwrhtml/mm 4829a1.htm.

191 **to less than 3% in 2010:** Tippett, "Mortality and Causes of Death."

191 **Better hygiene, cleaner water:** Laura Helmuth, "Why Are You Not Dead Yet?," Slate, September 5, 2013, https://slate.com/tech nology/2013/09/life-expectancy-history-public-health-and-medical -advances-that-lead-to-long-lives.html. This Slate series included a "Wretched Fate" interactive game to look at your chances and method of dying based on different time frames, including 1890, the date of Professor Clark's speech.

191 *every fifth child . . . would have died:* Average life expectancy in 1900: E. Arias, J. Xu, and K. D. Kochanek, "United States Life Tables, 2016," *National Vital Statistics Report* 68, no. 4 (2019), 49, table 20.

191 **"We under-invest in the services":** Interview with John Auerbach, June 2019.

191 **$88.9 billion, just 2.5%:** A. B. Martin, M. Hartman, B. Washington, and A. Caitlin, "National Health Care Spending in 2017: Growth Slows to Post-Great Recession Rates, Share of GDP Stabilizes," *Health Affairs* 38, no. 1 (January 2019), 102, exhibit 5. You might be wondering why this doesn't look like the 1:1 upstream-to-downstream proportion highlighted in the first chapter. Recall that

the upstream portion included expenditures that tend to make people healthier, such as pensions, unemployment insurance, public housing, and more. Here we're talking specifically about the amount spent on population health, which is concerned with reducing the incidence of death and disease. In other words, "upstream health" is a superset that includes, as a small portion, public health.

191 **"if you do your job, they cut your budget":** Interview with Julie Pavlin, August 2018.

192 **"We'll pay $40,000 a year for the price of insulin":** Interview with Patrick Conway, August 2019.

192 **world-leading access to MRI scans:** Note from Dan: After much fruitless digging, I have not been able to locate the original source that sparked this comment. My memory was that the author(s) were bragging about the MRI access. It's possible that I heard it in a speech. As for the fact itself—that the US is one of the world leaders in MRI scans—see the following source (and to be clear, they are *not* bragging about this): I. Papanicolas, L. R. Woskie, and A. K. Jha, "Health Care Spending in the United States and Other High-Income Countries," *JAMA* 319, no. 10 (2018): 1024–39.

193 **Take the case of Poppy + Rose:** Interview with Diana Yin, January 2019.

193 **suffered lower-back injuries:** Occupational Safety and Health Administration, "Healthcare: Safe Patient Handling," https://www.osha.gov/SLTC/healthcarefacilities/safepatienthandling.html.

194 **nursing homes could cut:** Centers for Disease Control and Prevention, "Ten Great Public Health Achievements: United States, 2001–2010," *Mobility and Mortality Weekly Report*, May 20, 2011, https://www.cdc.gov/mmwr/preview/mmwrhtml/mm6019a5.htm?s_cid=fb2423.

194 **founded in the 1970s by David Olds:** Andy Goodman, "The Story of David Olds and the Nurse Home Visiting Program," Robert Wood Johnson Foundation, July 25, 2006, 7–8.

195 **The program he created, NFP:** Details about the program drawn from several sources: Nurse-Family Partnership, "Nurses and Mothers," https://www.nursefamilypartnership.org/wp-content/uploads/2018/11/Nurses-Mothers.pdf; Nurse-Family Partnership, "Overview," https://www.nursefamilypartnership.org/wp-content/uploads/2019/07/NFP-Overview.pdf; Goodman, "The Story of David Olds," 11; Joan Riemer, "This Nurse Helps New Moms When They're Most Vulnerable," *Woman's Day*, January 8, 2019, https://www.womansday.com/life/real-women/a25805099/nurse-family-partnership-facts/; T. R. Miller, "Projected Outcomes of Nurse-Family Partnership Home Visitation During 1996–2013, USA," *Prevention Science* 16, no. 6 (2015): 765–77;

Michelle Andrews, "'Pay for Success' Approach Used to Fund a Program That Supports New Moms," Shots: Health News from NPR, August 9, 2017, https://www.npr.org/sections/health -shots/2017/08/09/542110282/pay-for-success-approach-used-to -fund-a-program-that-supports-new-moms.

196 **Three major randomized controlled trials:** T. R. Miller, "Projected Outcomes of Nurse-Family Partnership," 777; Nurse-Family Part-nership, "Research and Outcomes," https://www.nursefamily partnership.org/wp-content/uploads/2018/11/Research-Trials-and -Outcomes.pdf.

196 **a return of at least \$6.50:** Ted R. Miller, *Nurse-Family Partner-ship Home Visitation: Costs, Outcomes, and Return on Invest-ment,* HSBA (September 2012; revised April 30, 2013), https://www .researchgate.net/publication/264972035_Nurse-Family_Partner ship_Home_Visitation_Costs_Outcomes_and_Return_on_Invest ment_Executive_Summary.

196 **Reducing preterm births . . . criminal offenses . . . SNAP:** Miller, "Projected Outcomes of Nurse-Family Partnership," 765–77.

197 **roughly \$10,000 per woman served:** Nurse-Family Partnership, "Nurse-Family Partnership: Outcomes, Costs and Return on Invest-ment in the US," 2019.

197 **the "wrong pocket problem":** Pay for Success, "What Is the 'Wrong Pockets Problem'?," Urban Institute, https://pfs.urban.org/faq/what -wrong-pockets-problem.

197 **a "pay for success" model:** South Carolina's Department of Health and Human Services, "Fact Sheet: South Carolina Nurse-Family Partnership Pay for Success Project," 2016, https://www.scdhhs.gov /sites/default/files/021616%20SC%20NFP%20PFS%20Fact%20 Sheet.pdf.

198 **"the most obvious thing in the world":** Interview with Christian Soura, November 2018.

198 **look at the list of players involved:** Nonprofit Finance Fund, Pay for Success, "South Carolina Nurse-Family Partnership," Decem-ber 7, 2017, https://www.payforsuccess.org/project/south-carolina -nurse-family-partnership.

198 **the negotiations involved answering:** Interview with Christian Soura, November 6, 2018, 00:06:29.

198 **offer services to an additional 3,200:** South Carolina's Depart-ment of Health and Human Services, "Fact Sheet: South Carolina Nurse-Family Partnership Pay for Success Project."

200 **"The home service industry":** Interview with Brandon Ridenour, February 2019.

201 **Medicare spends a fortune:** Perry Undem Research & Communica-

tions, *The Revolving Door: A Report on US Hospital Readmissions*, Robert Wood Johnson Foundation, February 2013, 3, 34.

201 **Meet the Accountable Care Organization (ACO):** CMS.gov, Centers for Medicare & Medicaid Services, "Accountable Care Organizations (ACOs)," https://www.cms.gov/Medicare/Medicare-Fee-for -Service-Payment/ACO/index.html.

202 **"Before ACOs, doctors didn't get paid":** Interview with Farzad Mostashari, August 2019; "Our Company," Aledade, https://ale dade.com/our-company/.

202 **I talked with Jonathan Lilly:** Interview with Jonathan Lilly, August 2019.

203 **"capitation," a payment model:** "Capitation Payments," Investopedia, https://www.investopedia.com/terms/c/capitation-payments .asp; "How Kaiser Permanente Providers Are Paid," https://healthy .kaiserpermanente.org/static/health/en-us/pdfs/cal/ca_how_provid ers_are_paid.pdf; Kaiser Permanente, "About," 12 million: https:// about.kaiserpermanente.org/who-we-are/fast-facts.

203 **Kaiser Permanente (KP) is unusual:** J. Pines, J. Selevan, F. A. McStay, M. George, and M. McClellan, *Kaiser Permanente–California: A Model for Integrated Care for the Ill and Injured*, Center for Healthcare Policy at Brookings, May 4, 2015, https://www .brookings.edu/wp-content/uploads/2016/07/KaiserFormat ted_150504RH-with-image.pdf.

203 **At Geisinger Health System:** Andrea T. Feinberg, Jonathan R. Slotkin, Allison Hess, and Alistair R. Erskine, "How Geisinger Treats Diabetes by Giving Away Free, Healthy Food," *Harvard Business Review*, October 25, 2017, https://hbr.org/2017/10/how-geisinger -treats-diabetes-by-giving-away-free-healthy-food.

204 **$3.5 trillion health care industry:** Yasmeen Abutaleb, "US Healthcare Spending to Climb 5.3 Percent in 2018: Agency," Reuters, February 14, 2018, https://www.reuters.com/article/us-usa-health care-spending/us-healthcare-spending-to-climb-53-percent-in-2018 -agency-idUSKCN1FY2ZD.

204 **Nike's 2018 global revenue:** "Nike Inc., Reports Fiscal 2018 and Fourth Quarter and Full Year Results," June 28, 2018, https://news .nike.com/news/nike-inc-reports-fiscal-2018-fourth-quarter-and -full-year-results.

Chapter 12: The Chicken Little Problem:
Distant and Improbable Threats

207 **1999 as a VHS tape:** *Y2K Family Survival Guide with Leonard Nimoy*, 1999, https://www.youtube.com/watch?v=EEhEQEG43RU.

208 **John Koskinen was the man tasked:** The Y2K preparation story comes from two interviews with Koskinen in May 2019 and an excerpt from an unpublished draft of his memoir. Other details not from those sources are noted below.

210 **The Federal Reserve ordered $50 billion:** Bert Caldwell, "Bank Regulators Feel Confident Federal Reserve Prints Extra $50 Billion in Currency," *Spokesman Review*, December 4, 1999; Ruth Simon, "Wall Street Deploys Troops to Battle Y2K—Nervous Investors Hoard Cash Gold as Chaos Hedges," *Wall Street Journal*, December 22, 1999.

211 **lost touch … with some intelligence satellites:** President's Council, *The Journey to Y2K: Final Report of the President's Council on Year 2000 Conversion*, March 29, 2000, https://itlaw.wikia.org/wiki/The_Journey_to_Y2K:_Final_Report_of_the_President%27s_Council_on_Year_2000_Conversion.

211 **delayed paychecks, stalled payments, repeated charges:** Ibid.

211 **"Low-level Windshear Alert Systems":** Ibid.

211 **" 'Must not have been a problem' ":** Interview with John Koskinen, May 2019.

212 **"arrive with a yawn":** David Robert Loblaw, "Millennium Bug Is a Misnomer," *Just a Number* blog, 1999, http://www.angelfire.com/oh/justanumber/whatitis.html.

212 **"You Got Conned":** David Robert Loblaw, "You Got Conned and I Told You So," *Globe and Mail*, January 6, 2000, https://www.theglobeandmail.com/opinion/you-got-conned-and-i-told-you-so/article765168/.

212 **"The reason nothing happened":** Interview with Martyn Thomas, March 2019.

213 *which one keeps you up at night?*: Interview with Madhu Beriwal, March 2019.

213 **the bottom of a bowl:** Richard Campanella, "How Humans Sank New Orleans," *The Atlantic*, February 6, 2018, https://www.theatlantic.com/technology/archive/2018/02/how-humans-sank-new-orleans/552323/.

213 **In the years after 9/11:** Christopher Cooper and Robert Block, *Disaster: Hurricane Katrina and the Failure of Homeland Security* (New York: Henry Holt, 2006), author's note.

214 **a contract for $800,000:** Ibid., 2 and 6.

214 **The assignment:** Create hurricane response plans: Madhu Beri-

wal, "Preparing for a Catastrophe: The Hurricane Pam Exercise," Statement Before the Senate Homeland Security and Governmental Affairs Committee, January 24, 2006.

214 **taking 53 days to complete:** Ibid., 2.

214 **convened approximately 300 critical players:** Ibid., 4.

214 **"Though there is plenty of time to flee":** Christopher Cooper and Robert Block, *Disaster: Hurricane Katrina*, 1.

215 **"no fairy dust":** Ibid., 19.

216 **a chart comparing the simulation to the reality:** Madhu Beriwal, "Preparing for a Catastrophe," 6.

216 **account by journalist Scott Gold:** Scott Gold, "Trapped in an Arena of Suffering," *Los Angeles Times*, September 1, 2005, https://www .latimes.com/archives/la-xpm-2005-sep-01-na-superdome1-story .html.

217 **points of difference between Hurricane Pam and Hurricane Katrina:** Chart, Madhu Beriwal, "Preparing for a Catastrophe," 7.

218 **"difference between the two is contraflow":** Interview with Madhu Beriwal, March 26, 2019, 00:23:50.

218 **"Contraflow" is an emergency procedure:** "Hurricane Evacuation Contraflow Videos," Texas Department of Transportation, https:// www.txdot.gov/driver/weather/hurricane-contraflow-vids.html.

218 **the prior year during Hurricane Ivan:** "Mass Evacuations: Using Multiple Contraflow Loading Points," US Department of Homeland Security, Lessons Learned.

218 **stranded . . . for up to 12 hours:** Ibid.

218 **And then Ivan veered east:** Tony Reichhardt, "Hurricane Ivan Highlights Future Risk for New Orleans," *Nature*, September 22, 2004, https://www.nature.com/articles/431388b.

219 **overhauled its contraflow plans:** "Mass Evacuations: Using Multiple Contraflow Loading Points," US Department of Homeland Security, Lessons Learned.

219 **printed up 1.5 million maps:** Johnny B. Bradberry, "Written Testimony Before the US Senate Committee on Homeland Security and Governmental Affairs," January 31, 2006, 4.

219 **drivers were stopping:** "Mass Evacuations: Using Multiple Contraflow Loading Points," US Department of Homeland Security, Lessons Learned.

219 **Blanco ordered contraflow to begin:** Bradberry, "Written Testimony," 8, 9.

219 **The traffic flows were far better:** Ibid., 10.

219 **more than 1.2 million people were evacuated:** Ibid., 11.

219 **"we saved thousands of lives":** Interview with Ivor van Heerden, March 12, 2019, 00:30:05.

220 **multiple additional exercises:** Beriwal, "Preparing for a Catastrophe."

220 **"unable to come up with money":** Christopher Cooper and Robert Block, *Disaster: Hurricane Katrina*, 21.

220 **$62 billion in supplemental spending:** "FEMA Budget So Complex It Defies Consensus," Associated Press, September 24, 2005, http://www.nbcnews.com/id/9460436/ns/us_news-katrina_the_long_road_back/t/fema-budget-so-complex-it-defies-consensus/#.XPV8RYhKhDE.

220 **Phishing schemes:** *2019 Verizon Data Breach Investigations Report*, https://enterprise.verizon.com/resources/executivebriefs/2019-dbir-executive-brief.pdf.

221 **a vendor called KnowBe4:** Interview with Don Ringelestein, May 2019.

221 **use a student's information for years:** Ibid.; "Education Technologies: Data Collection and Unsecured Systems Could Pose Risks to Students," Federal Bureau of Investigation, Public Service Announcement, September 13, 2018, https://www.ic3.gov/media/2018/180913.aspx.

222 **5% in recent attempts:** Interview with Don Ringelestein, May 2019, and subsequent correspondence and phishing security test data.

224 **"The Vulnerable World Hypothesis":** Nick Bostrom, "The Vulnerable World Hypothesis," 2018, https://nickbostrom.com/papers/vulnerable.pdf.

225 **there are DNA "printers":** Rob Stein, "DNA Printing, A Big Boon to Research, But Some Raise Concerns," NPR, May 7, 2015, https://www.npr.org/sections/health-shots/2015/05/07/404460240/dna-printing-a-big-boon-to-research-but-some-raise-concerns.

225 **"So we recall the fate of Atlantis":** *Y2K Family Survival Guide with Leonard Nimoy*, https://www.youtube.com/watch?v=EEhEQEG43RU.

226 **A self-defeating prediction:** "Self-Defeating Prophecy," https://www.oxfordreference.com/view/10.1093/oi/authority.20110803100453214.

226 **founded the Future of Humanity Institute:** To learn more about Bostrom's work, check out this fascinating profile: Raffi Khatchadourian, "The Doomsday Invention: Will Artificial Intelligence Bring Us Utopia or Destruction?," *The New Yorker*, November 23, 2015, https://www.newyorker.com/magazine/2015/11/23/doomsday-invention-artificial-intelligence-nick-bostrom.

226 *Click Here to Kill Everybody*: Bruce Schneier, *Click Here to Kill Everybody: Security and Survival in a Hyper-connected World* (New York: Norton, 2018).

227 **"at risk from Moon germs":** Michael Meltzer, *When Biospheres Collide: A History of NASA's Planetary Protection Programs* (US National Aeronautics and Space Administration, 2010), BiblioGov, 215.

227 **It was the era of the Cold War:** Nuclear fallout shelters: Robert Klara, "Nuclear Fallout Shelters Were Never Going to Work," History, October 16, 2017, updated September 1, 2018, https://www.history .com/news/nuclear-fallout-shelters-were-never-going-to-work; biological warfare: Joshua Lederberg, "The Infamous Black Death May Return to Haunt Us," *Washington Post,* August 31, 1968, https:// www.nlm.nih.gov/hmd/lederberg/pdf/bbabtv.pdf; Cuban Missile Crisis: "Cuban Missile Crisis," Wikipedia, https://en.wikipedia.org /wiki/Cuban_Missile_Crisis; duck and cover in schools: Sarah Pruitt, "How 'Duck-and-Cover' Drills Channeled America's Cold War Anxiety," March 26, 2019, https://www.history.com/news/duck-cover -drills-cold-war-arms-race.

227 *The Andromeda Strain:* Michael Crichton, *The Andromeda Strain* (New York: Centesis Corporation, 1969).

227 **warned of two types of contamination:** Michael Meltzer, *When Biospheres Collide,* 18.

227 **"Backward contamination" . . . "forward contamination":** Erin Mahoney, "New Report Addresses Limiting Interplanetary Contamination During Human Missions," NASA, November 2, 2016, updated August 6, 2017, https://www.nasa.gov/feature/new-report -addresses-limiting-interplanetary-contamination-during-human-missions.

227 **Lederberg labeled "exobiology":** Michael Meltzer, *When Biospheres Collide,* 32.

227 **"Exobiology profoundly influenced":** Caleb Scharf, "How the Cold War Created Astrobiology: Life, Death and Sputnik," *Nautilus,* January 21, 2016, http://nautil.us/issue/32/space/how-the-cold-war-cre ated-astrobiology-rp.

228 **Planetary Protection Officer:** https://sma.nasa.gov/sma-disciplines /planetary-protection.

228 **The office still exists:** Interview with Catharine Conley, May 2019.

Chapter 13: You, Upstream

229 **In 2005, Tricia Dyal's husband:** Unless otherwise noted, the Daddy Doll story comes from interviews with Tricia Dyal in January and July 2019, an interview with Elena Grace Dyal in January 2019, and this article: Noelle McGee, "Ex-Danville Woman's Toys Bring Comfort

to Military Children," *(Champaign, IL) News-Gazette*, December 2, 2007, https://www.news-gazette.com/news/ex-danville-womans -toys-bring-comfort-to-military-children/article_89ace243-46da -51a9-a52a-e6e295b28902.html.

230 **more than 1,000 Daddy Dolls:** Stephanie Heinatz, "Dolls Help Children of Deployed Parents," *Chicago Tribune*, September 12, 2001, https://www.chicagotribune.com/news/ct-xpm-2006-09-12 -0609120147-story.html.

230 **Hug-a-Hero Dolls:** Company website, https://daddydolls.com /HugAHero.

231 **"it makes a difference for them":** Interview with Liz Byrne, January 2019.

231 **founding father of astrobiology, Joshua Lederberg:** Caleb Scharf, "How the Cold War Created Astrobiology," *Nautilus*, January 21, 2016, http://nautil.us/issue/32/space/how-the-cold-war-created-as trobiology-rp.

232 **Jake Stap, a tennis coach:** Pagan Kennedy, *Inventology: How We Dream Up Things That Change the World* (New York: Houghton Mifflin Harcourt, 2016), introduction, ix–x.

233 **"After twenty-five years of marriage":** From survey response submitted by Steve Sosland in December 2018 and subsequent follow-up via email.

234 *"Be impatient for action":* Interview with Maureen Bisognano, July 2019.

234 **think of advocates like Sally Herndon:** The story of Project ASSIST in North Carolina is adapted from a column I wrote with my brother years ago. Chip and Dan Heath, "Why True Grit Matters in the Face of Adversity," *Fast Company*, March 2011, https:// www.fastcompany.com/1722712/why-true-grit-matters-face-ad versity.

234 **mandating that 20%:** North Carolina General Statute 367 (1993), North Carolina General Assembly, https://www.ncleg.net/Ses sions/1993/Bills/House/PDF/H957v5.pdf, 2.

240 **The federal government had a rule:** Interview with Patrick Conway, August 2019; description also on CMMI website, https://innova tion.cms.gov/about/.

240 **were tracking the Diabetes Prevention Program (DPP):** Unless otherwise noted, the story of the work to expand the DPP comes from interviews with Darshak Sanghavi, April 2019, and Patrick Conway, August 2019, as well as Sanghavi's telling of the story in a presentation: Darshak Sanghavi, "Quality Talks 2018," YouTube. https:// www.youtube.com/watch?v=-LYWUqc2mSc, November 8, 2018.

240 **challenged to do two things:** Research Behind the National DPP,

Centers for Disease Control and Prevention, https://www.cdc.gov /diabetes/prevention/research-behind-ndpp.htm, accessed October 9, 2019.

240 **one-third less likely to develop type 2 diabetes:** Ibid.

241 **a letter was delivered to CMS's chief actuary:** Unnamed actuary, "Subject: Ethical Concerns in Using Lifetime Costs for Scoring Proposals," official correspondence to CMS Chief Actuary, December 15, 2015.

243 **legal language being added to government regulations:** Paul Spitalnic, "Certification of Medicare Diabetes Prevention Program," Office of the Actuary, CMS, March 14, 2016.

243 **"Try and leave this world":** Robert Baden-Powell, Introduction, Scouts.org, https://www.scout.org/node/19215?language=en.

Index